The 2020 Presidential Campaign

The 2020 Presidential Campaign

A Communications Perspective

Edited by Robert E. Denton Jr.

ROWMAN & LITTLEFIELD
Lanham • Boulder • New York • London

Published by Rowman & Littlefield
An imprint of The Rowman & Littlefield Publishing Group, Inc.
4501 Forbes Boulevard, Suite 200, Lanham, Maryland 20706
www.rowman.com

86-90 Paul Street, London EC2A 4NE, United Kingdom

British Library Cataloguing in Publication Information Available

Library of Congress Cataloging-in-Publication Data
Names: Denton, Robert E., Jr., editor.
Title: The 2020 presidential campaign : a communications perspective /
    edited by Robert E. Denton Jr.
Other titles: Twenty-twenty presidential campaign
Description: Lanham : Rowman & Littlefield, [2021] | Includes
    bibliographical references and index. | Summary: "As he has done since
    1992, Robert Denton gathers a diverse collection of communications
    scholars to analyze communication trends of the recent presidential
    campaign. Topics include early campaign rhetoric, the nomination process
    and conventions, candidate strategies, debates, advertising, the use of
    new media, news coverage of the campaigns"— Provided by publisher.
Identifiers: LCCN 2021010678 (print) | LCCN 2021010679 (ebook) | ISBN
    9781538156285 (cloth) | ISBN 9781538156346 (paperback) | ISBN
    9781538156308 (epub)
Subjects: LCSH: Presidents—United States—Election—2020. | Political
    campaigns—United States—History—21st century. | Communication in
    politics—United States. | Rhetoric—Political aspects—United
    States—History—21st century.
Classification: LCC E915 .A13 2021 (print) | LCC E915 (ebook) | DDC
    324.973/0905—dc23
LC record available at https://lccn.loc.gov/2021010678
LC ebook record available at https://lccn.loc.gov/2021010679

∞™ The paper used in this publication meets the minimum requirements of American
National Standard for Information Sciences—Permanence of Paper for Printed Library
Materials, ANSI/NISO Z39.48–1992.

This book is dedicated to Judith S. Trent. As a doctoral student and then as a new PhD, Juddi served as a mentor and then colleague assisting me in the journey of my academic career. She invited me to participate in programs, review books for journals, supported leadership positions in regional and national academic divisions, reviewed manuscripts, and, as I later learned, wrote letters of support for promotions and awards. Throughout my entire career, she has been confirming, collaborative, nurturing, and encouraging. Juddi was one of the founders and giants of the subdiscipline of political communication. She was a pioneer in the studies of women in politics and provides the foundation for exploring the early campaign or surfacing phase of presidential elections. Her work in the field surrounding the New Hampshire primary is legendary. I am most grateful for her years of mentoring, modeling, informing, and encouragement. With my utmost admiration, gratefulness, and love.

Contents

Preface

> Every four years a gong goes off and a new Presidential campaign surges into the national consciousness; new candidates, new issues, a new season of surprises. But underlying the syncopations of change is a steady, recurrent rhythm from election to election, a pulse of politics that brings up the same basic themes in order, over and over again.[1]

Forty years ago, as a new doctoral graduate student, I was struck by the above quote and work of noted political science scholar James David Barber. Every modern presidential campaign is different, yet the same. Since 1992, I have edited a volume on the presidential election. In all the previous volumes I have noted that every presidential election is historic from policy, issues, and cultural perspectives. The 2016 presidential election was so unique and historic in many ways. Could the 2020 presidential campaign be as historic as 2016? Well, yes, it was indeed.

- Nearly 160 million people voted in the 2020 presidential election, 25 million more than in 2016.
- Turnout rate for eligible voters was 66.5 percent, the highest since 1900.
- Kamala Harris was the first female elected to serve as vice president of the United States as well as the first Black and Asian woman to serve.
- Joe Biden received over 80 million votes, the most received by any presidential candidate.
- Donald Trump received 74 million votes, the most received by any previous incumbent running for reelection. He received 11 million more votes than in 2016.
- Joe Biden is the oldest president elected and to serve at age 78 (Reagan was 77 on his last day in office).

There are other interesting facets to this election. The election occurred during the backdrop of a global pandemic, an economic crisis, and widespread protests. Even receiving the largest number of votes for an incumbent, Trump is only the third president in recent history who failed to win reelection. He got 95 percent of the Republican vote and increased his support among black voters by 50 percent and Hispanic voters by 35 percent. Down ballot, Republicans flipped a surprising fourteen seats in the House to be just ten seats away from parity with Democrats. Equally surprising, in thirteen of the seats, the winners are women or minorities. Perhaps not surprising is that Trump's approval rating is the most partisan of any president in the modern era. In late summer, his job approval was 87 percent among Republicans and just 6 percent among Democrats. The 81-point gap is the largest recorded and most significant considering the gaps of 67 points for Barack Obama and 58 points for George W. Bush.[2]

Despite the record number of votes for Biden, he won the record low of 17 percent of counties in the nation. Surprisingly, given the magnitude of the victory, Trump actually came within 42,918 votes of an electoral tie (vote margins in Arizona, Georgia, and Wisconsin) and 65,009 votes to reaching the magic 270 electoral votes. Biden is the fifteenth vice president to become president but just the sixth to do so by election rather than by assassination, resignation, or death.

We came out of the election still very much a deeply polarized nation in terms of beliefs, attitudes, values, race, gender, income, geography and political ideology, and party. And by looking at the results, the "blue" areas of cities and suburbs became bluer and the "red" areas of small towns and rural areas became redder. Pew Research Center reported that 83 percent of registered voters indicated that it "really mattered" who won this year's presidential race. Another record. In 2016, it was 74 percent, and in the controversial 2000 election between George W. Bush and Al Gore, it was just 50 percent. Pew also found in postelection that Trump's and Biden's supporters disagree not only on political priorities but even on core American values. Eighty percent of Biden supporters and 77 percent of Trump supporters indicated that they fundamentally disagree with the other side's "core American values and goals." Just 20 percent indicated that the differences are just about politics and policies. In fact, to indicate the intensity of the divide, 90 percent of Biden's supporters and 89 percent of Trump's supporters said there would be "lasting harm" to America if the other candidate won the election.[3]

As unbelievable as it may seem, Rasmussen polling found that 24 percent of American likely voters think Biden voters are America's biggest enemy, tied with China as our nation's number one. Twenty-two percent view Trump voters as the nation's biggest enemy, while only 10 percent view Russia and 7 percent North Korea as our largest threat. By party, 37 percent of

Republicans identified Biden voters and 35 percent of Democrats identified Trump voters as the nation's number one threat. Nonaffiliated voters consider China, Biden voters, and Trump voters equally a threat to the United States.[4]

It is essential to note that the chapters in this volume focus only on the general election phases of the campaign. The vast majority of the chapters were completed well before Election Day and certainly before the faithful, alarming, and tragic January 6, 2020. There is some mention of media coverage of charges of election "fraud" and "irregularities" in chapter 6 but only initially as issues of media coverage. Thus, by and large, the postelection period up until inauguration day is not part of this volume with the exception of an Epilogue that acknowledges what will certainly perhaps be "the" historic phase of this presidential campaign. As of this writing and as the manuscript goes to press, many issues and questions are emerging. Each day new revelations are surrounding January 6, 2020. It will take some time to sort out and understand the full ramifications of postelection concerns. There will undoubtedly be many articles and books focusing on the postelection period of 2020 and into 2021.

For communication scholars, Dan Nimmo, one of the fathers of political communication as a field of study and mentor, argued that the essence of politics is "talk" or human interaction. The interaction may be formal or informal, verbal or nonverbal, public or private, but always persuasive, forcing us as individuals to interpret, to evaluate, and to act.

I have argued for decades that presidential campaigns are our national conversations. They are highly complex and sophisticated communication events: communication of issues, images, social reality, and personas. They are essential exercises in the creation, recreation, and transmission of "significant symbols" through human communication. As we attempt to make sense of our environment, "political bits" of communication comprise our voting choices, worldviews, and legislative desires.

The purpose of this volume, as were all the others, is to review the 2020 presidential campaign from a communication perspective. The chapters are clustered within three sections. The first section contains chapters that focus on major areas of political campaign communication in the 2020 election to include the nominations, the conventions, the debates, political advertising, social media, and media coverage of the campaigns. The second section provides a couple of fascinating elements of the campaigns to include candidate branding and the politics of food in the campaign. The final section summarizes the campaign finance and its pact in the election and explains the vote in 2016. The analyses presented here go beyond the quantitative facts, electoral counts, and poll results of the election. Thus, each chapter focuses on a specific area of political campaign communication. All the contributors are accomplished scholars. Most have participated in past volumes.

In chapter 1, Craig Allen Smith and Kathy B. Smith explore the surfacing stage of the presidential contest by analyzing the theoretical nature of the surfacing phase and the candidates' approaches to it. While the authors conclude that the rhetorical functions of this critical phase endure, the fragmented news environment demands attention to an array of audiences, issues, and key primary states. The changing party rules of nomination clearly influence the outcome of the evidential nominee, and it is essential for candidates to adapt to the rules and expectations. In the end, Biden survived because his challengers fragmented their efforts.

In chapter 2, Theodore Sheckels focuses on the 2020 party conventions. Of course, COVID-19 drastically and historically impacted the conventions, moving them to virtual and online events. As a result, from a rhetorical perspective, both conventions were much the same as their predecessors in terms of the deliberative, epideictic, and constitutive goals. However, production values came more to the forefront of consideration. Trump enjoyed a short-lived "bounce" in the polls. In 2020, both parties were generally successful in accomplishing their goals. It seems Trump may have swayed some undecided voters, whereas Biden called upon supporters for action in opposing Trump.

Ben Voth examines the debates of 2020 to include the primary debates and the presidential debates in chapter 3. The Democrat primary debates featured one of the largest onstage debates in American history, with twelve candidates. The primary debates exposed the divide between the more moderates among the Democrats and the more left or socialists wing of the party. The general election debates were largely structured where moderators actively checked the incumbent president and provided valuable benefits to the challenger. Three planned debates became just two debates. Although Trump did better in the second debate, journalist moderators largely reduced them to confront press conferences. Voth concludes the chapter with ten suggestions and reforms that could improve debates with the goal of understanding policy and differences between the candidate.

Political advertising in the 2020 presidential campaign, like everything else, was impacted by the social context of division, social unrest, and the pandemic. Perhaps surprisingly, John Tedesco and Scott Dunn found that because of the pandemic and Americans spending more time at home, the campaigns relied on advertising more heavily in 2020 than in 2016 to reinforce and mobilize voters. The election cycle set a record of spending across television, radio, and digital platforms. Tedesco and Dunn provide an overview of advertising expenditures by campaigns and political action committees and analyses of the major themes and strategies of the Biden's and Trump's campaigns. They identify the themes in ads that revealed the personal qualities, accomplishments, and issue positions candidates wanted to promote and the unfavorable aspects of their opponents. Interestingly, the attack ads were less personal than in 2016. Trump relied on more contrast and comparative ads compared to Biden's positive ads providing reasons for supporting his candidacy. The authors conclude with implications and questions for consideration for the 2024 presidential campaign.

The role and influence of social media continue to grow and now virtually dominates electoral politics. John Hendricks and Dan Schill review the role and impact of social media in the 2020 presidential election. They provide a detailed look at the use of digital media in both campaigns. In addition, they focus on the influence of specific platforms and the problematic issue of the spread of misinformation. The authors conclude with the need to find solutions to the problems of misinformation and deceptive practices on social media in campaigns.

In chapter 6, I provide an overview of the issues and characterizations of how the news media covered the 2020 presidential campaign. In doing so, it is essential to understand the transformation of the practice of journalism in America and the increasing influence of social media. In a survey of news articles and opinion pieces about media coverage, five themes emerged. Unfortunately, the media, broadly defined, are partners in the growing division and polarization of America. Tribal and partisan journalism with the self-appointed censors of social media impact who runs, who elected, and even the nature of our democracy.

Lisa Burns and Courtney Marchese provide an interesting and insightful examination of political branding in the presidential campaign in chapter 7. Not surprisingly, Trump and Biden presented very different brands. They analyze how esthetics contributed to the branding efforts of the campaigns by examining the visual messaging strategies represented in their design choices, social media imagery, and merchandising. Trump's rugged individualism and antipolitician narrow focus kept his messaging consistent, appealing, and motivating his base. Biden's broader appeal capitalizing on anti-Trump sentiment allowed his campaign to reach a wider base as well as independent voters. Digital engagement with voters requires attention to design- and image-based messaging strategies. The authors argue that design- and image-based messaging strategies will increase in importance as political branding must adapt to the digital age.

In chapter 8, Emily Contois explores the politics of food in the 2020 presidential campaign. It is the news media that gives attention to stories that focus on local specialties offered in dinners, state fairs, and the mishaps of improperly eating a hotdog, pizza, or Philly steak sandwich. After discussing how the candidate enhances authenticity through food and dining choices, Contois further examines how food's symbolic meaning constructs an identity for candidates and voters. She concludes with how actual food policy shapes political campaigns and argues that food issues should be more central to candidate messaging and media coverage in campaigns.

Cayce Myers examines the impact of campaign finance on the 2020 presidential campaign in chapter 9. Fundraising efforts by both parties were sophisticated and targeted, utilizing social and digital media for both large and small donations. Presidential and congressional races spent double that of 2016 for a total of $14 billion. The number of small donations is growing and becoming a larger portion of campaign spending. Technology allows for the mining and aggregation of contributor data that enhances and maximizes donations. In 2020, Democrats maintained the advantage in fundraising, and the pandemic had little effect upon either party's efforts. For Democrats, the importance of fundraising was very apparent during the primary season, especially with so many candidates. When looking across congressional and Senate races, money alone is not enough to win. Candidate quality and message still very much matter.

The study of political campaign communication focuses on the elements of the political environment, messengers, messages, channels of communication (print, radio, television, social media, and so on), audience, and effects. In the final chapter, Henry C. Kenski and Kate Kenski explain the presidential vote in 2020 by examining the overall political communication environment, the electoral rules of the election (including the Electoral College), the importance of party identification's relationship to the vote, an overview of how the candidates were perceived on favorability and temperament, and the demographic bases of the presidential vote. The public went into the election polarized, in the middle of a pandemic with historic early and mail-in voting. Biden benefited from independent voters and defectors among previous Trump supporters. His support improved over Hillary Clinton's performance among Democrats, liberals, and women.

There is no question that this election campaign will generate a great deal of analysis and scholarship, especially in light of the political environment and the postelection controversies culminating in the events of January 6, 2021. As already mentioned, I would offer a word of caution that these chapters are an early and first look at the election. I look forward to future scholarship focusing on this election. We live in one of the most politically polarized times in our nation's history. It appears that the nation is in a time of political realignment, generational transition, and continued communication technological advancements. The form and nature of our human interaction and mediated communication impact who runs, who is elected, how we are governed, and the very culture and identity of our nation. Presidential campaigns communicate and influence, reinforce and convert, motivate, and educate. Former mentor and early scholar of political communication Bruce Gronbeck argued that campaigns "get leaders elected, yes, but ultimately, they also tell us who we as a people are, where we have been and where we are going; in their size and duration they separate our culture from all others, teach us about political life, set our individual and collective priorities, entertain us, and provide bases for social interaction."[5]

As I have argued in the past in nearly every volume dealing with political communication, I believe strongly that political communication scholars should remember that *more* communication does not mean *better* communication. More technology does not mean more *effective* communication. For well over 200 years, America has incrementally and too slowly tried to move toward a more "inclusive" democracy. We have also witnessed unparalleled advances in communication technologies beyond belief just a decade ago. Yet, for well more than a quarter of a century during a time of increased opportunity for participation and information, sadly, citizen political awareness, knowledge, and understanding has declined. A democracy cannot stand without an informed and engaged citizenry.

The central task is how to cultivate an active and democratic citizenry. The challenges are real. Civic responsibility and initiative should once again become a keystone of social life. It is my hope that perhaps by better understanding the role and process of communication in presidential campaigns, we may somehow improve the quality of our "national conversations."

Acknowledgments

I have had the privilege to edit over twenty volumes over the years. There are always challenges working with a very smart, busy, and diverse group of scholars. However, I have actually come to enjoy the process. This project was no exception. Since 1992, I have edited a volume on the presidential campaigns from a communication perspective. The analyses go beyond the quantitative facts, electoral counts, and poll results of the elections. Each chapter focuses on a specific area of political campaign communication. This project brought together colleagues and friends, "new" and "old." All the contributors are accomplished scholars and are recognized as experts in their area of analysis. Virtually all of the contributors have participated in at least five of the previous volumes, several in all six. I am most fortunate to work with such an outstanding group of scholars. Once again, the contributors have made this a most rewarding and enjoyable endeavor. I genuinely appreciate their participation in this volume. I also value their friendship.

I want to thank my colleagues in the School of Communication at Virginia Polytechnic Institute and State University (Virginia Tech). As now a continuing and long-term administrator of various sorts over the years, I am grateful to my colleagues for their continued collegiality and encouragement, as well as for their recognizing the importance of maintaining an active research agenda. Thanks also to Robert Sumirchrast, Dean of the Pamplin College of Business, whose support allows my continued association with the Department of Marketing and the college. I am also most grateful to Lura Belmonte, Dean of the College of Liberal Arts and Human Sciences, who understands the importance of the "right mix" that makes the job of School Director a privilege and pleasure. I am fortunate, indeed. They both are outstanding mentors and administrators.

Finally, as always, countless thanks to my wonderful wife, Rachel, a true blessing, friend, colleague, and partner in my life. And, I also must pay homage to my now-grown sons, Bobby and Chris, who have their own wonderful spouses Christen and Sarah. The boys and Rachel have always been tolerant of the countless hours in the study, perhaps too tolerant and too many hours. Together with the five, plus our dog, little Abby girl, enrich and fulfill every moment of my life.

POLITICAL CAMPAIGN COMMUNICATION IN THE 2020 PRESIDENTIAL CAMPAIGN

Chapter 1

Setting the Stage

Surfacing for 2020

Craig Allen Smith and Kathy B. Smith

Election to the presidency requires winning a majority of the electoral votes awarded via states' general elections. Access to all state ballots is automatic only for Republican and Democratic nominees who are selected through their parties' primary and caucus processes. First, however, one has to reach the caucuses and primaries prepared to compete for the nomination, and that part of the process is known as "surfacing." The purpose of this chapter is to explain the theoretical nature of the surfacing puzzle and to assess the 2020 candidates' approaches to it.

TRENT'S THREE DIMENSIONS OF "SURFACING"

Judith S. Trent defined "presidential surfacing" in 1978 as "the series of predictable and specifically timed rhetorical transactions which serve consummatory and instrumental functions during the pre-primary phase of the campaign."[1] Rhetorical transactions trade symbols for resources such as attention, affiliation, money, and votes. Predictable rhetorical transactions include speaking, fundraising, polling, advertising, organizing, and briefing the media.[2]

Trent identified three instrumental rhetorical functions of surfacing: establishing expectations of the candidates, the emergence of important issues or themes of the campaign, and determining frontrunners and serious contenders.[3]

Establishing Rules and Expectations

"Any attempt to understand 'surfacing,'" Trent wrote, "must begin by viewing the concept within the total context of a campaign and within the constraints imposed on the . . . scene by party and federal rules changes."[4] Such rules are themselves rhetorical creations: verbal constructions developed, authorized, and enforced by parties, legislatures, and courts to constrain the thoughts, choices, and actions of candidates and their supporters.[5]

Trent wrote that the Federal Election Campaign Act of 1974 and the Democrats' McGovern–Fraser reforms changed the character of surfacing.[6] Therefore, "any rhetorical examination of . . . the first act . . . ultimately becomes a study of the ways in which candidates accepted or did not accept, understood or did not understand the constraints and functions of the drama."[7]

Thus, when Trent wrote of "establishing expectations of the candidates" she was referring to the changing legal and procedural requirements set for them by those regulating the electoral process and to candidates' abilities to understand, to accept, and to adapt their rhetorical transactions to those legal and procedural requirements. Because election campaigns (unlike social movements) are rule-governed rhetorical activities, those changing rules define the instrumental functions that candidates must perform.

Many legal and procedural requirements changed during the ten presidential elections since 1976: the rise of political action committees (PACs and super-PACs), additional campaign finance legislation, court decisions, party formulae for allocating delegates, the primary calendars, primary debates, and the development of criteria for inclusion in them. Candidates' understanding and acceptance of those changing constraints shape their strategic choices and the timing of their actions.[8]

Emerging Issues and Themes

The second function of surfacing is the development of issues and themes. Trent wrote:

> As the early *candidates* crisscross the country, they begin to come to grips with the issues which are on *people's* minds, begin to address themselves to these issues, begin to formulate "solutions" to the problems which seem compatible with popular perception, and with the help of the *media* begin translating these problems or positions into national issues (emphasis added).[9]

The interdependent actors performing those functions have themselves evolved as surfacing became a three-year national conversation.

Participants in our national political election conversations and interactions include campaigners, citizens and reporters. The latter serve as "narrators" of events and electoral process. Each participant has their own unique and specific agenda.[10] The campaigner's role is performed by considerably larger teams than we saw in the 1970s. Ten presidential campaign cycles developed issue polling, demographic analysis, issue PACs, and other ways for campaigners and citizens to share their problems and concerns, hopes and dreams, and likes and dislikes. Citizens now cluster into a variety of publics with varying degrees of organization, ideological commitment, identity, money, time, and volunteers. The national media Trent described have become a variety of reporters—journalists, scholars, pundits, pollsters, entertainers, and bloggers—who, like the chorus in Greek tragedies, observe and narrate the campaign for their audiences.[11]

Aspiring candidates need rationales for running that differentiate them from one another, citizens wonder which candidates share their concerns, and reporters need the dramatic tension generated by those conflicting rationales. Some candidates' rhetorical transactions articulate widespread public concerns, whereas others try to cultivate public concern for less appreciated problems. Some argue that leaders are not addressing the important problems, but when those leaders seem to be handling the important problems, campaigners often redefine the problems.

This issue surfacing is important from three theoretical perspectives.[12] Agenda-setting research suggests that the sheer amount of media coverage a topic receives influences the perception of importance of the topic. The more the media focuses and mentions an issue or topic, the more likely citizens will view the topic or issue as a factor for determining support or opposition of a campaign. Framing research suggests that this coverage provides audiences with alternative definitions and narratives that contextualize their choices. Priming research suggests that this coverage orients audiences toward some preferences and behaviors rather than others. So when aspirants can attract substantial media coverage of their positions, they can reframe public perceptions of problems, alter the agenda of public concerns, and prime their audiences for voting.

But agenda-setting theory was new in the 1970s. When its theorists argued that citizens perceive as most important those topics most reported in the media, they were talking about a more homogeneous media environment than we have today. When Trent explored surfacing in the mid-1970s, Americans got their news from newspapers, radio, and three prime-time network newscasts. But changes in the media environment were lurking. As radio listeners valued the clarity of their music, they turned to FM stations, leaving AM radio to find a new format. Political talk shows featuring conservatives such as Rush Limbaugh became popular in the 1980s. The Cable News Network (CNN) was not founded until 1980, with CNBC, Fox News, MSNBC, and others still to come. Then came personal computers and social media. By the turn of the century, Americans could choose how and where to find their news, and their choices created differentiated audiences.[13]

The newer media fragmented the national audience. Topics covered in one fragment of the media environment cannot set the agenda for citizens who ignore it, although some news sources can influence indirectly other sources' news agendas. Because every medium is a link among some citizens, some campaigners, and some narrators (but not others), our changing patterns of media use have changed the interface of candidates and issues in ways not visible from the 1970s. Because we now get our news from a variety of sources, our agendas are set, our issues are framed, and our behaviors are primed by different news sources. Put differently, a fragmented and polarized media environment now sets divergent agendas, frames different issues, and primes different behaviors for their audiences. Today, we must consider the interface between issues and media by asking which citizens learn about which problems from which reporters.

Trent did not suggest metrics for tracking issues and themes. One such metric is the Gallup organization's monthly report on citizens' perceived "Most Important Problems."[14] By comparing Gallup's polls over time, we can see how the surfacing conversation influenced the national issue agenda. In addition, the Pew Research Center's reports on politics and media use in the United States suggest which citizens rely on which news sources.[15] By combining Pew and Gallup analyses, we can see which audiences learn about which problems from which news outlets, thereby setting their agendas, framing their problems, and priming their responses.

Determining Serious Contenders

Trent's third surfacing dimension was "the process of selecting front runners and separating serious contenders from the not-so-serious."[16] This entailed "persuading the national media that one is a viable enough candidate to deserve attention."[17] So the same national narrators who shaped the issue conversation also anointed the parties' frontrunners. But the McGovern–Fraser reforms and the 1974 financing law convinced Trent that "Quite apart from persuading the national media that one is a front runner . . . a candidate now must emerge from the surfacing period as a possible leading contender through successful grass roots organizing and fund raising."[18] Therefore, visibility is necessary for surfacing but viability for the primaries is the goal, and viability requires endorsements, funding, and grassroots organizing sufficient to register in public opinion polls.

Achieving viability for the primaries requires progress on a variety of instrumental functions including understanding the laws and rules for campaigning, announcing the candidacy, building a campaign staff, creating an issue agenda, raising money, recruiting volunteers, establishing contacts and a media presence, and registering in public polling.[19] Some campaigners perform those instrumental functions well enough to survive and advance to the primaries, but many do not.

Trent used the 1976 New Hampshire campaign to study how candidates positioned themselves for subsequent primaries. Jimmy Carter won that

primary after campaigning in Iowa, making him the first candidate to surface in Iowa. By 1988, the Iowa precinct caucuses for county delegates had
become a significant surfacing moment. For the next eight cycles, Iowa
played a significant role in candidate surfacing without directly allocating
any of Iowa's convention delegates. Although a first-place finish in Iowa
won no delegates, nobody finishing below fifth in Iowa has ever been
nominated. Despite widespread criticism of Iowa's byzantine process, low
turnout, and racially unrepresentative voters, most campaigners sought to
validate or to jump-start their national campaigns in Iowa.

Campaigners began visiting Iowa shortly after the midterm elections
because they could meet local influentials and mobilize supporters for the
lightly attended precinct caucuses. After George W. Bush won the 2000
electoral vote despite losing the popular vote, Democrats almost immediately
went to Iowa. Aspiring candidates now begin surfacing in Iowa as soon as the
last presidential vote is in.

Iowa's role in surfacing raised another question: how does one surface for Iowa? Primary debates came earlier and earlier. But, who could
debate? Attention soon turned to qualifying for the debates that could
influence Iowa that could influence New Hampshire that could influence
later primaries.

In short, Trent's notion of identifying serious contenders has endured but
its dynamics have evolved. In the 1970s, the media anointed frontrunners
by mentioning them and assigning their best reporters to cover them. Their
choices were informed by the opinions and endorsements of party leaders and
by-polls. Over ten presidential campaigns, the number and variety of national
and state polls have exploded.

Trent did not suggest a metric for identifying serious contenders. But
today, we can use four available metrics. One is candidates' fundraising success as reported quarterly to the Federal Election Commission.[20] A second
metric is the number of endorsements from elected officials such as those
aggregated by *538.com*.[21] The final two are national and Iowa polls as aggregated into RealClearPolitics' rolling average of recent polls that corrects for
imbalances among conflicting polls.[22] By considering the aspiring candidates' rankings on endorsements, fundraising, national and Iowa polling, we
can see which candidates are meeting the instrumental surfacing functions to
achieve viability.[23]

In short, we are about to explore the ways in which a three-year national
conversation among citizens, campaigners, and reporters reshaped for 2020,
the legal and procedural campaign environment, citizens' perceived problems and preferred media for information about them, and the candidates'
instrumental success in attracting endorsements, funding, and polling support
nationally and in Iowa.

WHAT WERE THE RULES AND
EXPECTATIONS FOR 2020?

The process of understanding, accepting, and adapting to the laws and rules begins by considering how a majority of the party's convention delegates are to be won.

Republican Rules for 2020

The Republican rules for 2020 allocated 2,440 of their 2,550 convention delegates through primaries and caucuses. Although contests after April 1 could be winner-take-all, more than enough delegates for nomination were available in the earlier proportional primaries and caucuses. State formulae could require anywhere from 20 percent of the votes to 50 percent to qualify for delegates.[24] The threshold for Republican challengers was very high.

Republicans in thirty-seven states changed their rules in ways that facilitated renomination. Five states—South Carolina, Arizona, Kansas, Nevada, and Alaska—canceled their primaries, effectively awarding all of their delegates to President Trump. The 2020 Republican rules clearly disadvantaged challengers to their incumbent.

Democratic Rules for 2020

Democrats responded to their 2016 defeat by acting on Sanders' complaints about "Superdelegates"—the elected representatives and party officials who had made up 15 percent of the 2016 delegates. The 2020 rules renamed those officials "automatic delegates" and did not allow them to vote on the first ballot, meaning that a first-ballot nomination would depend entirely on someone winning a majority of the delegates through primaries and caucuses. Delegates would be proportionately distributed among all candidates surpassing 15 percent in a primary or caucus; candidates below 15 percent received no delegates.

Rather than discouraging challengers, the Democrats' 2020 rules made it even more difficult for any candidate to clinch the nomination. They scheduled as their first four contests Iowa, New Hampshire, Nevada, and South Carolina that combined to offer only 7.7 percent of the delegates needed for the nomination. If one candidate could win 86 percent of the votes in all four states, they would have only 155 of the 1,991 required delegates (assuming that they survived until Iowa's June state convention to collect their Iowa delegates). But mathematically, the 15 percent threshold meant that as many as six different candidates in each of the four states could win delegates.

In short, Democrats ensured that surfacing would continue until the delegate-rich primaries would be held in March. Two strong candidates could face a protracted battle. But three or more serious contenders could deny anyone a first-ballot majority and force a second convention ballot on which the 716 automatic delegates (17 percent of the new total) could vote.

The Democrats coupled their delegate rules with criteria for inclusion in their debates. Participation in the June 2019 debate(s) required candidates to poll only 1 percent in three authorized national or early-state polls or to have donations from at least 65,000 individuals (with at least 200 from 20 different states).[25] Mathematically, as many as 100 aspirants could meet the polling requirement and fundraisers could adapt to the rules. Twenty aspirants qualified for the first two nights of debate. The rules became increasingly stringent, with invitations to the November 2019 debate extended only to candidates with donations from at least 165,000 donors and 3 percent support in national polls or 5 percent in the first four states.[26] These criteria formalized fundraising and polling as instrumental goals of Democratic surfacing in 2020.

The parties' rules set different stages for aspiring candidates. Any Republican challenging the president for renomination would need to win 20–50 percent of the votes in the proportional state primaries to win any convention delegates at all. Then, they would need to defeat the president in proportional and winner-take-all primaries by a margin sufficient to overcome his lead from the five states that canceled their primaries. The president would need to satisfy only 50–80 percent of Republican primary voters to fend off any challenge, and his approval among Republicans averaged 87 percent.[27]

The Democrats provided a very different path. They would need only 1 percent in selected polls or 65,000 donors to debate, but later those standards would become more stringent. Then, they would need to outlast their competitors to win at least 15 percent in four diverse states (that offered few delegates to matter) in order to compete in the delegate-rich March primaries. Those who understood and accepted the Democratic rules realized that they needed to reach March with the resources needed to campaign nationwide.

WHICH MEDIA REPORTED WHICH ISSUES TO WHOM IN 2020?

The emerging issues and themes for 2020 occurred in a media environment unimaginable in the 1970s. Let us consider the problems and the news sources through which citizens learned about them.

The Most Important Problems

When Trump was elected, Gallup found four Most Important Problems: the general economy (16 percent), dissatisfaction with government (13 percent), jobs (9 percent), and race relations (8 percent).[28] But, there was no consensus on the importance of those problems, with 54 percent of Americans naming other problems.

Given the Republican rules and the president's approval among Republicans, Trump could run on his strength—the economy. But partly because of his success, fewer Americans considered either the economy or jobs to be "most important problems" by the end of 2019.

On the other hand, by late 2019, "dissatisfaction with government" had doubled to 27 percent and took first place as an impeachment vote loomed. Gallup found increased dissatisfaction on both sides of the aisle because each party was dissatisfied with the other's governing.[29]

Although the percentage of respondents naming race relations as most important dropped 2 percent, it advanced it to the third most important problem.[30] Joining dissatisfaction with government and race relations in the four most important problems were immigration (second at 18 percent) and health care (fourth at 5 percent).[31]

The Democratic surfacing conversation did less to alter the issue rankings than to redefine three issues. First, Trump had run on his plan to build a border wall paid for by Mexico, and he later stoked fears of immigrant caravans approaching our border. But, Democratic surfacing redefined the immigration issue to highlight the Trump administration's separating of families at the border that "put children in cages" as well as his immigration bans that were overruled by the courts.

Second, Democrats had spent a decade defending Obamacare from Republicans' efforts to "repeal and replace" it. But as Obamacare's shortcomings became increasingly apparent, some surfacing Democrats sought to replace it with Medicare for All. Their arguments cultivated Democrats' concerns about health care in a way that left Obamacare under attack from Democrats as well as Republicans. In response, several Democrats continued to defend Obamacare by suggesting repairs and improvements.

Third, as the president touted his economic success, Democrats redefined that issue as well. Conceding that economic indicators had improved, they argued that the benefits were poorly distributed throughout the country. Trump's economy, they argued, was making the rich richer and the poor poorer. Fewer citizens expressed economic concerns in late 2019, but those concerns were changing. But the reframing of issues was not reported universally.

The Media Environment for 2020

By 2019, Americans lived in a fragmented media environment and learned about different problems. The Pew Research Center studied Americans' preferred news sources in late 2019 and found that 18 percent of Americans got their news from social media.[32] Among other media, Fox News was the most relied upon (16 percent), followed by CNN (12 percent); NPR (5 percent); ABC, NBC, and MSNBC (tied at 4 percent); CBS (3 percent); and *The New York Times* (2 percent). But notably, Fox News was preferred by 93 percent of Republican-leaning citizens, with all other sources preferred by Democratic-leaning citizens. Republican leaners also watched the three network newscasts (the only national television news available when Trent studied surfacing), but they were less reliant on them than were Democratic-leaning viewers. In addition to the network newscasts, Democratic-leaning citizens preferred getting their news from MSNBC (95 percent), *The New York Times* (91 percent), NPR (87 percent), and CNN (79 percent).[33]

Citizens' news preferences were reflected in their reported trust and distrust. Pew found that 66 percent of liberal Democrats trusted *The New York Times*, as opposed to 10 percent of conservative Republicans. Rush Limbaugh was the third-most trusted source for conservative Republicans but the second-most distrusted source among liberal Democrats.[34] Their findings suggest that polarized audiences rely upon and trust different news sources that necessarily set different agendas, frame problems differently, and prime different behaviors.

Clearly, the 1970s media environment for surfacing had fragmented and realigned into four identifiable news cultures. As President Trump campaigned for reelection, those inclined to support him watched Fox News, listened to Limbaugh, and saw some network newscasts. Those who opposed Trump watched MSNBC and CNN, listened to NPR, read *The New York Times*, and watched some network newscasts. In between, many Americans watched the network newscasts and generally ignored the niche news sources favored by pro- and anti-Trump camps. Meanwhile, more people got their news from selective social media sites. As we divided our attention, we heard divergent narratives about different candidates and different problems.

The rules that routed President Trump and his 87 percent Republican approval toward renomination found Fox News as the perfect channel to reach his supporters who watched and trusted it. This was an ideal pathway to the nomination, but because only 16 percent of Americans watched Fox News it did not bode as well for the general election campaign. As Democratic rules fostered a wide-open contest, Democratic-leaning citizens turned to a variety of trusted news sources, including MSNBC, CNN, NPR, and *The New York Times*, but not Fox News.

In short, Americans turned to multiple news sources to learn about different issues and candidates. The fragmented media environment and changes in Gallup's "Most Important Problem" set the perceptual frameworks for the events of 2020. Narratives of Trump's impeachment and acquittal fueled dissatisfaction with the government in different ways for different audiences. Soon COVID-19 would further increase the salience of health care concerns while triggering an economic collapse that further increased the salience of jobs and economic problems. Later, the killing of George Floyd and subsequent protests increased the salience of race relations. All of those problems would look different to different audiences because they generated competing narratives in virtually discrete media environments.

WHO WERE THE SERIOUS CONTENDERS FOR 2020?

Campaigns derive from incumbency. Is there a sitting president unchallenged for (re)nomination? In the last 20 elections, incumbents were 11–4 as Johnson, Ford, Carter, and Bush were challenged for renomination and lost.[35] Both parties have presumptive frontrunners, one of whom may be the incumbent; everyone else has an uphill climb.

The Incumbent: President Trump

Incumbents must unify their base and discourage challengers. President Trump solidified his base from the start and punished "disloyal" Republicans. Although his job approval languished below 50 percent well into primary season, his Republican support averaged 87 percent well into 2020.[36] William Weld, Joe Walsh, and Mark Sanford ran but gained no traction; Weld somehow won an Iowa delegate, but Trump won all the rest and cruised to renomination.

The president criticized his intelligence agencies, spoke of "Deep State" opposition conspiracies, blasted Democrats and liberals, undercut and fired his own appointees, and sent provocative tweets that all combined to generate critical mainstream news coverage. That heavy criticism enabled him to tell his base that they were under attack. That master narrative framed various events—the government shutdown over funding for the border wall, the Mueller investigation of Russian interference in 2016, the confirmation hearings for Brett Kavanaugh, and the impeachment trial over Ukraine—and challenged Republican leaners to rally around him or lose power. Those who might abandon him would face Trump supporters' wrath in their primaries. By the time COVID-19 spread, Republicans had no alternative to their incumbent, even if followers of the Lincoln Project and Republican Voters Against Trump wanted one.

Trump's 2020 surfacing demonstrates the power of incumbency and its elasticity. Incumbents need not tout their accomplishments if they can blame others for thwarting their efforts. Incumbents need neither independents nor opponents to surface; they need their base. Incumbents, who cultivate among their allies a fear of losing power, can consolidate ambivalent supporters. They need not do much else to surface and win renomination.

The Frontrunner: Joe Biden

Not all challengers to an incumbent start from scratch. Atop the first major surfacing poll (conducted in October 2018) were Joe Biden (33 percent) and Bernie Sanders (13 percent), followed by Kamala Harris (9 percent) and Elizabeth Warren (8 percent).[37] Frontrunners enjoy an advantage, but they often stumble when votes are cast.

Indeed, Joe Biden had twice failed to survive the surfacing phase, but he now had eight years of experience as Obama's vice president. By May of 2019, Biden still led comfortably in the national and Iowa polls as well as endorsements. But three concerns dogged him. One was that Biden had never survived the surfacing stage. Second, Biden had a reputation for misstatements. Finally, he was an old white male striving to build a coalition with the young, nonwhites, and females. Those concerns undermined his fundraising until donors could see results.

As the Democratic frontrunner, Biden needed to weather the storm of challenges. Televised debates have been unkind to incumbents and frontrunners; experienced and inexperienced candidates often appear comparable as time constraints hamper, requiring shallow answers, quips, and attacks. Nevertheless, Biden's endorsement lead increased, and his national lead over Sanders remained at 10 percent in December. But in Iowa, Biden fell to third behind Buttigieg and Sanders. Could Biden as frontrunner survive a mere top-five Iowa finish or would he again collapse? Twenty-seven other Democrats were poised to surface.

The "Also Rans"

Among the twenty-eight aspiring Democrats, five (Wayne Messam, Mike Gravel, Seth Moulton, Richard Ojeda, and Deval Patrick) never qualified for debates and could be considered candidates only by charitable observers. Did they not appreciate the rules or did they fail to meet them? Patrick announced his candidacy late in 2019 when it was too late to become viable.[38]

Thirteen aspirants qualified for some debates: Eric Swalwell, John Hickenlooper, Kristen Gillibrand, Jay Inslee, Michael Bennet, Steve Bullock, John Delaney, Beto O'Rourke, Tulsi Gabbard, Tim Ryan, Bill DeBlasio, Marianne Williamson, and Julian Castro. The presence of so many marginal candidates in debates demonstrated the inclusive nature of the Democrats' rules. Most of those debaters had their moments, but ultimately all failed to surface as viable candidates even for the early contests. That produced a Top Ten.

Michael Bloomberg's Paid Media

Michael Bloomberg ranked tenth on our combined metrics because he ranked last in fundraising. Instead, Bloomberg read the rules and chose to circumvent them. As a former Republican, mayor of New York-turned-independent, Bloomberg was positioned to attract non-Democrats for November, but that would require ballot access in all states and the major-party nominations were the best pathway to that. Recognizing that he would begin with few Democratic endorsements or supporters, his strategy was to reach the big March primaries by sidestepping fundraising, the primary debates, the Iowa precinct caucuses, and even the primaries in New Hampshire, Nevada, and South Carolina. Bloomberg, therefore, committed a billion dollars of his personal funds to his campaign rather than pursuing individual donors.[39] His barrage of advertisements propelled him to fifth in national polls and eleventh in Iowa polls and endorsements by December 2019.

But Bloomberg's strategy worked too well. How could the Democratic National Committee keep the #10 candidate out of their debates simply because he would not take money from donors? Faced with the new reality, the DNC waived its fundraising criterion and added Bloomberg to the last two debates. And that proved fatal.

Bloomberg's debate performances were disappointing. The Republican mayor of New York turned independent and now Democrat did not seem to fit with the others. His style grated with some, and his policies with others. The debates burst the suspense of his March face-off with the survivors. Although his campaign never fully recovered, Bloomberg's issue ads crossed the media environments and contributed to the issue-surfacing conversation.

The Rich Debaters: Yang and Steyer

Two wealthy businessmen in the Democratic field did take donations. Andrew Yang built his campaign around technology, wry stereotypes of Asian Americans (such as his "I like math" button), and a plan to send every American $1,000 a month forever. He was reserved in early debates, offering his plan as the solution to any problem. By December, Yang stood at 3.2 percent nationally and 2.5 percent in Iowa—soft numbers sufficient to rank sixth nationally and seventh in Iowa. But he ranked eleventh in fundraising and no elected officials endorsed him. Yang was within striking distance of a top-five Iowa finish that could have boosted him into contention.

Tom Steyer's early social media campaign to impeach President Trump cultivated a sizable list of anti-Trump citizens and introduced him to Democrats. But a late start prevented him from participating in the early debates. As the also-rans floundered, Steyer gained support. By December, he ranked first in fundraising but had no endorsements. His 2.5 percent in Iowa tied

Yang for seventh, but he ranked ninth nationally at 1.6 percent. Steyer had lots of money but no endorsements and little public support. Still, he was within striking distance.

Yang and Steyer raised $65 billion, second only to Bernie Sanders. But their combined 4.5 percent national polling and 5 percent in Iowa would not have lifted them into sixth place either nationally or in Iowa, and they had no endorsements at all. Together they raised funds, debated, and enhanced the Democratic conversation, but they failed to win substantial endorsements or public support. Yang and Steyer might have collaborated to enlarge their market share, or they might have attacked one another to clear this lane; they did neither, and both failed to achieve viability.

Black Senators Mattered: Harris and Booker

African-American voters have become crucial to Democratic candidates, as President Obama proved, twice. Democrats had two such aspirants in California Senator Kamala Harris and New Jersey Senator Corey Booker. Moreover, with race relations among the most important problems, both senators seemed serious contenders for the nomination. Both qualified for debates and became important participants in the Democrats' conversation.

Both senators were respected by their peers: among the 28 candidates' endorsements, Harris ranked second and Booker fourth. Both raised significant funds; Harris's $36.9 million ranked sixth and Booker's $18.8 million ranked eighth. Political endorsements and funding are two crucial resources for surfacing, but neither Harris nor Booker was able to parlay those resources into substantial public support.

In October 2018, 5 percent of CNN's respondents liked Corey Booker, but he rarely cracked 3 percent thereafter. Worse, by December, he still polled only 2.3 percent in Iowa, a consistent ninth-place standing in a predominantly white state where he would need to finish in the top five to surface. As other candidates came and went, Booker soldiered on at about 2.8 percent.

Kamala Harris had a different problem. From an initial 9 percent in October 2018, she climbed to 12.6 percent nationally and 13 percent in Iowa by July 2019, both good for fourth place. But by September, she had dropped to 5.7 percent nationally and 8.5 percent in Iowa. By December, she was gone. What happened?

In the second debate, Harris attacked Biden for having worked with segregationist senators decades ago. Her gamble to take down the frontrunner misread the situation and it predictably backfired for two reasons. First, surfacing favors those who pick off the marginal candidates. Harris (12.6 percent) attacked Biden (28.4 percent) and dented his campaign, but he retained first place and her numbers fell by half. She might better have attacked Pete Buttigieg (who trailed her by 1.8 percent and overtook her by September) or even

Booker (unpleasant and risky in another way) to clear the African-American senator lane. Second, the Democratic conversation necessarily revolved around "getting things done" by working across the aisle more effectively than Trump. Yet Harris attacked another senator for working across the aisle. Cooperation is difficult, but challengers must at least sing the hymns of collegiality during the campaign. In this regard, Harris jeopardized the Democrats' narrative and undermined her own image as an effective senator.

Had Harris and Booker joined forces, their endorsements would have tied Biden for first. Their combined fundraising would have placed third behind Sanders and Warren. Their July national polling would have been fourth, and their July Iowa polling would have been tied for second with Elizabeth Warren. Harris and Booker brought considerable resources to the surfacing campaign, but, like Yang and Steyer, they neither collaborated nor attacked each other to clear their lane. Instead, both fell back in the pack (spoiler alert: Harris was selected for vice president by the candidate she had attacked).

Heartlanders in Iowa: Buttigieg and Klobuchar

Minnesota Senator Amy Klobuchar and former South Bend, Indiana, mayor Pete Buttigieg were white Midwesterners with a sense of Iowa Democrats' values and concerns. Who could better use Iowa as a springboard to national campaigns? Klobuchar emphasized her record of moving bills through the Senate. By July, she was fourth in endorsements, by October, she was ninth in fundraising, and by December, her 6.5 percent in Iowa placed her fifth and put her in position for an important top five finish; but nationally she lagged at 2.6 percent.

Buttigieg's personal style and insightful debate comments earned respect, but his limited political experience undermined political endorsements. By November, he ranked seventh in endorsements and sixth in fundraising. By December, he led Iowa (22.5 percent) and his 9.2 percent national polls trailed only Biden, Sanders, and Warren. Buttigieg was poised to surface from Iowa.

Unlike the Yang-Steyer and Harris-Booker lanes, Klobuchar attacked Buttigieg for his inexperience. But she did so by arguing that no woman with his record would have fared so well. Was the problem his inexperience or citizens' sexism? Or was it a dog whistle about the gay candidate? Her attack resonated with many women but blurred her attack on Buttigieg.

The Progressive Planners: Sanders and Warren

Bernie Sanders was an ideological insurgent in 2016—the Democrats' Trump. Never a registered Democrat, Sanders gave Hillary Clinton serious competition in 2016. But unlike Trump, Sanders is an ideologue. Whereas Trump's hodgepodge of positions alienated staunch ideological conservatives, Sanders analyzed every problem in ideological terms, deduced a Democratic Socialist solution, repeated his proposals at every opportunity, and accepted no compromise.

By December of 2019, Sanders ranked second across our metrics. His reliance on small contributions ranked him first in fundraising and his polling ranked second nationally and in Iowa, but despite 29 years in the House and Senate he merely tied for fifth in endorsements. Sanders would surely finish among Iowa's top five to survive and advance.

Elizabeth Warren is a compelling presence, and by December she ranked second in endorsements, third in national polls, fourth in Iowa, and fifth in fundraising. She excels at diagnosing problems and devising policies to solve them. This quality is valuable in academics, bureaucrats, and elected representatives, and it had helped Warren to succeed in all three of those roles.

Warren's signature catchphrase became, "I have a plan for that." Her campaign website proclaimed, "Elizabeth is fighting to . . . [JUMP TO ALL PLANS]" where one would find eighty-one policy plans.[40] Those eighty-one plans unnecessarily complicated her campaign and begged us to ask how President Warren could possibly fight effectively for all of them.

Both Sanders and Warren pushed solutions to problems. But candidates do not solve problems; they strive to win voter support so that they can begin to solve problems. Debate students learn the importance of problem-solution reasoning and that plan attacks can win a debate. To advance a specific plan is to (a) commit to details that will not matter until there is legislation drafted in the congress and (b) to commit to defending attacks from all sides on those details that do not yet matter. Why do that?

Consequently—and this is crucial—*plans invite attacks*. The Democrats had no shortage of debaters, not counting investigative reporters, pundits, and Trump defenders. Every plan invites a feeding frenzy. That is why candidates typically call for directional changes that invite calls for mere specifics. Campaigners should articulate problems and the values important to those whose eventual deliberations would solve them, but Sanders and Warren advocated specific plans that could not matter until specific bills required their signatures.

Consider, for example, Sanders' "Medicare for All" proposal. President Obama had signed the Affordable Care Act, but he neither wrote it nor liked all of its provisions. The bill drew enough support to reach his desk, and that made it historic. Republicans attacked "Obamacare" in 2012, 2014, 2016, and 2018 seeking to "repeal and replace" it, and Democrats defended it. But by 2019, Sanders was the most vocal Democrat opponent to Obamacare. It did not go far enough to provide adequate healthcare for all Americans. He wrote a "Medicare for All" bill that received initial support from several of his fellow Democrat candidates.

Biden understandably defended Obamacare and proposed repairs to it, such as the public option alternative that had been scrubbed from the bill. Buttigieg captured that position in his "Medicare for all *who want it*" phrase that enabled him to echo Sanders while supporting Obama and Biden. It turns out that the Sanders Medicare for All bill provided for the elimination of all other private health insurance that did not appeal to the insurance industry, obviously; neither did it appeal to unions that had negotiated coverage for their members, nor to people satisfied with their coverage plans. Moreover, the bill had insufficient Democratic support to pass in the Senate would take years to institute and would cost trillions of dollars. Sanders' dramatic defense was to say, "I wrote the damn bill"—a catchy but odd way to advocate for it.

The elimination of private insurance is not inherent in the concept of Medicare for All—Medicare recipients can supplement their coverage with private insurance—but the Sanders Bill would have ended that option even for current Medicare recipients. Any candidate could have proposed tabling the Sanders Bill in favor of an amendment to the Medicare Act deleting the words "over 65." By autumn, most Democrats disapproved Medicare for All because they had only the Sanders Bill to consider. Sanders' "damn bill" undercut his ability to win the nomination by narrowing his vision to a specific bill that posed problems. Meanwhile, Biden, Buttigieg, and Klobuchar could use it as a wedge to oppose Sanders and support Obama.

The Sanders and Warren commitments to plans were both their strength and the source of their downfall. Their rhetoric invited others to question the plans that provided the rationales for supporting them. Sanders and Warren might have collaborated to unify progressives or attacked one another to clear their path to nomination; they did neither.

THE HOME STRETCH: NOVEMBER TO MARCH

By November of 2019, Biden led Warren and Sanders, who were dividing progressives. Buttigieg and Klobuchar were working in Iowa with Steyer and Yang right behind. Moreover, Bloomberg stood ready to tackle the survivors when the March primaries would allocate 61 percent of the delegates. But because Democratic rules would distribute state delegates among the candidates who win 15 percent of their primary votes, those three candidates (and more) conceivably could each win enough delegates to block Biden's path to a first-ballot nomination.

In November, Sessam, Messick, and O'Rourke suspended their campaigns, joining Swalwell, Gravel, Hickenlooper, Inslee, Moulton, Gillibrand, DiBlasio, and Ryan. Patrick entered the campaign. Bullock and Harris left in

December; Castro, Williamson, Booker, and Delaney left in January. That officially winnowed the field from 28 to 10 before Iowa.

The February 3 Iowa precinct caucuses were a debacle. Failures of the new reporting app delayed the results for days and further undermined Iowa's credibility with the national press. Buttigieg edged Sanders (26.2 percent to 26.1 percent) to win 14 delegates to 12; Warren, Biden, and Klobuchar rounded out the top five. Sanders and Warren needed only that top-five finish to validate their campaigns but frontrunner Biden could have used more, and questions about his viability increased. Buttigieg had bested Klobuchar despite her legitimate critique of his inexperience.

Buttigieg and Klobuchar needed Iowa's springboard for New Hampshire and beyond. But success in Iowa earns candidates increased national scrutiny from the press and their opponents. Historically, Iowa's winners get four days of momentum before a decline in New Hampshire.[41] Worse, candidates who go all in on Iowa can impoverish their ability to campaign in other states. Klobuchar and Buttigieg urgently needed to parlay their Iowa successes into a New Hampshire win that could attract a massive infusion of funding, endorsements, and volunteers.

President Trump delivered his State of the Union Address on February 4, and the Senate voted to acquit him of the impeachment charges on February 5. That trial had occupied Senators Sanders, Warren, Booker, and Klobuchar when they would otherwise have been campaigning.

On February 13, Sanders edged Buttigieg (25.6 percent to 24.3 percent) for nine New Hampshire delegates each, and Klobuchar (19.7 percent) won six; neither Warren (9.2 percent) nor Biden (8.4 percent) reached the 15 percent cutoff. Sanders won again in the Nevada caucuses on February 22, gaining 24 delegates to Biden's 9 and Buttigieg's 3.

Media coverage increasingly focused on Sanders' wins and Biden's apparent collapse. But in the race to 1,991 Democratic delegates, the score was Sanders 45, Buttigieg 26, Biden 15, Warren 8, and Klobuchar 7 with two thousand delegates yet to be decided. Yang, Bennet, and Patrick left the race, winnowing the field to seven. Next up: South Carolina.

House Majority Whip Jim Clyburn was considered the most influential African-American politician in South Carolina. On February 25, Clyburn issued his much-anticipated endorsement: Biden. "I've known for a long time who I was going to vote for. I'm voting for Joe Biden. South Carolinians should be voting for Joe Biden," said Clyburn. "We know Joe. But more importantly," he said, paraphrasing a Klobuchar line, "he knows us."[42,43,44,45] On February 29, Biden trounced Sanders from 48.6 percent to 19.8 percent and a 39–15 delegate victory in South Carolina. March had arrived.

On March 3—Super Tuesday—sixteen states and territories would vote to proportionately distribute 1,400 delegates. But before they could vote,

Buttigieg and Klobuchar left the race, winnowing the field to four. When the Super Tuesday votes were tallied and the 15 percent cutoff applied, the delegate count was Biden 646, Sanders 554, Warren 53, and Bloomberg 48. Warren and Bloomberg quickly left the race.

Fourteen days had drastically changed the Democratic race. Before Clyburn's endorsement on February 29, the national polls had Sanders leading Biden (29.6 percent to 18.8 percent) with Bloomberg (16.4 percent), Warren (11.8 percent), Buttigieg (11 percent), Klobuchar (4 percent), and Steyer (2.6 percent) playing catch-up. On March 9, Biden led Sanders 53.4 percent to 36 percent. The withdrawals had netted Biden a 34.6 percent increase and Sanders a mere 6.4 percent.

Biden and Sanders—the two frontrunners in CNN's October 2018 survey—had surfaced as the two viable candidates who would slug it out in the remaining primaries. No longer could a third candidate force a second ballot. But the Democratic primaries were quickly overshadowed.

Two thousand cases of a new virus were recorded worldwide, with 67 cases in the United States. As COVID-19 spread in March, it complicated both campaigning and voting. The earlier doubts about Biden seemed to wane, or perhaps doubts about Sanders were growing. Biden led Sanders by some 300 delegates after the Wisconsin primary. Sanders would end his campaign on April 8, making Joe Biden the presumptive Democratic nominee.

CONCLUSIONS

Although the 2020 election cycle was affected by the pandemic, it arrived as the surfacing stage was ending. We can therefore draw several conclusions about the theoretical nature of the surfacing puzzle and the 2020 candidates' approaches to it.

Our first conclusion must be to affirm the enduring political importance of presidential surfacing. The rhetorical functions of presidential surfacing identified by Judith S. Trent in 1978 endured. There can be no alternative to surfacing because no one can campaign until words have codified laws and rules, named candidates and conflicts, attracted staffers and reporters, energized supporters and opponents, gained ballot access, and raised money. The choices of words, media, and audiences are inherently rhetorical. By defining surfacing in functional terms—establishing legal and procedural expectations, emerging themes and issues, and identifying serious contenders—Trent encouraged us to understand the ways that innovative rhetors could respond to predictable rhetorical situations with creative rhetorical transactions.

Our second conclusion is that surfacing for 2020 differed greatly from the surfacing for 1976. Instead of a national media environment, we have a fragmented news environment in which different people learn different things. Instead of a few issues, we have an assortment of important problems as perceived by different sets of citizens, narrators, and candidates. Instead of using New Hampshire to surface for later primaries, candidates had to surface to make the debates. Instead of simply announcing and traveling the 2020, candidates created exploratory committees, built websites, and began fundraising. Instead of New Hampshire being the symbolic, low delegate springboard to the primaries, Iowa, Nevada, and South Carolina shared that role. Indeed, those changes might be enough to convince us that surfacing is no longer the same, were it not for the fact that Trent defined surfacing in enduring functional terms.

The third conclusion is that the parties' rules influenced the outcome. Republican rules helped insulate their incumbent from serious challenges. If their rules had resembled the Democrats' rules—1 percent in the polls and 65,000 donors—Trump might have been tested in primaries. That conversation might have altered the issues. Some Republican leaners might have ventured beyond Fox News. The Republican Party might have written a platform to guide the next four years. But none of that happened, and Donald Trump became the first incumbent president to lose after being unchallenged within his party.

Conversely, the Democrats' rules encouraged challengers through accessible debates, low cutoff for delegates, and four early contests for scant delegates. One might argue that the first four states were a temptation to squander resources that serious contenders would need in March, but how else could they prove themselves serious contenders for March?

Our fourth conclusion is that America is increasingly fragmented. News sources are attracting discrete audiences that cocreate different narratives. We increasingly rely on our self-selected social media for news that feeds our appetites. Then, we vote in primaries—or, at least, the most active partisans vote in their primaries (those in the center mostly watch). All the while the process spirals us toward more fragmentation. Perhaps the Bloomberg campaign provided a real service by advertising across a variety of media outlets. But what future candidate will spend a billion dollars doing that after seeing Bloomberg's experiment fail?

Our fifth conclusion is that candidates need to adapt to the rules and expectations. Trump, Biden, and Sanders were the early frontrunners, and they survived and advanced until March. Some challengers either failed to understand those expectations or failed to make reasonable efforts to meet them. Some people saw in the Democrats' inclusive rules and opportunities for public visibility despite their lack of preparation for the job they sought. In earlier times, those challengers would have been shut down by the party bosses, but today they can use the rules to find the limelight.

A related problem faces people who seek seriously to lead the nation. Rarely do aspirants take down a frontrunner because frontrunners have a head start in familiarity or cash or in credibility among politicians, or possibly all three. Aspirants need not knock out frontrunners as Swalwell and Harris tried to do. Instead, they need to be among the frontrunners when the big-delegate primaries are held. Bloomberg tried to use his money to do that but stumbled in the debates.

Biden survived, in part, because his challengers fragmented their efforts. Four pairs of candidates made it into the top ten. The Rich Debaters, the Black Senators, the Heartlanders, and the Progressive Planners could have pooled their considerable resources to move forward as four substantial factions. In a field of five—Biden, Steyer/Yang, Harris/Booker, Buttigieg/Klobuchar, and Sanders/Warren—all five mathematically could have won 20 percent of the votes and cleared the 15 percent delegate threshold in every state. Doing so might have kept Biden from the nomination. But in all four cases, they failed either to collaborate or to clear the competition from their lane, and ten candidates fragmented the vote and yielded delegates to the frontrunners. Future campaigners—especially Democrats, given their rules—need to better understand the value of strategic retreat to pursue their shared objectives with combined resources.

The 2020 frontrunners—Trump and Biden—advanced and survived some thirty challenges. They did so by better adapting their rhetorical transactions to the rules, to the fragmented media environment, to perceived problems, and to their competitors. Both would go on to get more votes than any other candidate in American history. But even before their votes were certified, the 2024 surfacing conversation had begun.

Chapter 2

The 2020 Conventions

As Productions, a Departure;
as Rhetorical Exercises,
Business as Usual

Theodore F. Sheckels

The quadrennial political party conventions are doubly deliberative, epideictic, and constitutive events, but the balance among these rhetorical qualities
varies. One of the two ways in which the conventions can be deliberative has
so dominated the media's view over the most recent decades that the media
have tried to signal the conventions' insignificance. But the media have been
somewhat blind to all of the rhetorical work that the conventions do; the conventions do not just select the party's nominee.

The traditional deliberative function is, of course, just that—to select nominees. The increasing importance of primaries and caucuses, aided by party
reform measures, has almost eliminated this function.[1] We, after all, have
not seen a second ballot at a convention since 1952. However, even though
the smoke-filled rooms are gone and most delegates are now selected by voters, there is still the theoretical possibility of the nominee being chosen at the
convention, not in advance. The Republicans thought that they might see that
in 2016 because there were so many seeking the nod; the Democrats thought
the same in 2020 with an even larger cast of aspirants. But a single candidate
emerged in both instances, causing some in academe to suggest that political and
media dynamics make it highly unlikely that a single candidate will not emerge.

The other deliberative function is to gain support—to persuade voters to
cast their ballot for the nominees. Vigil has suggested that conventions seek
to facilitate identification between nominees and voters while denying such
a connection between their opponents and voters.[2] This Burkean frame is,
of course, not the only way to parse the persuasive rhetoric: one could consider the logos and pathos or the persuasive quality (i.e. the fidelity) of the
constructed party narrative. Regardless of rhetorical methodology, one could
study and assess the arguments the parties offer to garner support.

The epideictic function is related to this second deliberative one. To win voters, the parties praise themselves and their candidates while blaming the opposition party and its candidates for the ills besetting the nation. The dominance of this kind of partisan rhetoric is what convinced the media that the conventions were not newsworthy, although one might suggest that seeking support through praising and blaming is news, not just propaganda.

The constitutive function is an important one largely not on the media's radar screen.[3] As any student of political history will affirm, the major political parties have evolved. Some would even argue that they have crossed paths, with the once progressive Republicans becoming conservative and the once conservative Democrats becoming progressive. In the 1940–1990 period, there was clearly a moderate-conservative divide in the GOP. With Wilkie in 1940, Dewey in 1944 and 1948, and Eisenhower in 1952 and 1956, the moderates won the nomination on the basis that they could win in November; then, the party moved rightward, climaxing twice with Goldwater in 1964 and Reagan in 1980. Meanwhile, the Democrats saw a leftward drift, culminating with McGovern in 1972, and then, after his disastrous defeat, a good bit of wobbling between centrist (Carter, Clinton) and left-leaning (Mondale, Obama) candidates. Perhaps, on the Democratic side, the battle for the nomination between incumbent Carter and Massachusetts Senator Edward M. Kennedy in 1980 best shows the divide. In such a volatile context, quite often the convention not only reflects the party's definition but does the rhetorical work to define the party. The RNC in 1964 is a good example, as is the 1984 DNC.

So, in examining any set of conventions, a rhetorician should consider these functions. The first deliberative function is, once again, probably irrelevant: we know who the nominees will be—months in advance except for the vice presidential nominee, typically announced weeks in advance. So, a rhetorician has the other three functions to consider: deliberative—i.e., persuading voters; epideictic—praising and blaming in a more ceremonial, less substantive manner; and constitutive—telling Democrats and Republicans who they are. Rarely, however, are the three equally important. So, an initial question is which of the three, deliberative, epideictic, or constitutive, will dominate each party's gathering. And, if the others are present, what is the balance among the rhetorics?

In the convention hall, party faithful address the party faithful. But, in the television era (1948 onward), there has almost always been an awareness of a larger audience watching. Although it is possible that a convention tries to address all in this audience, the reality is that any given gathering will segment that audience and address some a great deal, some a bit, and some not at all. The most usual pattern will have convention speakers addressing the party base more than persuadable others, but the balance varies from year to year.

And, the "persuadable others" might be further divided into demographic categories.

The year 2020, however, raises yet another question—one unique to the year. The year 2020, is, of course, the year of the COVID-19 pandemic, and it initially prompted very different plans from the two parties. The Democrats, scheduled to convene in Milwaukee, chose to stage a largely virtual meeting. The predictable speeches would be given, but there would be no large gatherings, certainly nothing like the grand ones at stadia that Kennedy staged in 1960 and Obama reprised in 2008. The Republicans, scheduled to convene in Charlotte, chose to relocate to Jacksonville when the governor of North Carolina balked. As the COVID-19 pandemic surged or resurged in Florida, the GOP proceeded to plan a "normal" convention. The fact that they were meeting in a large group and the fact that they were largely ignoring the face mask recommendations of governments became something of a political statement that, eventually, Trump had to disavow. Arguing that the upsurge in COVID-19 cases in Florida was something of a surprise, he shifted the gathering to online. The Republicans were weeks behind the Democrats in thinking through the dynamics of an online event. Perhaps to compensate, Trump decided to use the White House and the Washington Monument as backdrops. The former choice represented an unprecedented (perhaps illegal) use of the White House: most incumbents have respected the distinction between being president and being a political party's candidate for president.

Both parties, then, found themselves in the position of putting on a show. One might say that such is the case for all modern conventions, but 2020 would be different. In other years, the parties stage a show, but it occurs in the context of an arena (and sometimes a city where events other than the show are transpiring). The media will also create offstage events by conducting interviews in the convention hall booth or in other locations. And, of course, the media personalities will talk, turning themselves into offstage distractions to the parties' planned show. In 2020, there would be no arena, no city streets, and no booths. Media personalities might conduct competing interviews or talk over the planned show, but the likelihood, looking toward the gatherings, was that the novelty of what the parties were doing would keep their planned show centerstage. There was probably a felt difference on the part of the media between interrupting a news event and interrupting what looks more like a planned television program. They do the first all of the time, but the second would seem odd—like departing from an ongoing Broadway play to interview the choreographer or offer comments on the special effects.

Questions, then, about show *qua* show will be more important than in most years. Yes, one can argue (as I have) that Hillary Clinton put on a better show than Donald Trump in 2016, but the show *qua* show questions, secondary in 2016, will be front and center in 2020.[4]

Related to the necessary modifications prompted by COVID-19 is another matter of media coverage. Historically, the media have been interested in covering a deliberative convention. They have yearned for one that would make big decisions (the identity of the nominees); they have settled for ones where the players were trying to sway voters. The latter was thought in the late 1970s to not be especially newsworthy. The same negative judgment was made by media toward any epideictic function a convention might have, while a constitutive function was not even recognized. Thus, beginning in the late 1970s, the television media reduced coverage. A cynic might argue that the reduction had as much to do with the burgeoning of cable television and the availability of alternative programming. But, either way, media coverage diminished. Then, as cable television news channels developed, it increased again. Now, I would argue it became tiered, with daytime, early evening, and 10 p.m.–11 p.m. EDST as three media zones with different audiences.[5] This zoning affects convention planning—by candidates and media. The year 2020, changed the situation somewhat, for the conventions have chosen to operate more or less in a two-hour block from 9:00 p.m. to 11:00 p.m., but the traditional networks (CBS, NBC, ABC, and Fox) have stuck with their 10:00 p.m.–11:00 p.m. window. The result is that these networks joined the planned program halfway through.

So, in 2020, we had two tiers, not three. Tier one was 9:00–10:00 (beginning a bit earlier for the Republicans), and this was preceded by "talk" on cable channels, which began their advertised coverage at 8:00, not 10:00. Since much of the convention programming is prerecorded and, thus, already viewed by the cable commentators, the "talk" was based on what will indeed occur, not on guesses or a preliminary copy of a speech. So, the 8:00–9:00 period, perhaps termed a "pre-tier," has an odd feel insofar as it was both, in sports terms, pregame coverage AND a report on all the plays and the final score.

Tier one began the show *per se*, but only on cable, with an audience somewhat more politically savvy and somewhat more partisan. Tier two, which is the second half of the show, was on cable and traditional network news. Thus, the audience changed and became somewhat less savvy and somewhat less partisan. This audience change midway through the program presented a planning problem for those staging the conventions. These planners also dealt with the awkwardness caused by some in the audience seeing only the second hour. Imagine if viewers only saw the second half of a television drama. If planners are trying to offer not just the usual "show," which they know will be interrupted by media, but a "show" more likely to be shown with minimal interruptions and, thus, with a higher degree of show *qua* show planning, the fact that the audience will expand and change halfway presented a challenge. Who speaks in the first hour, who in the second. How do you build a theme and, then, build it again? How do you program the precise moment of the shifting (since having the traditional networks join in the middle of a speech or in the middle of a theme would be awkward and not especially effective)? How do you simultaneously build a two-hour momentum and then a one-hour one?

Put another way, without much time for planning, the parties—or the candidates' "people"—in 2020 had to put together more of a true show than ever before with the very unusual constraint of having a mid-show audience shift. This situation required that planners be very media-savvy, and it also required that the critic know a bit more than usual about television and film production techniques. Previous planners, for example, did not have to worry about the basics of cinematography (length of the shot, type of the shot) or editing (fades? jump cuts? match cuts?), but 2020 planners presumably did because they were putting on a two-hour show, not a convention to be covered as a news event. So, one needs to assess what the planners did and how successful their production choices were.

A penultimate question should also be considered. Arguably, Trump's 2016 convention was poorly executed. It had far fewer speakers than the DNC, it had only a loose overall or nightly theme, and it had embarrassing moments, notably Melania Trump's plagiarism on Night One and Texas Senator Ted Cruz's refusal to endorse Trump on Night Two.[6] Given this 2016 failure, would the Trump people "get it right" in 2020?

The questions suggested thus far are what a rhetorician would focus on, but the media are not rhetoricians. The media gravitate to what they perceive as "the story," and their insistence on "the story" being THE story often makes it so. Thus, a last important question to ask of the 2020 conventions is what the media chose to stress—and ignore.

This chapter will thus proceed from DNC to RNC, exploring the following topics: (1) their deliberative function, (2) their epideictic function, (3) the targeted audiences, (4) their constitutive function, (5) their rhetorical success (or failure), (6) their production elements, (7) their success (or failure) as a production, and (8) how media may (or may not) have skewed "the story" by its choices of what to stress in coverage. The chapter will conclude by, first, comparing the two "gatherings" and, second, speculating on how the 2020 conventions will alter future ones.

THE DEMOCRATIC NATIONAL CONVENTION

Deliberative Rhetoric: Arguments for Biden/Harris

Night One (Monday) was announced by its emcee as dealing with three important issues that Trump had failed to address: the COVID-19 pandemic, the economic downturn, and racial injustice. The speeches and presentations were in service of making the twinned argument that a problem exists and Trump has failed. Then, Alabama Senator Doug Jones added the issue of voter suppression, newly prominent because it seemed that the U.S. Postal Service was slowing the mail (or at least making people believe as much). Former First Lady Michelle Obama picked up on the voter suppression issue, arguing that voting was essential, especially on the parts of those who chose not to vote in 2016.

Night Two featured less-focused attacks on Trump's presidency along with tributes to Joe Biden's character. Then, after 10:00 p.m., the focus sharpened and was on healthcare and the conduct of foreign affairs, both arguable areas of Trump's failure. The DNC's approach to issues—and deliberative rhetoric—seemed cumulative: three on Monday, two more on Tuesday, and three more—gun violence, immigration, and women's advancement on Wednesday. Both race relations and economic distress then resurfaced as the DNC began to lose its sharp organization. Thursday repeated earlier arguments and added what the Democrats would do to help veterans and support the LGBTQ community.

Epideictic Rhetoric: Praising Biden, Blaming Trump

There were many emotional moments in the DNC show. Joe Biden was praised repeatedly—for his service, resilience, and empathy. Perhaps more striking were stories of those victimized by racism, the pandemic, and gun violence. Although former Arizona Congresswoman Gabby Giffords, a victim of gun violence, spoke herself, more often the victims' stories were told by surviving family members. Trump was implicitly and explicitly blamed for these victims' plights.

Audiences

The issue appeals make it clear that the DNC had specific groups of voters in mind: African Americans, those suffering because of either the pandemic or the economic downturn, immigrants, women, veterans, and members of the LGBTQ community. The balance among these target groups was not even: African Americans, for example, received much more attention than LGBTQ citizens. The most striking group, however, was none of these but rather disaffected Republicans. There was a parade of Republicans on Monday night (former New Jersey Governor Christine Todd Whitman, former Hewlett-Packard CEO Meg Whitman, former New York Congresswoman Susan Molinari, and former Ohio Governor John Kasich); then, on Tuesday, Sally Yates, who served in the Trump Justice Department, Colin Powell, who served as George W. Bush's Secretary of State, and Cindy McCain, speaking on behalf of her late husband, Arizona Senator (and 2008 GOP nominee) John McCain, reinforced the message. That message was both anti-Trump and pro-Biden, but the pro-Biden part was based on Biden's character and willingness to work across the aisle, not on Biden's policy positions. This Republican presence was sufficiently striking for some progressive Democrats to complain; however, most would probably declare it strategic.

Constitutive Rhetoric

One might argue that focusing attention on an audience of disaffected Republicans would be a distraction from the convention's constitutive rhetoric, but it could also be considered a second instance. Biden's "people" were trying to constitute a nominally Republican group with strong reservations about Trump—"Republicans for Biden"—at the same time they were trying to constitute Democrats along certain lines. The pitch to Republicans, although strategic, might well have stolen time away from the more predictable task, which may have been more difficult than planners forecasted. It was—and is—difficult to assess the extent of a split in the party between a more progressive wing and a more moderate one. If there is indeed a marked split, then the convention's rhetoric, by focusing on Trump's failures, Biden's character, and disaffected Republicans, may have offered both too little reflective of the liberal wing's views and too little that sought to reconcile left and middle in a shared party definition.

Rhetorical Success or Failure

The question of success or failure is, of course, tied to the DNC's goals. The major ones were to depict Trump's presidency as a failure, to highlight Joe Biden's many years of service (readying him to lead), and to stress Joe Biden's character. The material used in the eight-plus hours of televised coverage (four-plus on the traditional networks) seemed to hit on the third more than the first two, and on the first more than the second.

Why? Those planning the DNC knew that, with a stress on all that was wrong in the nation, they ran the risk of staging a very negative convention, one reminiscent of the 2016 RNC. Dumping on Trump over and over would have just made the negative feeling more intense, so they tried to stress Trump's failures without making attacks too much of the televised program. The planners knew that much of Biden's record was boring history and that there were actions in that forty-plus year span that could be spun to Biden's disadvantage absent a lengthy explanation stressing the full context. So, they highlighted a few accomplishments and kept the rest of the Biden record vague. The planners were betting that the character issue would, ultimately, carry the day, because so many voters—even those who had voted for Trump in 2016—had reservations about the president's character.

Polls suggest that the DNC produced a "bounce," but not much of one.[7] Was that an indication of failure? Probably not because, in 2020, so much of the support seemed locked-in by Summer. There simply were not many voters ready to change their minds about either Biden or Trump. "Bounce," then, may well be an irrelevant measure in 2020. More crucial may be how well Biden met the rhetorical goals outlined above.

"The Show"

One watching the DNC had no standard by which to judge it. It seemed to move forward at a good clip—so much so that the networks rarely interrupted for commentary. It also featured a number of well-staged events. Some were effective because of their strong emotional appeal—the daughter of a COVID-19 victim telling the audience that her father's only preexisting condition was support for Trump, Cindy McCain noting her late husband John's praise of Biden's bipartisanship, a Parkland high schooler and Gabby Giffords on gun violence, and Delaware Senator Chris Coons' story (and clip) on Joe Biden's visit to Charleston, South Carolina, after the church shooting there. Some also had both that appeal and a touch of the theatrical—a choir of children singing the National Anthem on Monday, John Legend and Common performing "Glory," thirteen-year-old Braden Harrington's account of how Biden helped him overcome stuttering.

There were many such moments. Perhaps more striking, especially in contrast to the RNC, is how the DNC honored the convention traditions while giving them a new, virtual twist. There were nominating and seconding speeches; there was a roll call of the states. Defeated rivals spoke; former presidents spoke; and the prospective First Lady (and a past one) spoke. Most striking was probably Tuesday night's "Different Kind of Keynote." It was delivered not by one but by multiple up-and-coming members of the party, culminating with defeated Georgia gubernatorial candidate Stacey Abrams. Keynotes run the gamut from philosophical (Jordan in 1976 and 1992) to partisan (Cuomo in 1984 and Richards in 1988).[8] This "different" one fell on the partisan end of the spectrum—and tended to be more focused on specific policy matters than the norm. That the multivoiced keynote may or may not have fit the genre was, however, less important than the fact that the convention honored tradition by having one and that the DNC gave it a polyphonic twist made possible by the gathering's being virtual not live.

"The Show"'s Success or Failure

Hofstra University communication professor Mark Lukasiewicz cited the DNC's variety and energy in assessing it as a production success.[9] Trump's convention, according to Syracuse University television scholar Robert Thompson, suffered from having far too many people walk up to the microphone in Melon Auditorium in Washington, DC.[10] In defense of Trump's gathering, a proponent will argue that the DNC had too many "Hollywood" types, whereas the RNC featured more "average Americans." It is difficult to count the "average" because the term is ill-defined, but both conventions featured many. And, if one counts the DNC's four actress emcees, maybe it did draw more from Hollywood, although the RNC might have drawn more from sports and definitely drew more from the candidate's family. In 2016, the difference in how many spoke and who spoke between the DNC and RNC was dramatic; in 2020, probably not.[11] And, if the DNC had a better flow and fewer at-the-lectern moments, it lacked the presidential ceremonies and the White House backdrop. Both had fireworks: Trump's were more majestic, shot up over the Washington Monument; but Biden's over the top of a Wilmington shopping mall had "average person" appeal. (Wilmington, DE, is not Hollywood.)

Media Skewing

The DNC adhered closely to the announced 9:00 p.m.–11:00 p.m. time slot. Each night, there was a very clear sense of beginning, with the pledge of allegiance and/or the National Anthem and then the introduction of the night's hostess. The DNC used a sequence of American actresses—Eva Longoria, Tracee Ellis Ross, and Kerry Washington, and—adding in some Colbert-worthy humor—Julia Louis-Dreyfuss. The use of a hostess gave the nights a strong sense of being a program. There was also, on the part of planners, a sense of the 10:00 p.m. mark at which media coverage would expand from just cable news to cable and traditional network.

On Monday, viewers heard the National Anthem beautifully sung by a multistate choir of children. Then, they heard Georgia Congresswoman Gwen Moore, Washington, DC, Mayor Muriel Bowser, South Carolina Congressman James Clyburn, and New York Governor Andrew Cuomo. The stress was on crises that Trump was handling poorly. After 10:00 p.m., viewers heard from more prominent Democrats—Michigan Governor Gretchen Whitmer and Minnesota Senator Amy Klobuchar—but other speakers, a set of Republicans and the two who concluded the evening, captured media attention. The Republicans were former New Jersey Governor Christine Todd Whitman, former Hewlett-Packard CEO Meg Whitman, former New York Congresswoman Susan Molinari, and former Ohio Governor John Kasich. They all argued for supporting Democrat Biden over Trump. The two end-of-day headliners were Vermont Senator Bernie Sanders, who followed the genre of a speech by a defeated rival perfectly, and former First

Lady Michelle Obama. Both delivered politically important messages, but Obama received more media attention. She explicitly appealed to those who did not vote in 2016 (including many African Americans) to vote in 2020. By downplaying Sanders, the media might have minimized the sense of a divided party.

On Tuesday, viewers saw and heard a "different kind of keynote." It did some of the rhetorical business a keynote typically does, and it was delivered (as is common) by the up-and-coming. However, the up-and-coming were sixteen-plus young Democrats, culminating with Georgia's Stacey Abrams, who was defeated in the gubernatorial race there amidst charges of voter suppression. Following Abrams, there were speeches from New York Senator Chuck Schumer, Caroline Kennedy and her son, former President Jimmy Carter, former First Lady Rosalyn Carter, and former President Bill Clinton. Each speaker talked about the failures of the Trump administration, Biden's character and the importance of voting in this election. The message blended talk of Trump's failures, Biden's character, and the need to vote (in a context in which voter suppression was feared). As 10:00 p.m. neared, both Biden and Sanders were nominated and seconded, and as the program passed 10:00 p.m., the DNC was moving through a lively roll call of the states. Much occurred that night before 10:00, but much media attention focused on the very brief address New York Congresswoman Alexandria Ocasio-Cortez gave nominating Sanders.

After the roll call, the gathering heard from 2004 nominee John Kerry, former Republican Secretary of State Colin Powell, and the widow of the 2008 Republican nominee John McCain. The number of Republicans speaking at the DNC was drawing some criticism from progressives, so the media focused more on Cindy McCain's presence (and that of other Republicans) than their bipartisan message. Then, all attention focused on Dr. Jill Biden, who did what most future first ladies do: talked about the personal story and personal traits of her husband.[12] Her stress and the media's stress was on the hardships that Joe had experienced and triumphed over.

On Wednesday, the DNC perhaps did not do a good job with the 10:00 p.m. point. The DNC began the night with speakers stressing gun violence, violence against women, and civil rights. As 10:00 p.m. was approaching but still before that time, 2016 nominee Hillary Clinton spoke, and as the traditional networks joined in, House Speaker Nancy Pelosi was speaking. Then, right after 10:00, was Massachusetts Senator Elizabeth Warren. Striking up to 10:10 was that the speakers, regardless of precise topic, were all female—something the media did not choose to stress. Then, viewers heard from Barack Obama, followed, after routine nominating and seconding speeches, by the vice presidential nominee, California Senator Kamala Harris. Obama and Harris both spent much time urging younger voters to vote. Harris, whose speech received both the most attention and most praise, spent time introducing herself to the American people (not unusual for the genre) and then equally praising Biden's character and indicting Trump's character and actions.

The DNC featured many noteworthy speakers. The media focus was therefore somewhat diffuse. However, most stressed as the gathering moved through its initial three days were Michelle Obama, Jill Biden, and Kamala Harris—three women. Curiously pushed a bit into the background were the two Clintons and Barack Obama.

On Thursday, the pre-10:00 p.m. array feature speakers female and male including 2020 presidential aspirant Andrew Yang, Delaware Senator Chris Coons, Atlanta Mayor Keisha Lance-Bottoms, New Jersey Senator (and 2020 aspirant) Cory Booker, Wisconsin Senator Tammy Baldwin, and Illinois Senator Tammy Duckworth. They raised multiple topics. Duckworth talked about combat veterans, allowing her to segue into former South Bend, Indiana Mayor (and 2020 aspirant) Pete Buttigieg (a veteran), who segued into another mayor, former New York Mayor (and 2020 aspirant) Michael Bloomberg. The highlight of this period, 9:00 until 10:20, was probably not any of these many speeches, all of which were effective and (in the case of the four defeated rivals) in line with generic expectations, but John Legend and Common's moving rendition of "Glory," which they had composed for the film *Selma*. After 10:20, the focus was clearly supposed to be on nominee Biden, but the show was almost stolen by thirteen-year-old Braden Harrington, a young boy whom Biden had helped overcome his stuttering, something Biden had overcome as a child. Biden, not always a great speaker, delivered a carefully crafted speech that will probably be remembered less for its policy proposals and more for its pathos. The media, intrigued by the thirteen-year-old, nonetheless focused on Biden's message and style as the DNC closed with fireworks outside in a mall parking lot near Wilmington, Delaware.

THE REPUBLICAN NATIONAL CONVENTION

Deliberative Rhetoric: Arguments for Trump/Pence

The RNC rhetoric focused on what Trump had done and what Trump will do. It also offered Trump doing things in the present moment—pardoning and conducting a naturalization ceremony. According to the rhetoric, Trump had acted effectively to combat COVID-19, free hostages, improve the economy, protect the unborn, promote the advancement of women, combat the opioid epidemic, promote school choice, and support those serving in the military and their families. Testimony supported each claim. Whereas the rhetoric dealing with "Trump Past" was diffuse, that dealing with "Trump Future" was rather focused on how he would maintain law and order in America.

The "Trump Past" rhetoric came across, at times, as an implicit defense against charges opponents were making. The "Trump Present" performances stress that he *is* president and acting daily. The "Trump Future" rhetoric is different. It does vaguely suggest Trump will act and Biden will not, but it relies much more heavily on a fear appeal than logical argumentation with its stress on explication and proof. In other words, the audience does not know what exactly Trump will do and why it will succeed, just that Biden will, somehow, encourage lawlessness and disorder.

Epideictic Rhetoric: Praising Trump, Blaming Biden

The epideictic rhetoric at the RNC was not subtle. At every turn, either Trump was being praised for his actions or Biden was being indicted. There were suggestions that Biden was not the actor Trump is—that he was hiding in his basement, not standing in the arena. But stronger were suggestions that he, although a good person, has been co-opted by the radicals in the Democratic Party. Thus, he was a stalking horse or a Trojan horse for socialism.

Audiences

Much of the RNC's rhetoric was directed at Trump's base. There were nods at disaffected Democrats—for example, former South Carolina Governor Nikki Haley recalled how Democrat Jeanne Kirkpatrick spoke in support of Reagan at the 1984 RNC—but nothing to parallel the Republican parade at the DNC. More in view were "swing" voters who might be swayed by the fear over rioting and crime many evoked. Support for Trump among "suburban women" had proved tepid in 2016—and GOP weakness in this demographic was apparent in 2018. The RNC rhetoric assumed this group was volatile and could be swayed to support Trump by a "law and order" message similar to that deployed by Richard Nixon in both 1968 and 1972.

Constitutive Rhetoric: And Who Are These Republicans?

Just as the DNC was lacking much by way of constitutive rhetoric, so was the RNC. But the explanation for the RNC's deemphasis may be different. The DNC was, arguably, trying to smooth over the split in the party between moderates and progressives by not stressing either side. The RNC was not dealing much at all with the question of what the party stood for, for the focus from beginning to end was on Trump, not the Republican Party.

It is easy to assess the party conventions just in terms of how they weigh in the presidential race, but, in their constitutive function, they have effects beyond that contest. After the DNC, "down ticket" Democrats may well have had to specify their tilt as they campaigned—or try to be both progressive and centrist. After the RNC, "down ticket" Republicans have no other identity than being pro-Trump (or, at their risk, anti-Trump). This failure to constitute the party in any terms other than support for Trump will certainly affect their campaigns and may weaken their chances for victory if voters want a better sense of what these candidates will do on various issues.

This problem is not unique to Republicans in 2020. Many other conventions have focused on the candidate more than the party. Whether that focus hurt or helped has depended on the incumbent's strength. Democrats in 1964 were certainly not hurt by that year's DNC focusing on Lyndon Johnson (with glances at JFK). So, the absence of party-focused constitutive rhetoric at the 2020 RNC may be a problem only where a pro-Trump identity is a liability.

Rhetorical Success or Failure

Neither party convention got a big "bounce" in 2020, but the RNC did fare better than the DNC, although the "bounce" was short-lived. Its existence, however, suggests that some undecided voters were swayed by accounts of Trump's successes or his presidential displays, or his fear messages. Something in the RNC's rhetorical mix hit home enough for some prospective voters who were leaning against Trump (or neutral) to, at least for a moment, lean toward him.

Striking, however, is how short-lived the "bounce" was. The explanation may well be tied to what the media did in the days following the RNC and what communication researchers know about fear appeals. The media returned to covering the COVID-19 epidemic, and that coverage muted (if not refuted) the RNC's pro-Trump claims. And, fear appeals work well only if both threat and the efficacy of the proposed response are high.[13] In the case of the "law and order" message at the RNC, the former might well have been high but, given the lack of specifics in Trump's message about what he would do, the efficacy might have been low.

"Bounce," by definition, deals with winning new support, not strengthening existing support. It is on this latter count that Trump's convention might be judged a rhetorical success. The numbers attending Trump rallies and his ability to generate last-minute enthusiasm prior to November 3 through them strongly suggest a base that could be whipped into action. Much of the RNC rhetoric might be categorized as "rally" rhetoric. So, if it worked just prior to November 3 in increasing day-of votes for Trump, it might be presumed to have worked at the RNC in solidifying his base.

"The Show"

Since the Republicans were planning on live events, first in Charlotte and then in Jacksonville, and were late to shift to a virtual meeting, they had less time to prepare "the show." Arguably, this tardiness could have resulted in an inferior production. Did it? Four contrasts with the DNC are quickly evident.

First, the RNC featured more speakers walking to a lectern and speaking, with the vast majority doing so in Mellon Auditorium, a federal government facility that private entities may rent. Thus, the RNC looked more like a traditional convention. But, in proceeding with so many such speeches, the RNC might have been perceived as less innovative or creative.

Second, when the RNC was creative, it was traditionally so. The DNC, as noted earlier, transformed the traditional univocal keynote into a chorus among many party newcomers. The RNC, on the other hand, played not with the speeches as forms but with where they were delivered. So, Melania Trump spoke from the redesigned White House Rose Garden; Mike Pence spoke from Fort McHenry in Baltimore; and Donald Trump spoke from the White House South Lawn. These choices were indeed rhetorical: the site added something to the speech, but the speech itself remained intact as a text.

Third, the RNC did not proceed at as quick a pace as the DNC. The slower pace permitted television audience members to take breaks. It also gave the networks, both traditional and cable, an opportunity to insert more commentary. And, that commentary tended to extend beyond the brief breaks, resulting in some of the RNC show not being broadcast. In many cases, that commentary was negative—for example, many "fact checks" on what Trump supporters had just said or references to inconsistencies in the Trump's RNC message. So, allowing this commentary might have had a negative effect on how viewers were interpreting the RNC speeches.

Fourth, the RNC departed significantly from convention expectations. As noted earlier, the DNC tried to blend the traditional with new approaches. So, there was a roll call of states and a keynote address, although both were performed differently. The RNC, on the other hand, moved the entire nominating, seconding, and voting process outside the televised convention. There were no defeated rivals since Trump was largely unchallenged for renomination, but rivals from 2016 were strikingly missing. No Cruz, no Rubio, and no Jeb Bush. Rand Paul spoke but briefly and at a poor time. Only Ben Carson (in Trump's cabinet) received a good one. And, of course, Kasich had spoken at the DNC. There was no former president: one presumes George W. Bush either was not invited or declined. There was no keynote address. The modern keynote begins with both parties' conventions in 1932. Since then, only the 2016 RNC has omitted such a speech. The 2020 RNC repeated the 2016 omission.

The denial of the expectations probably did not have a rhetorical effect either way. In other words, no one in Trump's audience was cheering or jeering the absence of a roll call or a keynote. The omissions were likely either not noticed or dismissed as not especially significant.

One other departure was noticed—at least by commentators. And that is how Trump family members were used not so much to talk about what the Trump family members might know but to offer positive comments on his administration and negative comments on the Biden/Harris ticket. In other words, they delivered political speeches, not personal ones. Melania Trump did, occasionally, talk a bit more personally, as did daughter Ivanka, who introduced Trump on Thursday night. But even their addresses were more political than the norm for family members, and the speeches by Don Jr., Eric, and their significant others were quite political. Don Jr. seemed (to commentators) to be campaigning for a 2024 nomination, and Trump Sr.'s advisor and Jr.'s girlfriend Kimberly Guilfoyle's address on Monday was arguably the most brazenly political speech at the entire four-day gathering.

Did this departure from the family norm make a difference, however? In the minds of the Trump base, probably not. Those opposed to Trump were probably inclined to point to the parade of Trumps as evidence that there was a paucity of others to speak on his behalf, an observation perhaps valid in 2016 but probably not in 2020. Those undecideds watching the convention undoubtedly attended to the political messages the Trump family speakers delivered but may have wanted more on Trump's character since the DNC had so emphasized Biden's. There were testimonials to Trump's character—his empathy in order to match Biden's—but these came from average citizens, not Trump's family.

One other dimension of "the show" must be discussed: the RNC's appropriation of federal government space. Mellon Auditorium is available for private use; both the Washington Monument grounds and the Fort McHenry grounds are managed by the U.S. Park Service and can be, with permission, used for political events. The fact that all previous conventions have been held in large venues in various American cities has limited other sites just to stadia, used for the final address to impart grandeur and permit a larger audience. FDR used Franklin Field in Philadelphia, JFK used Los Angeles Memorial Coliseum, and Obama used Mile-High Stadium in Denver. One could argue that both political parties have avoided sites in the national capital as well as national historical sites rife with meaning based on the assumption that such sites would be inappropriate for partisan politics. Neither party ought to "grab" the Washington Monument, for it belongs to the nation. One could certainly argue that incumbents have been studiously careful not to flamboyantly use the trappings, let alone the lodgings, of office at a party gathering. They have been sensitive to the question of appropriateness and, in the case of the White House, the question of law, for the RNC's use of the White House may well have been a violation of the Hatch Act. Although a future Congress might investigate the RNC's use, the prosecution is unlikely. Trump supporters not only did not care that he was violating propriety or the law but perhaps applauded his use of incumbency. Trump's opponents were left to complain bitterly. Those undecided in the race probably professed indifference on the issue but may have been subtly affected by the visual presidential images the RNC projected.

"The Show"'s Success or Failure

The question of success or failure can be parsed in two ways. The first would be an assessment of "the show" *qua* show. Offering such goes beyond what a rhetorical critic usually does, so one needs to tread carefully. As noted earlier, media commentators (notably, television scholar Robert Thompson at Syracuse) found the DNC "tighter," suggesting it was "better produced." He also noted moments when the RNC seemed to "drag." Given that the Republicans had less time to plan, this assessment makes sense. Renting Mellon Auditorium and having many speakers march to the lectern there was an easy "fix." The venue looks impressive, as will the chosen White House locations and Fort McHenry. These decisions were, it might be noted, low-tech ones. Again, given their time constraints, the RNC planners may not have had the opportunity to plan anything as creative as the DNC's "Different Kind of Keynote."

The second would be an assessment of how voters responded. Absent polling data, one can only guess that the base found the show more than acceptable than those opposed to Trump. The latter were likely to nit-pick the "show," pointing to the very odd combination of too many traditional at-the-lectern speeches and too many departures from convention norms. The former was not likely to notice these matters—or care about them.

If there had been a major problem with either program design or execution, then both would be addressing it, mocking it, or excusing it, but nothing of this magnitude was apparent. There were, for example, no multiple minutes of "dead air," no distorted video feeds from Fort McHenry, no back-to-back speeches saying contradictory things. (There were, however, some internal contradictions—as noted earlier—among speakers who claimed Trump had solved a problem and those who claimed Trump would solve a problem and those who claimed there was no problem.) So, the conclusion for 2020 is that, if the DNC was indeed a better "show," that proved insignificant.

Media Skewing

If we consider the RNC as beginning at 9:00 p.m. EDST and concluding at 11:00 p.m., then there were eight hours of programming. It tended to begin earlier, and, on Thursday, it concluded well after 11:00. So, actual programming was probably closer to ten. Obviously, not all that happened in these hours would be stressed when the media shifted from covering events as events to covering the RNC as a news story. The latter would mean that the media would choose what to stress and what to ignore. Even those who watched the entirety would be likely to adapt to this media framing.

On Monday, the RNC seemed somewhat aware of the 10:00 p.m. moment when media coverage would expand. Before, there were many effective speakers, designed to touch on a number of topics—COVID-19 response, racism in America, the need for law and order. After, the focus was on three speakers, all of whom seemed to be as much campaigning for 2024 as campaigning in 2020: former South Carolina Governor and U.N. Ambassador Nikki Haley, son Don Jr., and South Carolina Senator Tim Scott. Both Haley and Scott received positive media coverage, but it was a speaker from the less important 9:00–10:00 slot who stole the show. That was Kimberly Guilfoyle, Trump Sr. aide and Trump Jr. girlfriend. Her vehement attacks on the Biden/Harris ticket skewed media coverage on Day One toward the negative.

On Tuesday, the RNC again was somewhat aware of the 10:00 p.m. mark. Before, several speakers and multiple issues (the economy, abortion, advocacy for women, the opioid crisis, and crime). No single moment stood out (and Tiffany Trump's speech got lost). After using post-10:00 time for a White House ceremony granting citizenship to a (deliberately) diverse group of now-citizens, the focus shifted to Secretary of State Mike Pompeo, who received more coverage for where he spoke, Jerusalem, which he was visiting on official government business, than anything he said. Then, with the question of Pompeo's having violated the Hatch Act being discussed by pundits, the focus shifted to Melania Trump in the White House Rose Garden. As noted earlier, her speech was atypical for a First Lady—perhaps precedented by outgoing First Lady Michelle Obama in 2016—insofar as it addressed more the president's policies than his personal qualities. It was also out-of-sync with much of the convention rhetoric insofar as it offered a positive view of the nation. Media coverage focused more on her than either Pompeo or the naturalization ceremony.

On Wednesday, once again, the RNC showed an awareness of 10:00 p.m. Before, multiple speakers; multiple themes. After 10:00, there were fewer speakers, with the attention focusing on law and order (but also a bit on civil rights). The media were now occasionally cutting away from the RNC to cover events in Kenosha, Wisconsin, where there were BLM demonstrations and some violence, and Hurricane Laura churning away in the Gulf, but returned for a video tribute to Vice President Pence and his speech. Over the decades, the vice presidential nominee's acceptance speech has evolved, as a genre, into an address that attacks the opposing ticket very aggressively. Pence did so, but he also spent time speaking about Trump's accomplishments. When attacking, he stressed the law and order theme, arguably aided by what was transpiring on the streets of Kenosha.

So, based on media skewing, Monday was Guilfoyle; Tuesday was the First Lady; and Wednesday was Pence. The latter two were probably in accord with RNC planning; the first, a surprise, one that tilted the convention in a negative direction. One would surmise that the RNC wanted a balance between positive and negative, but media coverage, liking controversy, might have pushed the anti-Biden/Harris message into prominence.

Thursday evening was Donald Trump's to shine. All that was staged as a lead-in faded very quickly once Trump made his grand entrance and proceeded to the lectern on the White House's South Lawn. Throughout his presidency, Trump had fared better with media commentators when he stuck to his script. However, he scored highly with many in his base when he went off-script and used rhetoric that might be categorized as "rally rhetoric." This evening, he largely stuck to his script, but striking in that script was the inclusion of some "rally rhetoric." That rhetoric gave the speech a dark quality. In contradiction to the beautiful setting, Trump stressed how disturbing Joe Biden's America would be. He made some positive comments about his actions as president, but the media stressed the negative picture.

The media also stressed the speech's length, for it was indeed long. Not even Bill Clinton, known for his duration, had gone on as long as Trump did. Nominees almost always ignore the 11:00 p.m. EDST end-time given by the networks, daring them to cut the speech off, but Trump did so flagrantly. So, arguably in response, some media commentary stressed how long the speech was more than what it said.[14]

DNC VERSUS RNC IN 2020

Much of this essay has been descriptive, noting what occurred and often putting what occurred in the tradition of the political convention. Political communication scholars are interested in such details, but other scholars and those who come to this essay casually probably are more interested in the question of comparative success. When writing on the 2016 conventions, I found it relatively easy to judge the DNC to be the superior event. In addition to bumps caused by Melania Trump's plagiarism on Night One and Ted Cruz's failure to endorse on Night Two, the 2016 RNC exhibited poor planning on several counts. It struck me as having been planned by people who did not know enough about planning such an event. In 2020, the situation was different.

The shows were different, but the ultimate assessment is probably tied to neither the "show" dimensions (John Legend and Common performing "Glory" vs. White House trappings) nor how many speakers and who they are. Rather, the ultimate assessment is probably tied to whether the two gatherings succeeded in meeting their rhetorical goals. Let me focus on four.

Constituting Party Identity

Neither convention was especially successful in telling Democrats or Republicans who they were. Perhaps, the fact that the DNC offered "a different kind of keynote," and the RNC offered no keynote at all partially explains the failure. Constituting the party has long been a function of the genre. But other factors probably contributed more. The DNC was dealing with a party divided between progressives and moderates. Wanting both wings to be pleased, the DNC dodged the task of reconciliation. The RNC was dealing with a different dynamic: a party, so the convention would suggest, that had been so captured by Trump that he was the dominating personality and issue. In other words, the RNC was much more Trump's convention than that of the Republicans. The domination of a political convention by an incumbent is not unprecedented: one can point to Johnson in 1964, Nixon in 1972, and Reagan in 1984. But, when the domination occurs, the party comes out of the gathering over-defined—for good or for ill—by the top of the ticket.[15]

Balancing the Negative and the Positive

The DNC wanted to stress the nation's dire problems, crises Trump had failed to address; and the DNC wanted to stress the hope, Joe Biden, largely because of his character offered. The DNC, in my judgment, succeeded. Part of why it succeeded was its subtle movement during the four days from more negative to more positive. Another part is the strong ways the gathering ended each night. On Monday, it was Michelle Obama; on Tuesday, Jill Biden; on Wednesday, Kamala Harris; and on Thursday, Biden himself. Each gave a strong speech that evoked both applause and hope. The hope was rooted in the fact that four people, perceived as so caring, were involved in the nation's resurrection from the darkness.

The 2020 RNC was certainly more positive than the 2016 gathering. Whether truthful or not, it told of Trump's successes and brought on stage many who expressed their appreciation of the man. The gathering, however, wanted to stress how frightening "Joe Biden's America" might be; the gathering wanted to evoke fear as it voiced a "law and order" message. This message might have injected too much negativity into the gathering. Its concluding messages (Tim Scott, Melania Trump, Mike Pence, and Donald Trump) were sound with some effective moments, but the sheer length of Trump's may have undermined it. He also seemed, as is his wont, to go off script into a "rally mode." Much of this was actually in the script, but, whether off or in, he began mixing overly broad claims with much negativity. Noteworthy, perhaps, is that, whereas Biden never mentioned Trump by name, Trump mentioned Biden by name more than forty times. This naming gave the speech an attacking "feel," fireworks and an opera performance afterward notwithstanding.

Defining the Problem

Both party conventions discussed many issues, but both had a single issue they wanted to stress as *the* problem most pressingly facing the nation. The DNC chose the COVID-19 epidemic, which—Democrats argued—Trump had handled very poorly. The RNC chose the threat to law and order posed by BLM and others who were taking to America's streets to demonstrate. Arguably, both conventions succeeded in pointing to *the* problem in the eyes of those in their bases.

The DNC convened with its members already convinced that COVID-19 was a major problem and that Trump had catastrophically failed to address it. DNC speakers, then, just had to remind them. Beyond the base were many who were skeptical about the pandemic: some thought it was a hoax; some thought it was being exaggerated by the Democrats and the media. If they had a problem in sight, it was the weakening economy, weakening because of Democrat-led, media-fueled overreaction to COVID-19.

The RNC did not want the weakened economy to be *the* problem because Trump wanted to be able to argue that the economy was incredibly strong before the pandemic struck and was becoming incredibly strong again because of his leadership. The RNC—and Trump—wanted *the* problem to be the threats to law and order posed by demonstrators and by their calls to "defund" the police. The RNC rhetoric, then, needed to effect a shift in the focal point for many of its members. Needing to do so may explain why speakers, including Trump, were so heavy-handed in portraying "Joe Biden's America" as a lawless place.

Arguably, both parties defined *the* problem for their base. (Trump may have, in the short term, gone beyond his base.) The DNC assumed little risk in so defining the nation's primary concern, for they could place all of the blame on Trump and offer compassion and hope. The RNC assumed more risk because they were going negative without having a clear solution to the law and order problem other than not electing Biden.

Meeting the Major Goal

That the RNC did not maintain as good a negative-positive balance as the DNC may in large measure be because the RNC's major goal was to stress how "Joe Biden's America" would be one of rioting and crime with the police "defunded" and, therefore, not there to help. The RNC wanted to paint Biden as, if not radical himself, controlled by radical elements, but the "law and order" message had become more important in Trump's planning, for it gave him a fear-invoking crisis to distract from the fear-invoking COVID-19 crisis. The RNC certainly did succeed in stressing this message, arguably putting the Biden campaign on the defensive after the RNC concluded. One might also argue that every media story about rioting helped Trump sustain the message and hamstring the Biden campaign.

The DNC's major goal had been to present Biden as a devoted, caring man. The gathering's rhetoric accomplished this goal. In 2000, studies showed that people voted heavily based on character: George W. Bush came across as a "good guy"; Al Gore was not only stiff but also prone to misrepresent the truth. Bush won on character. Might that happen again in 2020, with the Democrat on top this time? The DNC was banking on it: the rhetoric highlighted Biden's competence, but it stressed his character. In 2016, many voters may have "held their noses and voted for Trump." Could the Biden campaign not only present Trump as generally odious but more specifically portray him successfully as uncaring and irresponsible as the COVID-19 crisis struck the country?

Although the Democrats left their virtual gathering with all feeling more upbeat than, perhaps, those watching the RNC did, the key question may be this last one related to the two parties' major goals. Both parties achieved them. The question then becomes which party assessed the dynamics of the 2020 election better as they moved from virtual conventioneers to general election campaigning. In other words, which central message would win over more voters?

THE FUTURE OF POLITICAL PARTY CONVENTIONS

The 2020 conventions, insofar as they were virtual, might have some thinking that 2024 might be more like 2020 than the many election years before. That neither convention was a failure might add fuel to the ideas, as might the production possibilities the parties only barely tapped. In other words, might the 2020 emergency solution have suggested a new, less expensive, and quite a creative forum? Commentators are suggesting that the emergency might alter business travel and higher education permanently.[16] Might the same be true for these time-honored gatherings?

In considering this final question, one has to understand that the political party conventions are both media events and live events. This year's were, for the most part, just media events. Yes, there were people at the White House, at Fort McHenry, and—for Biden's convention—in a mall parking lot. But the true audience for both gatherings was the television one. That audience probably does not care if a speech is live or recorded and might actually prefer something akin to the DNC's "A Different Kind of Keynote" or its scenic roll call to the usual fare. So, if one thinks of the conventions primarily as media events, there might be a case for going virtual from here on out.

But the conventions are also live. As such, they have a different audience and they serve a different purpose. They are pitched to those who are the most politically active. They connect these people; they rally these people. In terms used by performance studies scholars, they are examples of *communitatis*, something we might see at a social movement rally or a sporting event, or a rock concert. I doubt the 2020 conventions served any of these communication functions well. Those who usually experience those functions (but did not in 2020) are, of course, the ones who will decide whether to be live or online in 2024. They then may make a selfish decision and reembrace the hoopla and the energy, or they may recognize that these functions served by the live convention are important, for those connected and rallied in enthusiasm are the lifeblood of American politics. Like it or not, they drive the quadrennial process. So, to preserve what they do, the conventions are likely to be back in the respective arenas come in 2024. That said, the successes of 2020 might inspire some online additions or substitutions, giving the next conventions something of a hybrid quality.

CONCLUSION

One necessarily begins an examination of the 2020 conventions expecting to talk about the differences. The reality, however, is that from a rhetorical perspective, they were much the same as their predecessors—that is, they had the same deliberative, epideictic, and constitutive goals and used many of the usual means to achieve them. There were a few new twists, but they altered the rhetorical dynamics minimally. In analyzing these gatherings, one must ask production questions not usually raised and assess the conventions more as "shows" than in past years. But the conventions have always had a "show" dimension in the television era, so 2020 simply increased that critical focus. And, neither gathering failed as a "show," even though the Democrats made more use of the virtual possibilities and featured a brisker pace due in part to superior editing. But this superiority seemed to matter little: perhaps the use of the White House as a scene trumped better production values or Trump supporters cared little about them.

So, if 2020's difference is not the central critical concern, one falls back on the usual questions of efficacy. The response to those questions is that both parties succeeded in meeting their goals, although both were weak when it came to defining what the party stood for. The two conventions had different "feels": the Democrats tried to evoke hope while being critical of the president; the Republicans tried to evoke fear while praising Trump. As a result, the Democratic convention seemed more positive than the Republican.

"Bounce" is not the only measure of convention success, but Trump's gathering did get a slightly larger "bounce" in polls than Biden's, but it faded. The difference, although negligible, may be tied to the immediate but fleeting power of fear appeals when the threat level is not matched by a similarly high efficacy level. The difference might also be explained by the volatility of the relatively few undecided voters at convention time. The total 2020 vote significantly surpassed that in 2016, and Biden's ability to capture more of these "new" voters than Trump probably explains the results. But that obscures how the undecideds tilted. Trump's last-minute rallies, rife with the same appeals as the convention, seemed to have the power to sway many in this group to produce a day-of-voting surge. That surge was much like the postconvention bounce, narrowing the predicted Biden margin significantly in many places.

The efficacy, then, of Trump's convention rhetoric—and preelection day rally rhetoric—should not obscure how Biden's convention rhetoric *may* have worked. It may not have produced a sizeable bounce; however, it may have encouraged those supporting Biden to act in line with that support and vote. It is a time-honored verity among political commentators that Republicans are more likely to actually vote than Democrats. Biden's rhetoric, delivered through an effective convention, may have altered that pattern, especially given how, in response to COVID-19, voting was (ironically) arguably easier to do in 2020 than in previous years.

There have been years when a critic could contrast the conventions: the one-party succeeded, the other did not. The years 1964, 1968, and 1972 come to mind. So, arguably, does 2016. But 2020 seems to fall into the larger category of years when both parties did well. Saying as much, however, should not obscure the possibility that they did well in different ways. Trump's may have swayed some undecideds; Biden's may have encouraged those who already supported him (or strongly opposed Trump) to act.

Chapter 3

Presidential Debates 2020

Benjamin Voth

Presidential debates represent one of the most potent persuasive forces in American presidential elections. Simply reviewing the audience sizes of various forums of political argument, nothing can match the impact of televised presidential debates in the twenty-first century. Presidential debates in 2020 were five times as popular as the primary debates. Primary debates were as popular as major political convention addresses. Understanding the presidential debates for 2020 requires the examination of three key areas: (1) presidential primary debates, (2) presidential debates in the presidential election, and (3) potential reforms for the presidential debate process.

Debate represents one of the most difficult forms of public communication. Debate requires a complex interplay of arguments with regulated structures. In general communication theory, the debate is among the highest of communication competencies and uniquely demanding of its practitioners. This would be a key part of German theorist Jurgen Habermas' important idea of communication competence.[1] Within a democracy, the debate is a crown jewel signifying free discourse and the capacities of dissent and disagreement.

In 1940, Republican Wendell Wilkie challenged President Franklin D. Roosevelt to a radio debate, but despite having an elite command of the airwaves through his Fireside Chats, Roosevelt declined.[2] The debates can make a significant difference for the two contestants. Since 1960, Gallup polling indicates noticeable persuasive effects. Only in the 1984 election did the October debates fail to register a change in the polling of the two major candidates (Reagan and Mondale). Poll changes since 1960 range from 12 points for President Bush in 2000 to one point for President Bush Sr. in 1988.[3] Empirical communication studies suggest about 7 percent of voters change from undecided to a candidate preference on the basis of debates.[4] Televised debates changed the nature of presidential elections beginning in 1960.[5]

For the 2020 election, the debates may certainly have played a critical role in deciding the election. The election was quite close and record numbers of voters participated in the election with more than 150 million voters.

PRIMARY DEBATES FOR DEMOCRATS
IN 2019 AND 2020

The Democratic Party field was quite large. Important frontrunners in the process of 2019 and 2020 included Senator Bernie Sanders, Senator Elizabeth Warren, Senator Kamala Harris, and Vice President Joe Biden. In many respects, the size and scope of the field resembled the Republican field of 2016 with many Democrats believing they could best represent the party against the incumbent president. One of the most surprising outcomes of the primary debate process was the early exceptional performance of Senator Kamala Harris. She was certainly one of the best debaters in the early primary process, but she was also was one of the first candidates to leave the primary process. Harris's aggressive attacks on Biden may have played an important role in the final decision to select her as the vice presidential running mate in the summer of 2020.

Two of Harris's primary attacks were: (1) sexual assault allegations against Biden were serious and credible and (2) Joe Biden defended historically racist practices such as segregation. Harris's standing as a black female candidate along with her public skills as a prosecutor provided a strong rhetorical combination on the debate stage. In the June 28 debate, Harris asked Biden: "Do you agree today that you were wrong to oppose busing in America?" Most analysts agreed that in early debates, Harris did considerable damage to the Biden campaign.

Most experts and candidates understood that Joe Biden was an expected and most senior candidate. The primary debates were deemed a proving ground about whether he still possessed the political acumen and stamina to take the Democratic standard of attack to incumbent President Donald Trump. Biden rarely excelled in the debates but also failed to flounder in a manner deemed insurmountable or catastrophic to the larger primary process providing a situational backdrop to the debates. His worst rhetorical wounds were inflicted by Senator Kamala Harris.

The primary debate series featured one of the largest onstage debates in history with twelve candidates for the October 15, 2019, debate in Ohio.[6] The Democratic primary debates were governed by a complex formula of fundraising targets, polling, and primary performance levels. These criteria established an objective basis for narrowing the field moving forward. The expectations were marred by a more flawed and arguably distorted process in

2016 that led to the premature ejection of three Democratic contenders and some apparent favoritism toward candidate Clinton when Donna Brazile fed primary town hall questions to Clinton in advance of the event by way of her role as a CNN commentator.[7] Ultimately, Biden survived both the debate process and the primary calendar to finally surpass Bernie Sanders as the final candidate for the Democrats. The debate and primary process solidified the argument rivalry between the moderates of the Democratic Party and the more galvanized socialist left that was energized by further rounds of racial politics derived from interpretations of police violence against black suspects.

General Election Debates

The general election debates were profoundly hindered by the COVID pandemic. Scheduled from late September to late October, four debates were to follow the now generic pattern established by the Commission on Presidential Debates since 1988. The second debate would be a vice presidential debate. The third debate that would have been the second debate between Biden and Trump was canceled due to contentions over the COVID guidelines. President Trump developed COVID shortly after the first presidential debate and procedures that added plexiglass and testing processes guided the debating process in October.

The first debate in late September was by far the most contentious and featured so many interruptions by both sides that it was nearly impossible for anyone to keep track. There was a little consensus of appreciation for the event and considerable consternation and disappointment. Biden told Trump to "shut up" twice and also referred to the president as a "clown."[8] Trump was known since 2015 for having a uniquely aggressive style, and it may be that the president knew that incumbents as a rule lose the first debate and sought to hamstring his challenger with interruptions, not unlike those unleashed by Biden against Paul Ryan in the vice presidential debate of 2012. More than 25 percent of the first debate was consumed by "cross talk," meaning that both candidates were speaking at the same time. By comparison, less than 1 percent of the second debate between Biden and Trump was consumed by "cross talk."[9]

An unusually prescient question emerged from the conclusion of debate number one. Moderator Chris Wallace, who did seem to favor Vice President Biden throughout the event, asked both candidates whether they would be willing to wait until the election was properly certified before claiming victory in the election. Wallace's unusual and unprecedented question was clearly rooted in an emerging theory about the election that absentee and mail-in voting would create a delayed partisan result favoring the Democrats. This would mean that President Trump would appear to win on election night but over time more late votes would shift the actual results in favor of Biden. Both candidates told Wallace that they would be willing to wait for certified results to claim victory. In reality, Biden would claim victory based on media calls and not certification a few days after the election. That irony animated a long legal process initiated by legal advocates sympathetic to the president and even indulging more than 15 state attorney generals supporting an investigation of voter fraud.[10]

In sum, the general debate process cast considerable doubt upon the Commission on Presidential Debates (CPD) organization that guided the presidential debates. The primary problem and concern arose from the selection and conduct of moderators. Chris Wallace did cross the 20 percent of time threshold in his opening to the process.

C-SPAN moderator Steve Scully was removed by CPD once it was confirmed that he was using his Twitter account to actively confer with antagonists of the president to prepare questions for his debate that was canceled.[11] There was considerable criticism that all of the moderators were evidently opposed to the president's reelection and displayed behaviors that favored the challenger, Vice President Joe Biden.

Kristen Welker moderated the final debate on October 22. The debate was watched by seventy-seven million viewers. President Trump had two additional minutes of speaking time compared to Biden. In the final analysis of the presidential debates provided by *USA Today*, they explained that moderator Kristen "had to interrupt" the candidates. This media phraseology justified their rhetorical intervention and provided an ideological framing for interrupting President Trump almost ten times as often as the challenger (48 to 5).[12] After the first debate, the CPD announced that microphones would be turned off at certain times to ensure that candidates would not talk over one another. Although this process was utilized, it was not clear why additional interruptions were needed by the moderator to prevent cross talk.

Suggestions for Improving Presidential Debates

Presidential debates exist as a televised tradition since 1960 in the United States, but the Commission on Presidential Debates presented for 2020 was flawed and should be reimagined. Moderators have evolved to be the center of attention rather than the candidates—who seize on the opportunity to deliver partisan points rather than a basis of dialogue. Our drift to "town hall" formats is an unfulfilling and unrevealing substitute for true debate.

Since the CPD took over the League of Women Voters' debates in 1987, viewership averages over 60 million.[13] By comparison, the Super Bowl gets 100 million, political conventions get 10–20 million, popular TV shows get

5 million, and even vice-presidential debates like the one between Sarah Palin and Joe Biden in 2008 can attract more than 70 million.

The most viewed presidential debate in history is the 2016 first debate between Donald Trump and Hillary Clinton, with more than 80 million viewers.[14] No other persuasive communication impacts these many people in the typical 90-minute format. They represent an important opportunity for the campaigns and the public to understand the positions candidates have on issues. Nonetheless, the CPD has reached an impasse in its capacity to conduct these debates.

Moderator problems are at the forefront of CPD shortcomings. From initial incidents such as Bernard Shaw asking about the possible murder of Michael Dukakis' wife Kitty in 1988 [15] to Candy Crowley's intervention in the debate between Obama and Romney in 2012,[16] moderators have skewed the basic expectations of a debate. The debate should ideally provide: (1) a previously known topic, (2) two opposing sides, (3) equal time for each side to present, and (4) a mechanism for decision. Chris Wallace, who moderated the first 2020 presidential debate, said a key to debate success is moderator "invisibility."[17] Moderators were not only visible but also occupied an increasingly disruptive function within the debate process that continued to emphasize that these events are not actually debates but iterative press conferences led by a journalist looking for ratings.

The rules for debates since 1987 consistently suggest limits for the candidates but fewer limits for moderators. This led to a trend of moderators occupying larger and more disruptive roles. In 2012, presidential debate moderators occupied a range from 8.1 percent by Jim Lehrer to 12.8 percent by Martha Raddatz.[18] In 2016, Lester Holt took 10.8 percent of the debate while Chris Wallace occupied 19 percent of the debate content in his final debate moderator role.[19] In the first debate of 2020, Wallace took 25 percent of the time—equating to about 20 minutes of the 90-minute debate (figure 3.1). Apologists maintain the disruptive nature of candidate interruptions—especially by President Trump—justifies this larger occupation. Future reforms could reduce this problem and restore the credibility of an important public venue for learning the differences between candidates.

Reforms that can be implemented to fulfill the purpose of these debates by 2024 are as follows:

1. Require a trifecta of debate professionals and the two major campaigns to negotiate the terms of the debate. Remove the journalists and media companies as a monopoly on the forum. Debates could take different formats and cover topics strictly approved by both campaigns. These should be debates and not iterative press conferences.

2. Compel moderators to exert minimal and relatively invisible roles in the debate, such as starting and stopping the clock or announcing the topic area. Moderators should not occupy more than 7 percent of the speech time in a debate and infractions should be punished with deductions to their compensation and public announcement of conduct errors. Severe infractions can lead to removal from moderating future debates. Utilizing nonpartisan debate professionals is desirable. The 2020 debates demonstrate moderators took more than 20 percent of all debate times (see figure 3.1).

3. Provide more generous opening statements by the candidates. Debates typically feature opening speeches known as constructive. These four to eight-minute speeches will allow candidates to build their position in the debate.

4. Allow candidates to cross-examine one another. Candidates want to challenge the opposing candidate directly rather than through an intermediary. Such cross-examination periods could last three minutes apiece. An impromptu version of this emerged in the vice presidential debate when Mike Pence deferred from his speech time to invite Kamala Harris to explain whether she and Joe Biden planned to pack to the Supreme Court. Harris's decision to answer and inability to frame a coherent response proved fruitful for Pence and a learning moment for the audience about an important political issue surrounding the Supreme Court.

5. Abolish the "town hall" as an official form of debate. This format is founded upon an illusion that regular citizens—sometimes falsely designated as "undecided"—are allowed to ask questions of their own choosing. On the contrary, the media members are chosen by the media, and the journalist-moderator reviews their questions in advance. In a "town hall" hosted by NBC this past week, the moderator asked more questions in the first twenty minutes than all of the citizens in the next forty minutes.[20] The president was in fact debating the moderator. When the format was conceived in 1992 academic designers viewed the format as ideal for helping challenger Bill Clinton defeat incumbent George H. W. Bush.[21]

6. Stop choosing moderators with evident partisan affiliations. The incident with Steve Scully, and his false suggestion that his Twitter account was hacked when he reached out to a strident opponent of President Trump, was an avoidable debacle since Scully was known to have been an intern with Joe Biden. Wallace's strident and lengthy lectures to introduce partisan questions were amplified by aggressive ideological remarks after the debate emphasizing that he found President Trump's disagreements with Vice President Biden unreasonable.

7. Encourage creative debate formats. In college and high school debates, team debate is popular. It would be possible to create a forum where the vice president works in tandem with the presidential candidate in

Table 1

2020 Presidential and VP Debate Statistics	Debate 1	Debate 2 VP	Debate 3	Debate 4
	Case Western University	*University of Utah*	*Miami, Florida*	*Belmont University*
Viewing Audience	73 million	37 milion	**Cancelled**	71 million
Date	9/29/2020	10/7/2020	October 15	10/22/2020
Moderator	**Chris Wallace**	**Susan Page**	**Steve Scully**	**Kristen Welker**
News Network	FOX	USA Today	C-SPAN	NBC
			Twitter misconduct	
percent speaking time	25.00%	25.00%	NA	21.00%
Estimated time	22m 30s	22m 20s	NA	20m
Democrat	**Biden**	**Harris**	**Biden**	**Biden**
total words	6450	7992		
Percentage	38.00%	46.00%		39.00%
Time speaking	33m 30s	34m 12s		37m 2s
words/minute	193	233.68		
moderator interruptions		12		5
Trump or moderator interruptions	21	42		50
CNN ORC poll	62	42		53
Republican	**Trump**	**Pence**	**Trump**	**Trump**
total words	6298	8393		
percent speaking time	38.00%	43.00%		41.0%
Time speaking	33m 30s	33m 35s		39m 1s
moderator interruptions		11		48
Biden or moderator interruptions	71	72		37
CNN ORC POLL	27	48		39

Figure 3.1 Overview and Candidate Comparisons in the 2020 Presidential Debates

the debate. Such interactions would be highly informative. In a sixteen-candidate field, two days of one-on-one debates could cut the field in half and feature quarterfinal debates and culminate in a final round debate for the championship. Such tournaments could be frequent and provide candidates with multiple opportunities. Candidates could focus on debates germane to differences with a specific opponent.

8. Utilize debate "tournament formats" to inform the public about large fields of primary candidates. Democrats and Republicans have recently created fields of more than a dozen nominees. In college debates, such entries are handled with a tournament process guided by preliminary head-to-head rounds that are scored and then divided into elimination rounds based on those debates. Candidates would debate one-on-one versus a variety of individuals.

9. Re-center the presidential debate process within the National Archives and Records Administration.[22] The United States under this legislation maintains more than a dozen presidential libraries with elegant facilities. They represent ideal forums for hosting presidential debate events and connecting history to the future of the presidency. The Reagan library successfully hosted a 2016 Republican primary debate.

10. Create a truly bipartisan advisory group for presidential debates. Former presidential candidate Bob Dole rightly observed that all of the Republicans currently serving on the CPD oppose President Trump.[23] Republicans have complained for more than a decade that the process disfavors their candidates.[24] The public deserves a credible deliberative process.

Do Presidential Debates Matter to the Larger Persuasive Campaign?

More than fourteen billion dollars was spent by the two primary parties to engage the American public in a tectonic sociological war about competing political ideas. In the sum of those events, it is possible to look at any portion of the at least eighteen-month process that leads to the 2020 presidential election and conclude that the small portion does not matter to the larger rhetorical calculus.[25] We know from 2020 exit polls that 13 percent of the public described themselves as making their decision in the last month of the election.[26] However, for we academic experts who parse the persuasion processes, the debates both in the primaries and in the general election period must stand as among the most important persuasive ingredients in any presidential campaigning. We also know in hindsight that the polls predicting a Biden landslide were wrong at both the national level and various swing state levels. Presidential debates do occupy an important role in persuading and galvanizing the public to vote for their candidate. Here are the key reasons for recognizing this important rhetorical reality:

1. More people watch debates than almost any conceivable form of candidate communication. This is true by a factor of at least three.

2. Debates inherently provide rhetorical contrasts often lacking in other channels, media, and forms of communication. These contrasts form the essential basis of voting.
3. Reactions to the debate in comedic outlets, media outlets, and social media forums are among the most significant parts of twenty-first-century campaigning. These reactions amplify the original importance of the debates.
4. Debates remain the ideal format for comparing candidates and potentially mitigating the dangerous alternative to credible politics: propaganda.[27]

These reasons continue to underscore the importance of presidential debates and their intimate connection to the larger legitimacy of representative democracy. The general American public is increasingly skeptical of the media framing mechanisms presenting political content. The ability to directly compare arguments between competing candidates is best accomplished by debates functioning in unfiltered formats where "fact checks" and moderator intervention is minimized. To pretend that such unfettered access to candidates and direct comparison is unrealistic is a dangerous form of intellectual gaslighting. Debates take place around the world and among children and adults. The debate process can help restore credibility to our twenty-first-century political process so badly damaged in the present.

CONCLUSIONS

Presidential debates remain one of the most important ingredients in the persuasive process leading to the most powerful public office in the world. Polling research in 2020 suggested that presidential debates were a noticeable factor in how candidates won or lost in 2016.[28] Without well-constructed debates, the natural tendency of political argument and its larger thinking process of ideology is to yield processes more common to propaganda. The 2020 presidential debates were structured through the moderator processes to check the incumbent president and provide a valuable insurgency to the challenger. The main reason incumbent politicians refuse to do public debates is that the first debate will inevitably elevate the challenger and help their campaign. In the American presidential debate process incumbents have lost every first debate since 1960. Incumbents typically recover and perform most strongly in the third and final debate. This round of presidential debates was reduced from three to two and mitigated the recovery of the incumbent. Most experts agreed that Trump's performance in the second debate was better than in the first. Americans should aspire to a better debating process that does not defer the deliberative characteristics of a debate in favor of an ideological iterative press conference designed to discredit the political party challenging the journalists' dominant narrative. Diminishing and even removing the journalist moderators would elevate the deliberative value of the debates and send a positive signal to all dissident communities around the world. The free and reasonable debate is the path to meaningful self-discovery and greater social improvements.

As commentators increasingly express alarm over First Amendment civil right guarantees of freedom of speech, American society is tending toward a reactionary ideological culture that seeks to reduce the wide-ranging political conversation of America to a duel between the Democratic Party and Socialist advocates such as Senator Bernie Sanders. President Trump endured one-sided media coverage throughout the election cycle, and that mediation was amplified as a propaganda goal in the selection and behavior of journalist moderators. President Trump was debating the moderators in both debates and was likely to debate a third if Scully had not been disqualified for his brazen partisan planning prior to the debate. Debate is the global antidote to propaganda. Propaganda is the prelude to injustice and violations of civil rights. Understanding the failings of the 2020 presidential debates should be a pretext to meaningful reform that makes intellectually honest debate the centerpiece of true representative democracies.

Jurgen Habermas' elusive communication competence[29] is found in the teaching of the debate so global publics are able to apprehend and resist propaganda denying the humanity of fellow human beings. The low discursive complexity of a world without debate breeds violence, injustice, and ultimately genocide. These are broader ramifications to specific solutions sought in the imaginative world of public debate. We must build, more broadly, a pedagogy of debate that disseminates discursive complexity. In this new pedagogy, the individual tendency to shrink and be silent in the face of discrimination and crimes diminishes, and the bravery and courage common to efforts to stop the worst of human harms rises. Fixing the American presidential debate process of the distortions plaguing it in election 2020 would be an important step forward for the nation and the world at large.

Chapter 4

Political Advertising in the 2020 U.S. Presidential Election

John C. Tedesco and Scott Dunn

Following the 2016 presidential election, when for the first time in several election cycles that expenditures by the two major-party candidates did not exceed expenditures from the prior presidential campaign, there were questions about whether 2016 was the start of a shift away from televised advertisements. Since digital ads allow microtargeting, or the ability to reach very narrow segments of the voting population, and social media provide direct candidate-to-voter communication, we wondered whether the shift away from television advertising would be even more discernible in 2020. However, perhaps with the aid of the public health pandemic that forced many Americans into work-at-home or shelter-in-place mandates, televised political advertising came roaring back in the 2020 presidential campaign.

The 2020 U.S. presidential election is historically significant and remarkable for many reasons, most likely to be remembered more for the after-election challenge. The political context included an impeached president, a public health pandemic and its economic fallout, civil unrest caused by the murder of George Floyd and the resulting Black Lives Matter social justice movement, the first African-American and Asian-American woman on a major-party ballot, and the confirmation process for Justice Amy Coney Barrett following the death of Justice Ruth Bader Ginsburg in the final weeks of the election. While these context features are important, it is the public health pandemic that most significantly impacted campaign communication. For example, the campaigns were unable to engage in the same amount of face-to-face or door-to-door voter registration and get-out-the-vote drives. Campaign events, such as fundraising dinners and candidate rallies had to be scaled back significantly, canceled, or reworked for online delivery. The predominantly remote and prerecorded party nominating convention speeches, for the most part, failed to capture the ceremonial atmosphere and celebration that typifies a nominating convention. The pandemic also impacted the voting process as states made adjustments to early voting, mail-in, and absentee voting procedures with the goal to offer voters a safe way to participate in the election. As the pandemic forced schools and universities to move instruction online and required organizations to allow many of their employees to work from home, in-home data use increased significantly.[1] In fact, the 38 percent increase in in-home data usage spanned streaming sticks, gaming consoles, televisions, computers, phones, and tablets.

Given the context for the 2020 presidential election, it is unlikely that historians will identify political advertising as one of the most remarkable or historically significant features of the election. But, political advertising is about making small shifts in the margins, so even if effective at mobilizing a small percentage of voters, "reaching Americans in their homes across a variety of consumable media was the key to persuading leaning or undecided voters."[2] The number of advertisements aired, the pervasiveness of advertising in competitive races, and the record amount of advertising expenditures suggest that advertising continues to play a central role in campaigns. Although this chapter does not measure advertising effects on voters, it does address the content of the candidate ads and prominent super-PAC ads aired across broadcast and digital platforms. With grassroots campaign communication hampered by the pandemic and the large majority of Americans spending more time at home, campaigns leaned on advertising more heavily than ever to reinforce or mobilize voters and potential voters.

Political advertising expenditures during the 2020 U.S. election cycle reached a record of $8.5 billion across television, radio, and digital platforms.[3] Although some of the spending estimates for the presidential campaign vary, AdImpact, formerly Advertising Analytics, reports more than $3 billion of the $8.5 billion was spent on advertising in the primary and general election phases of the presidential election. AdImpact's 2020 Political Cycle Review details political advertising expenditures by election level, media market, and media type. The Biden campaign ($652 million), the Democratic presidential primary campaign of former New York Governor Mike Bloomberg ($582 million), and the Trump campaign ($381 million),[4] which AdImpact identifies as the three campaigns with the highest advertising expenditures in presidential history, certainly contributed to the record level of expenditures. However, political action committees (PACs) raised and spent hundreds of millions during the general election phase of the campaign. Since the 2010 U.S. Supreme Court ruling on *Citizens United v. Federal Election Commission*, which determined that corporate independent political expenditure limits violated First Amendment rights of corporations, super-PACs have played an important role in the political advertising landscape. Wesleyan Media Project, which is an advertising tracking collaboration between The John S. and James L. Knight Foundation, the Democracy Fund, and Wesleyan University, identified significant advertising expenditures from a large number of PACs.

BIDEN CAMPAIGN AND PRO-DEMOCRAT PACS

The Biden for President campaign spent more than $617 million on advertising and the Democratic National Committee (DNC) contributed another $32 million. The Biden Victory Fund, which is a committee that raises money in coordination with the DNC, spent an additional $80 million to support Biden's campaign. Five pro-Democrat PACs (Future Forward, Priorities USA Action, Independence USA PAC, American Bridge 21st Century, and The Lincoln Project) combined to spend an additional $300 million to support the Biden campaign.

According to AdImpact, Future Forward PAC spent $118 million on advertising during the general election.[5] Some of the significant donors to Future Forward include Facebook co-founder Dustin Moskovitz and former Google CEO Eric Schmidt. Former New York City Mayor Michael Bloomberg created Independence USA PAC in 2012 to support candidates interested in bi-partisan cooperation. Independence USA spent nearly $70 million during the 2020 presidential election. Priorities USA was formed in 2011 to support Barack Obama's 2012 reelection campaign. It supported Hillary Clinton's 2016 presidential campaign and data suggests it spent about $70 million to support Joe Biden. American Bridge 21st Century, or AB PAC, was founded by Media Matters for America founder David Brock in 2010 and focuses on opposition research. Billionaire George Soros was the largest donor to AB PAC in its early years. AdImpact indicates AB PAC spent $41 million,[6] but Ballotpedia shows advertising expenditures exceed $50 million to oppose President Trump's reelection. Some additional pro-Democrat PACs sponsoring digital or television advertisements include a partnership between the Latino Victory Fund and Priorities USA Action, Unite the Country, and Republican Voters Against Trump.

TRUMP CAMPAIGN AND SUPPORTING PACS

The Democrats had a larger number of supportive PACs and they spent $164 million more than the pro-Republican PACs.[7] America First Action was established in 2017 to help the White House accomplish its issue agenda. America First Action is supported by wealthy donors, including Ike Perlmutter, chairman of Marvel Entertainment, and his wife Laura, and

Republican megadonor Timothy Mellon. American First Action spent more than $55 million on advertising, mostly in battleground states of Florida, Pennsylvania, Ohio, and Wisconsin.[8] Preserve America PAC was late to enter the 2020 political landscape. It was formed in August 2020 by pro-Trump Republicans aimed at stopping Joe Biden and the "radical left-wing." Preserve American PAC spent nearly $60 million against Biden during the general election. NRA (National Rifle Association) Victory Fund did not have the resources in 2020 to spend at the levels they have spent in the past, but others include Americans for Limited Government, Restoration PAC, and Committee to Defend the President. The Republicans continue to attract wealthy donors, while the Democrats were more successful in raising money through small donations.

The literature review will present a brief overview of some important political advertising research that will help frame our description and analysis of the 2020 ads.

CONTENT AND EFFECTS OF POLITICAL ADVERTISING

Political communication scholars have studied political advertising content and effects ever since the first presidential advertisements in 1952. Although the concept of "political advertising" is often associated with television spots, scholars have expanded the definition to include any political messages that are totally controlled by the sponsoring candidate or organization and distributed through mass channels.[9] This definition is expansive enough to include not only television and radio spots but also direct mail, posters, and pamphlets, as well as paid messages distributed through social media and other online platforms. By contrast, this definition does not include campaign events like speeches and rallies, which most voters (besides those who are physically present) experience only through the filter of the news media.

Although pamphlets and other campaign-created messages that would meet this broad definition of political advertising have existed since the early days of American democracy, the modern age of political advertising begins with the arrival of television advertising in the 1952 presidential campaign.[10] The role of advertising in campaigns grew quickly, with advertising costs becoming the major expenditure for campaigns and a cornerstone of their rhetorical strategies. In the twenty-first century, television advertising has continued to be a key aspect of political campaigns while digital advertising has increased in importance. Consequently, voters in states and districts with competitive elections often cannot escape political ads, whether they encounter them on television, social media, search engine results, advertising-supported streaming services like Hulu and Pandora, or online video games.[11]

Despite mixed evidence of political advertising's effectiveness,[12] campaigns continue to spend large percentages of their budgets on television and digital advertising. Advertising is attractive to campaigns because the campaigns not only control the content of the ads but also provide the ability to target specific publics with the ads. For instance, campaigns and interest groups typically buy television advertising time from network affiliates, allowing them to target distribution of the ad geographically, whether they want to target a specific district in a House of Representatives race or a select group of swing states in a presidential race. Direct mail and digital platforms allow "microtargeting" to people in very specific demographic and psychographic categories. While it is true that campaigns can get a lot of value from earned media, especially a candidate like Donald Trump, who attracts huge crowds at his rallies, the control over messages and audiences provided by advertising ensures that it remains a key component of political communication strategies.

Scholars have identified multiple categorical schemes for classifying political ads. One popular distinction is between positive ads (those that extoll the virtues of a candidate) and negative or attack ads (those that attack an opposing candidate). In addition to these two types, scholars have recognized the importance of comparative or contrast ads, which combine elements of the positive and the negative, as well as response ads that reply to an opponent's attack.[13] Research shows that political advertising has tended to become more negative over time, though that trend is far from linear, with somewhat more positive campaigns in 1960 and 2000, for instance.[14] This trend toward negativity has particularly accelerated due to the increased spending on advertising from groups not officially affiliated with the campaigns. This practice goes back at least to the Democrats for Nixon organization that ran negative ads against George McGovern in 1972.[15] The role of unaffiliated groups has accelerated in the twenty-first century as legal changes (e.g., *Citizens United*) have given such groups more leeway and incentive to run ads that are independent of the campaigns.[16]

The use of independent groups to fund political advertising offers at least two advantages over campaign-funded advertising. First, independent groups are largely exempt from legal limits on donations that apply to campaigns. Thus, a multibillionaire like George Soros can donate no more than $2,800 to a candidate's official campaign,[17] but he can donate millions of dollars to "super-PACs" that are virtually unregulated. The second advantage for independent groups is that they can run ads attacking a candidate without as much worry about a backlash hurting their preferred candidate. Many voters dislike attack ads, and campaigns fear that they will have the unintended consequence of turning off voters and discouraging them from voting for the sponsoring candidate. The evidence is mixed on whether attack ads boomerang and diminish the sponsoring candidate,[18] but the conventional wisdom is that this reaction is less likely to happen when an ad identifies an outside group as its sponsor.

The 2016 presidential election illustrated the trend of attack ads largely sponsored by outsides groups. Ads sponsored by Hillary Clinton's campaign were 34 percent positive, 50 percent negative, and 16 percent comparative, while ads from Donald Trump's campaign were 21 percent positive, 41 percent negative, and 38 percent comparative.[19] While those numbers indicate quite a negative campaign, they pale in comparison to the negativity that came from outside groups. There are so many groups sponsoring political ads that it is difficult to address all the groups and their ads, but based on the ads included in one analysis, about 90 percent of ads from groups supporting each candidate were negative.[20] Overall, 70 percent of the ads run by campaigns and outside groups in 2016 were negative, which is even more than the level of negativity in the 2012 political campaign, which was, in turn, considerably more negative than other recent campaigns.[21]

Besides the frequency of positive and attack ads, scholars have identified specific goals and strategies used in both types. The two most common functions of positives ads are to define the candidate's image for voters and to explain his or her position on issues, but such ads can serve a variety of other functions such as to reinforce positive feelings, to redefine or soften a candidate's existing image, to raise money, to present statistical or factual information, or to focus on shared public values.[22] A particularly important function is to associate the candidate with the characteristics of a "benevolent leader."[23] Negative ads are generally designed not only to associate political opponents with negative traits and failed or unsuccessful policies but also to set the opponent's "rhetorical agenda" and put the opponent on the defensive.[24]

Besides the positive or negative tone of the ads, scholars have noted the importance of distinguishing between ads that focus on policy issues versus those that focus on candidates' images. Although many ads have at least some content focused on both issues and image, ads generally focus more on one than the other.[25] This distinction provides important insights into particular candidates' advertising strategies. For instance, in 2016, pro-Clinton ads mostly focused on image, with most of those ads being negative or comparative, showing that the Clinton campaign and outside groups supporting her focused strategically on attacking Trump's character.[26] While Trump also ran a lot of ads attacking Clinton, his campaign also ran a substantial number of issue-focused comparative ads.[27]

The result of these strategic decisions from both campaigns was that low-information voters who rely largely on advertising saw comparisons of the candidates' issue positions presented in ways that were favorable to Trump with no equivalent comparisons coming from the Clinton camp.[28] The only consistent message voters got from pro-Clinton ads was that Trump lacked the character traits that would make for a strong president, which was a message they were already getting from media coverage of Trump.[29] This finding from 2016 is also interesting in light of research showing that negative ads have tended to be more issue-oriented historically, but the ads in 2016 show the exact opposite pattern.[30] It is possible that this result indicates a shift toward more negative image-advertising, though it is also possible that it is an anomaly from an election in which both major-party candidates were strongly disliked by the public.[31]

Based on the categories identified in this literature review, the authors examined all of the ads they identified as sponsored by the official Trump and Biden campaigns and the major outside groups that supported each candidate. The authors used an open-coding approach to identify the major themes and strategies that appeared in each set of ads. No definitive archive of ads in the 2020 election was available, so the authors built their own from the campaigns' YouTube channels, websites of outside groups, and Google searches. While it is not realistic to propose that we found every ad that was made supporting each candidate, we are confident that we found a large and representative enough sample for the purposes of this qualitative analysis.

MAJOR THEMES AND STRATEGIES IN BIDEN'S ADS

Joe Biden's campaign was very active posting both television spots and online-only adlike videos. Between September 1 and Election Day, the campaign posted more than 200 videos on YouTube that were less than two minutes long and resembled a traditional ad format, and our search unearthed other ads that only appeared on other social media sites or streaming services.[32] Despite the high number of ads, there were three (sometimes overlapping) main themes and strategies that emerged: Biden as a benevolent leader, indirect attacks on Trump, and personal testimonials.

Biden as Benevolent Leader

One of the most dominant themes of Biden's ads was the idea of Biden as a "benevolent leader." The ads often associated the former vice president explicitly with many of the elements of the benevolent leader framing identified by Joslyn: compassion, empathy, integrity, activity, strength, and knowledge. One example is an ad titled "Ser Humano,"[33] which starts with images of various former presidents engaging in compassionate or empathetic actions, such as George W. Bush putting his arm around a firefighter at the World Trade Center site and Jimmy Carter building a home (presumably for Habitat for Humanity). The second half of the ad shows Biden warmly shaking hands with, high-fiving, and hugging various ordinary Americans. As these images play out, a voiceover from former President Barack Obama states the importance of the Spanish phrase "ser humano," literally translated as "not only a human being, but to *be* one . . . it means caring for all and leading with empathy, no matter the challenges. It means showing compassion for your neighbor." Obama goes on to state this empathy and compassion "can never be optional."

The message of this ad is clear: empathy and compassion are essential traits that many previous presidents have embodied and that Biden will likewise embody. Of course, though the ad includes former presidents from both parties, one glaring omission is central to the message of the ad: Donald Trump. In fact, the ad may be a more effective anti-Trump ad than if Trump were actually named. By associating Biden with a range of (relatively) popular presidents and pointedly leaving Trump out, the message is clear: Biden has the kind of empathy and compassion that people expect in a president and that Trump lacks.

An ad called "It's about Us"[34] makes this comparison with Trump more explicit. As the viewer sees images of empty storefronts and people working in kitchens, hotels, and farms, Biden says in a voiceover, "Donald Trump fails the most important test of being an American president, the duty to care for you, for all of us." Biden makes a bold statement here—that compassion for the American people is not just an important trait in a president but also a consideration that should take precedence over any other leadership trait or policy position. Later in the ad, Biden says of Trump, "He's quit on you, he's quit on this country. . . . A president's supposed to care, to lead, to take responsibility." This statement invokes another aspect of the benevolent leader framing: activity. According to this ad, Trump's lack of compassion and empathy have led him to fail to support people in need during the COVID-19 pandemic and subsequent economic downturn, so he is not just uncaring—he's also inactive when action is needed most.

Another ad, "Rising,"[35] attacks Trump for lacking another characteristic of benevolent leaders: integrity. The ad alternates images of Biden addressing the camera directly with images of Biden greeting a diverse array of voters. Biden states, "Who we are, what we stand for, maybe most importantly, who we're going to be is all at stake. Character's on the ballot, the character of the country." The positive images of Biden contrast with the clear statement that the country's *soul* is at stake. The spiritual connotations of that word choice emphasize the stakes of the comparison he makes between himself and Trump. As with some previously examined ads, Biden does not use Trump's name, but he makes the target of the attack clear when he says, "This is our opportunity to leave the dark, angry politics of the past four years behind us."

As with the "Ser Humano" ad, Biden singles Trump out as the anomaly. The message of the visuals is that Biden is the kind of leader voters expect, which the text makes it clear that Trump is not.

Even ads that are ostensible "issue ads" promote Biden as a benevolent leader, especially ads that focus on the issue of health care. The clearest example is probably an ad called "Personal."[36] This ad starts with Biden briefly telling the story of the car accident that took the life of his daughter and first wife and left his two sons hospitalized and then the story of losing his son to cancer. He connects these stories to the health care issue, saying, "I can't fathom what would happen if the insurance companies had the power to say, 'The last few months you're on your own.'" He then makes the connection even more explicit: "The fact of the matter is, health care is personal for me, Obamacare is personal to me. When I see the President of the United State try to eliminate this health care in the middle of a public health crisis, that's personal to me too." In a similar ad titled "Lead," Biden promises, "If I have the honor of being president, I promise you I will lead," and then briefly outlines his health care policy proposals. He closes the ad saying, "I will take care of your health care coverage and your family the same way I would my own." In both of these ads, the surface-level focus on health care functions as a vehicle to deliver the real message, that Biden will govern guided by the principles of benevolent leadership. This approach blurs the traditional distinction between "issue ads" and "image ads."

Indirect Attacks on Trump

Many of Biden's ads also blur the distinction between positive and negative ads, and in ways that are subtler than the typical comparative ad. In previous campaigns, comparative ads tended to be basically split ads, with the first half attacking the candidate's opponent and the second half praising the sponsoring candidate.[37] Instead, Biden used indirect attacks that overtly praised him as a candidate while implying an attack on Trump without explicitly mentioning him. As previously noted, some of the ads that focused on Biden as a benevolent leader attacked Trump by omission, clearly suggesting that he lacks the qualities that Biden displays. Several other Biden ads use this strategy to indirectly criticize Trump in more specific ways. An example is an ad called "Empty Chairs in America because of COVID-19."[38] This ad's visuals feature a poignant montage of empty chairs at dining room tables, city streets, offices, a classroom, a stage, a porch, and a school gymnasium. In a voiceover, Biden reports the number of Americans who have died of COVID-19 and says that this death toll "means there are empty chairs at dining room tables and kitchen tables that weeks ago were filled with a loved one, a mom, a dad, a brother or sister." Both the visuals and text drive home for viewers the reality of the pandemic, which can seem remote for those who have not been affected personally. The attack on Trump comes as Biden's voiceover continues, "And so many of them didn't have to lose their lives to this virus," and then onscreen text reads, "Over 220,000 American lives lost because of failed leadership." As with several of the ads mentioned in the previous section, Trump's name is never mentioned, but it is clear that the ad lays the blame for the magnitude of the death toll at his feet for his lack of action in response to the virus.

Another ad called "Vote For"[39] has all of the surface-level characteristics of a classic positive ad. As an upbeat Nina Simone song[40] plays in the background, Biden's voiceover makes this simple, straightforward statement: "The days of divisiveness will soon be over. We can build a more perfect union. We can believe again." Meanwhile, the visuals show images of people hugging, protesting, and praying, along with iconic images of Americana like a rural church, a rodeo, a waving American flag, and a group of people with their hands over their hearts (presumably pledging allegiance to the flag). It also includes images of popular public figures John McCain and Ruth Bader Ginsburg. The text on the screen tells viewers to "Vote for empathy; vote for respect; vote for honor; vote for equality; vote for bravery; vote for love; vote for truth; vote for choice; vote for the planet; vote for justice; vote for leadership." While on the surface this looks and sounds like a positive ad, the reference to the "days of divisiveness" is a clear reference to the Trump administration, and it is hard to imagine any viewer not recognizing the implication that Trump is the opposite of everything the ad says they should vote for.

Personal Testimonials

Another common strategy used in Biden ads was the use of personal testimonials. While there were a number of ads highlighting well-known figures ranging from basketball star Chris Paul[41] to former First Lady Michelle Obama[42] to poet Nikki Giovanni,[43] these celebrity testimonials tended to appear late in the campaign and focus on get-out-the-vote efforts. These were dwarfed in number by ads featuring noncelebrities giving testimonials about how Trump's policies had affected their lives. These personal testimonial ads focused primarily on two topics: the effects of COVID-19 and racial justice.

Among testimonial ads about COVID-19, some focused on personal effects while others focused on how the pandemic has affected small businesses. The ad "Tell You"[44] took a humorous approach to the personal effects of COVID-19 that was likely quite relatable to many viewers. A woman identified as Margaret from Wisconsin starts to talk to the camera but is repeatedly interrupted by her children and unable to complete a sentence. As she tends to her children, the on-screen text informs viewers that "Margaret is a mother of four during the pandemic. She'd like to tell you that America needs real leadership with a plan to safely reopen schools." Although the tone is light in this ad, viewers who are dealing with children who are home from school during the pandemic can relate to Margaret's struggle to even get through a 30-second ad without interruptions. As with many ads cited previously, the ad also makes clear the contrast between Trump's handling of the pandemic and Biden's hypothetical handling of it (again, without naming Trump directly).

An ad called "My Mom" displays a more serious approach to presenting the pandemic's personal toll. In this ad, Marygrace from Archbald, Pennsylvania, recounts her mother's struggle with COVID-19 that eventually led to her death. In a particularly emotional detail, she reports that she had to use the FaceTime app to say goodbye to her mother. She then connects her experience to the president, saying that she thought the president would take the pandemic more seriously once he contracted the virus himself. With an impassioned tone, she says, "It is so disrespectful as an American who lost my mom to COVID to watch him downplay the virus. To see the president get top-notch medical care and not encourage a mask is heartbreaking." Interspersed with Marygrace's testimonial, the ad shows clips of President Trump addressing the nation after his recovery from COVID-19, saying, "I learned so much about coronavirus . . . Don't let it dominate you . . . Don't be afraid of it . . . Don't let it take over your lives." The clear goal of this juxtaposition is the make viewers connect the feelings of pathos that arise from hearing the story of a lost mother to the president's weak response to the pandemic, as reflected in his words.

A variation of this theme is seen in ads that focus on the effects of COVID-19 on small businesses. An example is an ad titled "Building Back Small Businesses,"[45] which focuses on a salon owner named Nefertiti in Detroit, Michigan. She talks about the important role salons play in African-American communities and how "COVID just put an end to all of that." More specifically, she states that her business has dropped by 75 percent and that many of her clients have died during the pandemic. She explicitly lays the blame on Trump, saying, "This current administration did not give us the information that they knew." She contrasts Trump's actions with Biden's "build back better plan," which she believes will help small businesses like hers get back on their feet. This phrasing connects to the "Build Back Better" branding that was prominent in campaign messaging around the time of the Democratic National Convention.[46] Although this branding was not seen as commonly in general election Biden ads as it was in convention speeches, this ad is one example of how it is employed strategically when specifically discussing the effects of COVID-19 on small businesses.

An ad that focuses on a different type of small business is "Totally Negligent,"[47] which features Rick from Lawrence County, Pennsylvania, who runs a farm that's been in his family for three generations. After expressing his love of the farming lifestyle, Rick shares that he voted for Trump in 2016, which he calls a "mistake." He goes on to say and discuss how Trump's handling of the pandemic has made it hard to make money as a farmer, saying, "President Trump, he's not responsible for this virus, nobody was going to be able to stop that, but he was totally negligent on how he informed the people." As in the previous ad, Rick draws an explicit contrast between how Trump handled the pandemic and how Biden would: "You know, with Joe Biden I think we've got a person that's got some compassion and he's got a real plan to get things going, turned around. You know, I made a mistake in '16, I won't make a mistake in 2020." This ad is also interesting for being one of the few featuring someone who voted for Trump and decided to vote for Biden, another theme that was more prominent at the Democratic National Convention than it was in Biden's advertising.[48]

The other major theme seen in personal testimonial advertising was racial justice. Perhaps the most powerful ad in this category was one titled "Elsie,"[49] about an African-American man by that name whose exact age is not given, but he says he "was born in the Great Depression." His grandson reports that Elsie was "the first black licensed plumber in eastern North Carolina." Elsie relates voting for the first time after the civil rights movement had secured that right for African Americans in the South: "They put a sticker on me. I wore that sticker till it wore out." Elsie's grandson connects the story with why he and his grandfather are voting for Biden: "I don't want to live through the era that my grandfather lived through. I want to live in a country for all people." Like several previously discussed ads, this one combines an uplifting explicit message about Biden with an implicit attack on Trump.

Direct Attacks in PAC Ads

As noted in the literature review, outside groups have historically run more negative ads than official candidate campaigns, and those groups that supported Biden in 2020 largely continued this pattern. Although these groups did run positive and comparative ads, the bulk of their ads were negative in a more direct way than those coming from the Biden campaign. One particularly hard-hitting ad is "Somos Patriotas,"[50] from Independence USA. The ad features Santiago D. Morales, a Cuban exile identified as a "member of Brigade 2506" and a "political prisoner for 18 years." After discounting the idea that people who support Biden are socialists or communists, Morales compares Trump to dictators Hugo Chavez and Fidel Castro. He then makes this bold statement: "We either vote for Biden or we bury democracy in this country." While the Biden campaign's ads regularly attacked Trump, even their more direct attacks stopped well short of associating the president with dictators or starkly stating that American democracy will be buried if Trump were reelected.

Another group that aggressively attacked President Trump was the Lincoln Project, a group of Republican leaders who opposed Trump and politicians associated with him.[51] One of their harshest attacks came in an ad called "Imagine,"[52] featuring former Maryland lieutenant governor and Republican National Committee chair Michael Steele. After recounting the plot to assassinate President Lincoln in Baltimore just before his inauguration, Steele says, "In the days ahead we may face a crisis of similar proportion, an outlaw president clinging to power and defying the will of the people." Steele goes on to encourage viewers to vote for Biden because the alternative is to "plunge our country into chaos." He closes the ad with the line, "America or Trump? I choose America." Again, Biden's official campaign ads made it clear that Trump had failed to be the kind of leader America needed, but only outside groups like the Lincoln Project used their ads to explicitly frame Trump as anti-American.

Overall, this analysis shows that much of the pro-Biden advertising was in fact anti-Trump advertising, though it did always take the form of classic negative, or even comparative, advertising. The Biden campaign itself used pointed but often indirect attacks to show that Biden would be the kind of benevolent leader that Trump was not, while outside groups delivered more pointed attacks.

MAJOR THEMES AND STRATEGIES IN TRUMP'S ADS

Identifying the universe of Trump 2020 political ads is a difficult challenge since the advertisements were not posted on the Trump campaign website and no official list exists. Trump's YouTube channel, iSpot.tv, and media websites were scanned to identify the range of paid political ads. A review of the advertising content reveals the Trump campaign focused on themes of American Comeback, Fear of Biden's America, and attacks on Biden and his family.

American Comeback: Jobs and Economy

President Trump's campaign made expensive advertising buy to air two television commercials during the Super Bowl LIV. The first ad, "Stronger, Safer, More Prosperous,"[53] begins with the anonymous announcer asserting "America demanded change . . . and change is what we got" with ceremonial images of Trump taking his Inaugural oath and images of American military strength. The announcer continues, "Under President Trump, America is stronger, safer, and more prosperous than ever before." Clips of news segments where different reporters are quoted in sequence, "best wage growth I think we've seen in almost a decade," then "unemployment rate sinking to a 49 year low," followed by "unemployment for African Americans fell to a new low" and "unemployment for Hispanics hit an all-time record low." The proclamations about unemployment for racial groups are made while images of racially diverse workers in American manufacturing are shown, giving the impression that media everywhere are singing the praises of Trump's job creation. The advertisement ends with Trump addressing a crowd and stating, "and ladies and gentlemen, the best is yet to come."

Throughout the campaign, this theme was repeated regularly. In fact, Trump named one of his ads, "American Comeback."[54] The advertisement begins with images of coronavirus vaccine vials in production as the announcer begins, "In the race for a vaccine, the finish line is approaching. Safety protocols in place. And the greatest economy the world has ever seen coming back to life. But, Joe Biden wants to change all that." Then, Biden is shown stating, "I will shut it down." The announcer resumes, "Why would we ever let Joe Biden kill countless American businesses, jobs, and our economic future when President Trump's Great American Comeback is underway?" The ad features images from an array of work settings and shows people getting back to work. Text on screen quotes CNBC, "Payrolls INCREASE by nearly 1.4 MILLION as the unemployment rate tumbles." This ad attempts to imply that Biden's policies to address our public health pandemic would result in significant loss of jobs and damage to our economy and its recovery.

In one of the last ads released by the campaign, "Strength,"[55] Trump addresses how America is renewing, restoring, and rebuilding following the public health pandemic and civil unrest. The anonymous announcer states, "Strength, it's a word we've heard a lot this year. Strength of the American people. Strength of the American worker. Strength of the American family. We've seen grit, determination, optimism, hope. We took the virus head on and now we are getting back to a normal life . . . the second shift, the dance lessons, and Friday night football." This portion of the advertisement opens with images of a battleship to exhibit America's strength, then shows images of family and children, manufacturing, medical workers, and parents teaching at home during the pandemic to demonstrate that America is moving forward despite the pandemic. Then, the ad contrasts with an attack that asserts, "But some want to tear us down. They don't believe in America's promise. Their ideas would kill jobs and drag down our economy." In the contrast, the images turn negative and show what appears to be looting, rioting, and an American flag on fire with closed and shuttered businesses. The ad returns to a favorable message, "We'll never give up on America. Not now, not ever. Because now is a time to renew our faith, restore our safety, rebuild our economy to keep winning. We faced our toughest challenge and we are overcoming it just like we always do. Because we believe in America." The advertisement ends with the Iwo Jima Monument in the foreground and the Washington Monument in the background, iconic American symbolism before the screen fades to the American flag.

Fear of Biden's America

Trump attacked Biden's policies and attempted to equate Biden with the radical left. Following a summer of civil unrest and Black Lives Matter protests, the call to defund the police became a focus of attention among liberals. Although calls to defund the police never included calls to eliminate funding, the defund-the-police calls were used to stoke fears of a lawless country and the absence of a police force to protect and serve citizens in times of emergency.

Trump's ad "911 Police Emergency Line"[56] shows images of an empty police office, social unrest, fires, looting, and protestors holding "defund the police" signs. The announcer, representing the voice of the 911 operator on an answering machine, states, "You have reached the 911 police emergency line. Due to defunding of the police department, we're sorry, but no one is here to take your call. If you're calling to report a rape, please press 1. To report a murder, press 2. To report a home invasion, press 3. For all other crimes, leave your name and number and someone will get back to you. Our estimated wait time is currently 5 days. Goodbye." Text in the ad reads, "Joe Biden's supporters are fighting to defund police departments," followed by "violent crime has exploded." The ad ends with the text, "You won't be safe in Joe Biden's America." This ad attempts to resonate with real fears that defunding the police would mean that help would not be available in a time of need. Despite the fact that Biden was clear that he didn't support defunding the police, this ad plays on the fears that he will be a pawn to the radical left. Although "Break In,"[57] another Trump ad, is similar in its attack, this ad is more subtle by indicating and suggesting that Biden would not be able to stand up to the radical left and will be influenced by them to defund police.

Trump's ad "Break In" dramatizes the issue by showing an elderly woman at home watching the news and depicting someone trying to break into her home. When she lifts the phone to call for help, the newscaster is heard saying, "Seattle's pledge to defund its police department by fifty percent, even including a proposal to remove 911 dispatchers from police control." An answering machine appears to answer the 911 call and the voice begins, "Hello, you've reached 911. I'm sorry that there is no one here to answer your emergency call. But, leave a message and we'll get back to you as soon as we can." This plays on fears that defunding police means eliminating police. This ad becomes misleading when the voice of Fox News reporter Sean Hannity is heard stating, "Joe Biden said he is absolutely on-board with defunding the police," followed by an out-of-context quote where Hannity tells the viewer to "listen closely" followed by a voiceover of Biden stating, "Yes, absolutely." Hannity stating that Biden is "absolutely on-board" is not true and the text on screen states, "Joe Biden wants to reduce police funding," followed by the text, "You won't be safe in Joe Biden's America."

Trump's ads also attack Biden's tax plan and suggest that Americans should be afraid of the taxes he will impose. In "The Real Biden Plan"[58] and "American Can't Afford Biden,"[59] Trump plays on fears of a significant tax increase directed toward the middle class, seniors, and small businesses. These ads also weave in fear of immigrants as a drain on our resources or competition in the workforce by suggesting that Biden would grant citizenship to 11 million undocumented residents. The ads suggest that taxes would increase while Biden extends free health care, Social Security, and Medicare for illegal immigrants that would be granted amnesty. "American Can't Afford Biden" is particularly misleading because it takes a statement from Biden out of context. When talking about the wealthy who appeared to benefit from Trump's tax policy by getting tax relief, Biden responded, "If you elect me, your taxes are gonna be raised, not cut," implying that Biden's plan represents the largest tax hike in history. The ad suggests that Biden is talking to the folks in the audience, not about the 1 percent.

Attacks: Biden Corruption

Trump's most blatant attacks accuse Biden and his son Hunter of lies and corruption. For example, in "Biden Lied,"[60] "Biden Corruption,"[61] and "Why Did Joe Biden Let Hunter Do It,"[62] Hunter Biden's dealings with Ukrainian and Chinese energy companies are presented as corrupt. In "Biden Lied," Hunter is asked whether he would be on the Board of Burisma if his last name was not Biden. After Hunter admits it is unlikely, the ad alleges that the former vice president lied to the American people and met with the Ukrainian executive that hired Hunter. The ads argue that Biden was complicit with Hunter getting deals because of his father's status and allege that the former vice president was lying about the lucrative deals and whether he benefited from them as well.

Positive Ads

While Trump did not appear to air the same volume of positive ads in 2020 as he did in 2016, the positive ads were strategic ads and capitalized on some of the economic indicators achieved in his presidency. Trump's positive ads messages promote the prepandemic economy, criminal justice reform, and appeal to racial minorities. One of the Super Bowl ads, "President Trump Got It Done,"[63] tells the story of Alice Johnson, who was serving a life sentence for a nonviolent drug offense. The ad states, "Alice Johnson was sentenced to serve life in prison for a nonviolent drug offense. Thanks to President Trump, people like Alice are getting a second chance. Politicians talk about criminal justice reform. President Trump got it done. Thousands of families are being united." The ad shows powerful images of Ms. Johnson's release from prison into the arms of supporting family and friends. She states, "With gratitude, I want to thank President Donald John Trump" while those greeting her cheer. "Man of His Word"[64] is a Trump ad that appears to be shot on location at a Trump rally. Testimonials are used in this ad, with an African-American supporter opening the ad with, "Look at our economy, look what he's done. I mean how can you not support the president." Then, an older African-American male states, "He's done more for the Black people than they realize. He gave us jobs when we didn't have none. Donald Trump is a man of his word." The ad cuts to a Latina in the crowd who states, "This is freedom. I was 9 years old and had to be in line to get 10 pieces of roll or bread. That is socialism. This is freedom. President Trump, thank you." The ad goes on to celebrate job creation, soaring income, and reduced poverty under Trump. The visuals in the ad show racial minorities at the rally and signs that state, "Cubans for Trump," "Latinos for Trump," "Women for Trump," "Veterans for Trump," and "Cops for Trump." The use of first-person testimonials from racially diverse Trump supporters enabled minority voters to express their reasons for supporting Trump.

Pro-Trump PACs

America First Action PAC and Preserve America PAC each spent more than $50 million on advertising to support Trump. America First Action began airing ads shortly after Democratic primary candidate and Vermont Senator Bernie Sanders dropped out of the race and Biden was the evident nominee. As is expected from third-party independent groups, America First Action ads were hard-hitting attacks on Biden's record. In the initial set of ads titled "Bad Folks,"[65] "Biden Origin,"[66] and "Forty Years,"[67] launched by America First Action targeting battleground states, Biden is associated with failed policies toward China. The ad narrator in "Bad Folks" states, "China is killing our jobs, stealing technology, putting America's health in danger." Biden is quoted as stating that China is not competition for the United States and that the Chinese are not bad folks. In "Biden Origin," the narrator indicates that "Joe Biden has led the charge" in making China great by allowing the Chinese to steal American manufacturing and hording emergency protective gear during the pandemic. The narrator ends with, "Now more than ever America must stop China and to stop China you have to stop Joe Biden." In "Forty Years," Biden is attacked for labeling Trump's ban on flights from China as xenophobic. Biden is criticized in the ad for saying he feels the same way about China now as he did in 1979: "that a rising China is a positive development." Trump blamed China for the "deadly epidemic" and concluded that he has been wrong on China for 40 years. After his initial set of ads regarding Biden's policy toward China, an additional ad called "China Prosperity"[68] echoed some of the arguments in the first wave of ads.

America First Action also painted Biden as too weak to stand up to the radical left. Similar to Trump's "911 Police Emergency Line," America First Action's "On Hold"[69] attacks Biden by alleging that he supports defunding the police. "On Hold" is a dramatized spot that shows a mother and child hiding from what appears to be a violent uprising. The 911 operator in the ad states, "You have reached 911 emergency services. Due to budget cuts and increased criminal activity, our agents are busy assisting other callers. The hold time is 17 minutes. Have a nice day." The ad plays on fears that Democrats want to eliminate critical police support in communities. In "Pandemic Tax,"[70] America First Action attacked Biden's tax plan as raising taxes on every income group, including middle-class retirement. Several other ads, including "Joe Biden's Tax Hike,"[71] attack the Biden tax plan.

Preserve America used testimonials from real citizens to attack Biden and his plans. In "Alyssa,"[72] Alyssa Cordova, the wife of a slain on-duty police officer, indicates that Biden lacks leadership because he had not condemned the violent protests. "Gillis"[73] features a testimonial from a retired Los Angeles Police Department lieutenant whose daughter was murdered by a gang for being the daughter of a police officer. In "Too Weak,"[74] Biden is portrayed as too weak to lead the country at a time when arson, looting, and lawlessness were rampant in cities across America. His insistence that the protest was peaceful was challenged with footage from Minneapolis, Seattle, Portland, New York, Chicago, and the ad ends with the tag, "He's the wrong man for these times." Preserve America also attacked Biden's record on jobs, out-sourcing manufacturing, and taxes. "Dave,"[75] an Iowa trucker and proud Teamsters Union member, provides a first-person testimonial where he asserts that Biden has been shipping American jobs overseas for more than forty years and will unleash the largest tax hike in history. "Dave" ends with the assertion that "Joe Biden will kill jobs and drive our economy into the ground."

CONCLUSION

Since the "Eisenhower Answers America" advertising campaign in the 1952 U.S. presidential election, political ads have been instrumental for presidential candidates. However, after the 2016 presidential election, which witnessed less in advertising expenditures than the 2012 presidential campaign, we questioned whether the emergence of other direct forms of communication between candidates and voters meant we would continue to see paid televised ads diminish as a portion of presidential campaign strategy. Since televised political advertising is so expensive, it would be understandable that campaigns would lean more heavily on digital advertising, which is not only less expensive but also more efficient in that it is better able to reach targeted audiences who share specific characteristics or positions. However, televised political advertising came roaring back in 2020.

It is unlikely that voters in any media market, even those most saturated with political advertising, would see all the ads that the candidates and their supporting issue groups or PACs produced. Projects like Wesleyan Media Project and AdImpact offer rich data on advertising expenditures and the number of ads aired in specific media markets. Although analysis of candidate or campaign message strategies cannot measure how ads impact voters, it does enable researchers to discover the favorable personal qualities, accomplishments, and positions candidates want to promote and it reveals the unfavorable or controversial aspects candidates want to expose about their opponents. Assessing themes in candidate ads helps reveal a candidate's strategy in a state or media market or with a particular voting segment.

While there were many examples of attacks in the 2020 presidential campaign ads, the attacks, in general, were not as personal. In 2016, Clinton and Trump employed ad hominem attacks frequently.[76] There were fewer blatant examples of ad hominem attacks in the 2020 ads, but they were used. While not a major theme across the ads, Trump's ads attacked Biden's cognitive ability by manipulating footage to suggest that some pauses or gaps in Biden's speech reflect a diminished capacity to think clearly or coherently or suggest that Biden needed a teleprompter to answer questions because he did not have the cognitive capacity to respond to reporters' questions. Like in 2016, Trump employed a large number of contrast or comparative ads in 2020. Although we discuss some positive appeals used by Trump, where he mostly underscored his economic record, these were not as pervasive for Trump as in 2016. Biden's campaign appeared more strategic than Clinton's 2016 campaign in that the Biden campaign made certain to offer voters a reason to vote for him. His positive ads discussed the policies that he would support and revealed his compassion, inclusiveness, and his goal to be president for all Americans. Clinton did not use sufficient appeals to discuss how voters would be better off with her as president, and that is not a mistake that the Biden campaign repeated. Although the record number of ads aired on television and digital channels and the record in expenditures were surprising, the ad content was less surprising. In fact, COVID-19 and the public health pandemic, impacts of the pandemic on the economy and jobs, social justice, defunding the police and police reform, and taxes dominated the ads just like they were dominant issues in the news.

It will be interesting to see what happens with advertising in 2024. We are in an interesting information environment where voters are able to avoid mediated messages altogether if they choose or to select media messages that massage their political views instead of challenging them. While candidates and campaigns like direct-to-voter communication that advertising allows, it is easy to observe how unmediated communication between candidates and voters can create problems. Unfortunately, the ads contained a lot of misleading messages, exaggerations, or blatant lies. Even if media organizations could fact check the contents of ads, there is doubt that the electorate would trust the sources critical of candidate messages. Restoring faith in media to perform the fourth estate function and to point out exaggerations, misleading messages, or blatant lies in advertisements is difficult when the electorate has such polarized views of media. Restoring faith in journalism is the single biggest challenge to our democracy since media have long played the role of holding elected officials accountable.

Will we continue to see personal attacks in 2024 political ads or will our election crisis of 2020 create an environment less tolerant of attacks? Will digital ads take a larger share of the advertising pie in 2024? Will audiences revert back to prepandemic media consumption patterns, which would make it harder for campaigns to reach voters through political ads? Will increased reliance on streaming services diminish the importance or utility of political ads? No matter what happens to advertise in 2024, let's hope that the candidates and voters alike do their part to preserve and protect our democracy.

Chapter 5

The Social Media Campaign of 2020

John Allen Hendricks and Dan Schill

As Election Day 2020 approached, voters had many concerns to factor into their voting decisions—mainly, a deadly pandemic that was escalating, an economic recession that was deepening, and systemic racial discrimination that was continuing to reveal itself in deadly ways. On Election Day, the United States Centers for Disease Control reported a staggering 231,988 people had died from COVID-19 and almost 9.3 million more Americans had contracted the novel coronavirus that had originated in Wuhan, China.[1] Both COVID-related statistics were the highest of any nation in the entire world. Because of an economy closed due to the COVID-19 pandemic, the United States Bureau of Labor Statistics reported more than 11 million Americans were unemployed. The number of Americans not in the workforce at the time but searching for a job was hovering at 6.7 million in October as Americans were preparing to choose their next president.[2] The Bureau of Labor Statistics reported an unemployment rate of 7.9 percent and a 3.9 million net job loss under the Trump administration.[3] Other than President Herbert Hoover during the Great Depression, Trump was the only president running for reelection with fewer jobs, overall, than when he entered. As Americans were sheltering in their homes during the early phase of the pandemic, they learned about the death of George Floyd, a 46-year-old African-American man from Minneapolis. Floyd was arrested by Minneapolis police officer Derek Chauvin for allegedly using a counterfeit $20 bill at a convenience store. Bystander video showed Chauvin with his knee on Floyd's neck, for more than 8 minutes, while Floyd was handcuffed and face down on the ground pleading with the officer that he could not breathe. Floyd eventually fell into unconsciousness and was carried away from the scene of the arrest on a gurney after he no longer had a pulse. He was pronounced dead approximately an hour after the arrest.[4] Outraged and horrified at what they witnessed and other racially motivated murders such as those of Ahmaud Arbery and Breonna Taylor, an estimated 15 million to 26 million people took to the streets, in urban, suburban, and rural areas, to protest against incidents of systemic, racially motivated violence, and police brutality.[5] Partially due to the outcry, Officer Chauvin was eventually charged with murder and arrested.

In addition to the 2020 presidential campaign being framed by a global pandemic, an economic recession and millions of Americans protesting racial injustice, the 2020 presidential election gave American voters two candidates with very different resumes and personalities that also influenced the manner in which they campaigned and the decisions voters ultimately made on Election Day. Donald Trump was a conservative New York City billionaire businessperson and reality TV star who had never held political office before running for president and who was known to be outspoken and brash. In contrast, Joseph Biden spent his entire adult life (nearly 50 years) in Washington, DC, as a progressive, moderate senator from Delaware and the vice president of the United States and was known to be a traditional, gaffe-prone politician. The two candidates campaigned for the White House from those two perspectives. However, despite their differences, both candidates embraced social media to communicate with the electorate.

Since 2008, when candidate Barack Obama firmly established the use of the Internet, social and digital media platforms have rapidly increased their centrality in each consecutive presidential election.[6] By 2020, due to the pandemic, social media use in political campaigns was integral to the communication strategy because the candidates were forced to move their campaigning primarily online for social distancing reasons. The candidates had to communicate with the voters where they were—online, at home. The *Washington Post*'s Ariel Procaccia explained:

> Nowadays the online world is home to millions of small communities; Facebook, Instagram, Twitter and other platforms have become social pressure-cookers. Especially in this pandemic-burdened time of homemade bread, homemade haircuts and homemade ballots (of the legitimate variety), social media gave America a socially distanced opportunity to make voting observable again. And voters could influence their friends to vote too, while they were at it. In 2020, a time-honored system of democracy may have thrived, against all odds, thanks in part to social media. It would be just another irony in a year that has had more than its fair share.[7]

Thus, despite claims of being conduits for misinformation and polarization, social media effectively became the 2020 election because it provided an avenue in which candidates were able to reach socially distanced Americans in the midst of a deadly pandemic. And, in 2019, the Pew Research Center found that a little more than 40 percent of Americans got their news from Facebook, 21 percent from YouTube, and 12 percent from Twitter.[8] Clearly, Americans use social media platforms to connect with friends and to access news.

CITIZENS AND SOCIAL AND DIGITAL MEDIA

In 2020, social media use was at an all-time high, with 72 percent of Americans of voting age using social media platforms and 69 percent of that demographic is on Facebook alone.[9] Social and digital media are now the most common pathways through which Americans get their political news.[10] In a 2020 survey from the Pew Research Center, one-in-four U.S. adults (25 percent) said that they get their political news primarily through news websites or apps, and about one-in-five (18 percent) reported that they follow politics mainly through social media (followed by cable television [16 percent], local television [16 percent], network television [13 percent], radio [8 percent], and print [3 percent]). Those who got their political information from these social and digital sources tended to identify as or lean to the Democratic Party, be younger and more ethnically and racially diverse, and have lower levels of education and income than those who relied on other platforms, such as network television and print. Regarding gender, those who relied most on social media were disproportionately more women than men (58 percent to 41 percent), while those most likely to use news websites and apps totaled more men than women (61 percent to 39 percent). Those who depended on social and digital sources also said that they were less likely to follow the 2020 election very closely and scored worse on fact-based current events quizzes, indicating lower political knowledge levels. Notably, these social-media-first voters were more likely than other media consumers to have heard about unproven conspiracy theories.[11]

Regarding specific apps and websites, search engines such as Google and podcasts were also relatively common ways Americans sought out political information.[12] Nearly two-thirds of Americans (63 percent) said that they often or sometimes get the news from search engines and 15 percent said the same about podcasts. Turning to social media, Facebook and Instagram were the most frequently used platforms for news: 64 percent of respondents said they had used Facebook to get news in the past week, compared to 23 percent who used Instagram, 13 percent who used Twitter, 11 percent who used Snapchat, 6 percent who used Reddit, and 5 percent who used LinkedIn. Google News was the most widely used news aggregator; more than one-in-three Americans (35 percent) reported using it often or sometimes (compared to the 13 percent who used Apple News, 4 percent who used Flipboard, and 2 percent who used Pocket).[13]

The Pew Research Center found that while Americans are broadly aware of newer digital platforms, few used these emerging outlets for news in 2020.[14] Specifically, 86 percent of U.S. adults were familiar with Internet streaming services, 75 percent with push notifications and alerts, 73 percent with smart speakers, 72 percent with streaming devices, and 63 percent with smartwatches. In terms of news use, among those who know about these technologies, push notifications were the most likely to be used for news, with 42 percent saying they often or sometimes get their news from these alerts on their phones. Large majorities of those who were familiar with smartwatches (79 percent), Internet streaming (67 percent), smart speakers (66 percent), and streaming devices (66 percent) never used them to access news.

In 2020, with the contentious presidential election, the global pandemic, one of the largest social protest movements in U.S. history, several natural disasters, and countless other news events, news consumption and ratings spiked as Americans tuned into the drama. A new term—"doomscrolling" or "doomsurfing"—was coined and popularized for the incessant consumption of negative news on social media and news apps, often to the detriment of the scroller's mental health. *Merriam-Webster* defined it as "the tendency to continue to surf or scroll through bad news, even though that news is saddening, disheartening, or depressing."[15] *The Washington Post*'s Elahe Izadi described the feeling of many Americans:

> Sleep? At a time like this? No way. So we stay up late, doomscrolling on our phones until our eyes dry out. During the day, we let television sets roar while we juggle jobs (if we are lucky enough to have them), children, dishes. We want to shut the news off, but we can't get enough.[16]

With phones in most pockets and unscheduled time at home, in 2020, Americans turned to the news and online media for answers during times of uncertainty and crisis.

SOCIAL AND DIGITAL MEDIA ADVERTISING

Facebook and Google experienced the majority of political ad purchases in the 2020 election, but other online platforms such as Hulu, Pandora, Reddit, and Spotify also saw political advertising.[17] Conversely, many platforms had significant restrictions or complete bans on political advertising, including Amazon, Bing, LinkedIn, Pinterest, Twitch, and TikTok.[18] Facebook technology enabled advertisers to microtarget specific consumers, or voters, and Trump used that technology to direct specific advertising to the particular people with whom the message would most resonate. Biden used less targeted advertising than Trump and tended to mostly use Facebook to seek donations.[19]

In total, the two major-party campaigns spent $1.67 billion on campaign television, radio, and digital advertising, of which $174.3 million went to Facebook properties ($89.1 million from the Trump campaign and $85.2 million from the Biden campaign) and $116.4 million went to Google properties ($56 million from the Trump campaign and $60.4 million from the Biden campaign).[20] The top states for Facebook advertising were Florida ($25.9 million total from both campaigns), Pennsylvania ($16.9 million), California ($12.1 million), North Carolina ($10.6 million), and Michigan ($10.5 million).[21] Political advertising was everywhere on social and digital media. For instance, in a multimillion-dollar ad buy, the Trump campaign purchased the YouTube masthead—the large ad that runs atop the country's most-visited website and one of the most high-profile spots on the Internet—for the final three days of the election, including Election Day.[22] Similarly, during the four days of the Democratic National Convention, the Trump campaign launched a multimillion-dollar digital advertising campaign to blanket YouTube, *The Wall Street Journal*, *The Washington Post*, FoxNews.com, and Hulu with unskippable ads as counterprogramming to the Democratic platform.[23]

With a total number of 2 billion active monthly users, YouTube emerged as a key player in the dissemination of political messaging during the 2020 campaign. There was such demand for political advertising time on YouTube that the platform ran out of space. Mark Bergen, of Bloomberg News, shared: "At times, YouTube is so inundated with election ads that it has been unable to place as much as three quarters of the amounts campaigns would like to spend on a given day."[24] The most sought-after ad purchases were the ones that viewers were not permitted to skip through.[25] Although not being able to target specific demographics as precisely as other social media platforms, YouTube advertising had some limited targeting abilities. Glazer and Haggin explained: "A YouTube ad can, for instance, be made to appear exclusively ahead of videos viewed by people identified as left-leaning voters in Polk County, Iowa."[26] YouTube implemented a new process for politicians to purchase advertising for the 2020 election by creating a tool called Instant Reserve that allowed campaigns to electronically purchase and reserve advertising time and space well in advance and not have to work directly with a salesperson.[27] Glazer and Haggin noted: "Political ads [on Google] are subject to additional scrutiny, from verifying the buyer's identity to embedding a disclosure in the spot stating who paid for the ad."[28]

The two campaigns had differing advertising strategies as evidenced in the tone and topics of their advertising. Generally, an analysis from the Wesleyan Media Project found that pro-Biden ads were positive or contrast, with only about 10 percent being pure attacks. On the other hand, pro-Trump ads were more negative and less positive. In the final week of the campaign, for example, over 60 percent of Trump's ads were pure attacks, and fewer than 10 percent were purely positive.[29] The issues mentioned in their campaign communication also differed. The most commonly discussed issues in Trump's ads were taxes, the economy, jobs, and prescription drugs. In contrast, Biden ads most frequently mentioned healthcare, jobs, social security, and infectious diseases. While their issues overlapped, Trump was more likely to emphasize taxes and the economy and Biden was more likely to focus on healthcare, social security, and the pandemic.[30]

The Biden campaign spent tens of millions of dollars on a national digital advertising campaign in the final days of the election in which they highlighted the personal stories of those impacted by the pandemic (such as frontline workers, small business owners, teachers, and farmers) in an attempt to persuade late-deciding voters in 16 battleground states.[31] While Trump continued to argue that Biden was a "Trojan horse" for the radical left and other issues, the Biden campaign consistently focused on the coronavirus pandemic and its effects on the economy and healthcare. An analysis by *Axios* using data from Bully Pulpit Interactive revealed that the Trump campaign frequently changed the topic of its Facebook advertising in response to current events and changing campaign dynamics. Instead of a single message, Trump spent millions of dollars on issues designed to rally his bases, such as the Supreme Court and conservative judges, "fake news" and targeting the media, law and order and policing, immigration, and the impeachment process and Special Counsel Robert Mueller.[32]

THE CANDIDATES AND SOCIAL AND DIGITAL MEDIA

Steve Passwaiter, vice president and general manager of Kantar, a campaign media analysis group, asserted: "Social media plays key roles in a campaign's outreach to voters. It's a great tool for fundraising, organizing, volunteering and Get Out the Vote (GOTV) efforts."[33] In accomplishing these roles, the Trump campaign trounced the Biden campaign in nearly every metric used to measure social media engagement.[34] For example, in the final 100 days of the election, Trump's official Facebook page received 354.4 million interactions (290.5 million reactions, 38.6 million comments, and 25.4 million shares), compared with 52.2 million for Biden's page (39.95 million reactions, 7.5 million comments, and 4.8 million shares), according to data from CrowdTangle, a Facebook-owned data platform.[35] The Trump campaign also posted more, with about 2,500 posts during that time period compared to about 1,000 from Biden. In April of the election year, President Trump's

106 million combined followers on Facebook and Twitter dwarfed Biden's 6.7 million.[36] The disparity was also evidenced on YouTube. In the final three months of the election, the videos on the Trump YouTube channel received over 551 million views, more than quintupling the 91 million streams of videos on Biden's channel.[37]

Donald Trump and Social and Digital Media

On a day-to-day basis, the Trump campaign was frequently shaped by, and directed to, an audience largely already existing on social media. As *Vox*'s Jane Coasten argued: "Trump is an Extremely Online person. Not only is he frequently active on social media (predominantly Twitter), but he operates in a world in which what he and others post, on Twitter or in the world of online media, is extremely important."[38] Donald Trump and his allies in conservative media created a distinct information ecosystem to maintain power and influence. President Trump heavily promoted conservative media outlets and their stars—such as Fox News, Fox Business Network, One America Network, Newsmax, Sinclair Broadcast Group, Gateway Pundit, The Daily Wire, The Daily Caller, Ben Shapiro, Rush Limbaugh, Donald Trump Jr., and Dan Bongino, among others—and the outlets returned the favor by giving airtime to Trump, broadcasting his rallies, and attacking Biden, his family, and his allies.[39] The "Make America Great Again" media system effectively had its own culture and set of beliefs. Ezra Klein from *Vox* described it as a unique *universe*: "To follow along with ease, you had to be deep into the Fox News cinematic universe, easily conversant in right-wing memes and conspiracies. Trump's campaign was angry, negative, and alarmist, but it was also just confusing, a reflection of the president's idiosyncratic interests and obsessions."[40]

The Trump campaign mastered Facebook in 2016 and enhanced its mastery of the social media platform in 2020. Allison and Egkolfopoulou asserted: "President Donald Trump uses Facebook like a Swiss Army knife— to raise money, amplify his message, and mobilize voters."[41] On an average day, Trump made about fourteen posts to his tens of millions of followers.[42] Conservative perspectives dominated political discussion on Facebook. For instance, the four public Facebook accounts with the most election engagement over the final month of the campaign were conservative voices— namely, President Trump, Fox News, Dan Bongino, and Breitbart, according to CrowdTangle data[43] (table 5.1).

It was Twitter that partially thrust Trump into the White House in 2016, and he continued using the social media platform throughout his presidency and the 2020 campaign. Like other social media, Twitter allowed Trump to communicate directly to his constituents. Timberg and Dwoskin estimated

Table 5.1. Top United States Politics Facebook Accounts by Interactions in Final Month of Election

Profile	Posts	Interactions	Share Voice
Donald J. Trump	490	88,319,862	15%
Fox News	968	64,160,271	11%
Dan Bongino	480	32,929,057	6%
Breitbart	1,413	26,008,492	4%
Occupy Democrats	1,115	19,530,260	3%
Joe Biden	345	16,304,362	3%
Team Trump	1,263	15,889,353	3%
Ridin With Biden	499	14,576,725	3%
The Hill	1,662	13,996,407	2%
Ben Shapiro	1,525	13,606,263	2%
USA Patriots for Donald Trump	554	13,210,394	2%

Note: All data from CrowdTangle. "Interactions" is defined as reactions, comments and shares. "Share Voice" is defined as the percentage of total interactions that belongs to a page or account on CrowdTangle's U.S. 2020 Politics list.

that Trump has sent more than 32,000 tweets since he entered political life.[44] He is a prolific tweeter and uses it to attack his opponents and declare his positions. During and after the campaign, Twitter flagged a number of Trump's tweets for "violating policies against the glorification of violence and misinformation about the civic process."[45] It prompted a tweet on November 6, 2020, from Trump saying: "Twitter is out of control, made possible through the government gift of Section 230!" (referencing Section 230 of the Telecommunications Act that designates social media platforms as internet service providers and shielding them from any legal responsibility from what is posted on their sites).

The Trump campaign introduced a mobile app that enabled it to gather data on the 2.8 million users who downloaded it. The app monitored supporter movement via IP addresses, gained access to the contact lists of the supporters, sold MAGA merchandise, and texted supporters campaign messages via the app. Burke observed that "The digital details the app collected can be put to multiple uses—to fundraise for the president's future political ventures, stoke Trump's base, or even build an audience for a new media empire."[46] In addition to accessing it via the Trump app, the president's supporters were able to watch a "Team Trump" webcast every night via Facebook, Twitter, or YouTube.[47] Khalid and Keith shared that these webcasts started "with a slick intro that's part campaign ad, part movie trailer, part cable news show open. Trump doesn't appear live, but glowing descriptions of him are constant."[48] The webcasts looked like a newscast with Trump family members and other political supporters. Khalid and Keith reported: "It looks like cable news, but in reality, it's more like an elaborate infomercial. Graphics in the lower third of the screen rotate through discount codes to buy Trump merchandise and prompts to download the Trump 2020 app or text the campaign."[49]

Joe Biden and Social and Digital Media

In many ways, Joe Biden's 2020 campaign was conceived as an antidote to four years of the Trump administration.[50] Ezra Klein referred to Joe Biden as "a quiet candidate in a loud time."[51] Trump had won the 2016 race in part by dominating media attention and the national conversation through inescapable bombast and seemingly endless social media content. The Biden campaign believed that a majority of the country was tired of the loudest voices in the room and fatigued by four years of inexhaustible disputes and grievances that the same strategy that propelled Trump to the White House in 2016 would ultimately cost him the election in 2020.[52]

Biden did not attempt to match and disrupt Trump's dominance on Facebook, Twitter, YouTube, and Reddit. As *New York Times* critic Amanda Hess described it, Biden's campaign had "negative online energy."[53] In its place, Biden portrayed himself as a practical moderate, who understood and could respond to a nation in crisis, thereby defusing President Trump's depiction of Biden as a radical liberal out to remake the country. Biden made this strategy clear in a May interview, saying in reference to President Trump: "The more he talks, the better off I am." In fact, the Biden campaign sold a T-shirt reading: "Tweet less, listen more."

However, temperate listening was not a natural fit for social media. *The New York Times'* Kevin Roose argued that Biden's style was a structural mismatch with Facebook and Twitter:

> Most of our online political communication takes place on internet platforms that are designed to amplify content that provokes strong emotional reactions, often by reinforcing tribal identities. Mr. Trump's unfiltered, combative style is a natural fit for the hyperpolarized audiences on Facebook and Twitter, whereas Mr. Biden's more conciliatory, healer-in-chief approach can render him invisible on platforms where conflict equals clicks.[54]

Instead of trying to "out Trump" Trump, Biden outsourced attacks to independent expenditure groups and instead ran a largely positive campaign characterized by gauzy, postpartisan advertising, small, socially distanced speeches, and uplifting social media content that felt pulled from a bygone era.[55] As *Wired*'s Kate Knibbs wrote: "Biden is a throwback, less instantaneously accessible and less interested in the internet as a site of connection."[56]

When the pandemic forced the campaigns to limit in-person campaigning and develop an all-digital strategy, the Biden campaign floundered. Biden's first virtual town hall was riddled with embarrassing technical problems and his podcast failed to find listeners and only lasted seven episodes.[57] Livestream events and interviews recorded in his makeshift studio in his basement that were posted to YouTube typically only received a few thousand views, a paltry number compared to those of Trump and his Democratic primary opponents.

While President Trump and conservative media thrived on Facebook, liberal perspectives were more common on Instagram, reflecting the younger and more progressive demographics of its users.[58] Looking first at the candidates' main Instagram profiles (@realdonaldtrump and @joebiden), Trump bested Biden on nearly every metric, including each week with the exception of election week, including followers (on Election Day Trump had 23.4 million followers and Biden had 5.9 million followers), video views (Trump had 254.7 million video views over the final 100 days compared to Biden's 134.3 million), and weekly and total interactions (Trump had 159.7 million likes and 3.7 million comments and Biden had 90.2 million likes and 2.6 million comments over the final 100 days).[59]

But below the topline accounts, many of the most viewed and shared Instagram posts were from the political left. With its focus on lifestyle and culture, the most popular accounts on Instagram in 2020 were entertainment, sports, and celebrity accounts, but several top creators frequently posted liberal viewpoints.[60] For example, the Election 2020 Instagram post with the most engagement was an October 28 post from singer and actress Ariana Grande instructing her followers to "vote for Biden" that received 7.36 million likes and over 55 thousand comments. Relatedly, an October 7 post from Taylor Swift about why she would be voting for Biden received 2.89 million likes, and a September 27 video post from Dwayne "The Rock" Johnson endorsing and interviewing Biden and Harris was viewed 7.91 million times and 1.26 million likes and over 118 thousand comments. The most viewed Instagram video was a September 19 clip defending voting for Biden from Alexandria Ocasio-Cortez that generated 10 million views and 1.68 million likes.[61] The Biden campaign actively solicited these celebrity endorsements through #TeamJoeTalks, a campaign to line up celebrity endorsements on Instagram such as from actors Misha Collins, Bradley Whitford, and Debra Messing, celebrity chef Tom Colicchio, and former presidential candidate Andrew Yang.[62]

The Biden campaign employed new platforms in their voter outreach. For instance, Biden surrogate Alexandria Ocasio-Cortez attracted more than 430,000 concurrent viewers to her first-ever Twitch stream. Twitch, a subsidiary of Amazon.com, is a video game live streaming site where people record and broadcast themselves playing games to a live audience online and had over 15 million daily active users in 2020. On her stream, Representative Ocasio-Cortez played the hit game *Among Us* for 3.5 hours while talking about healthcare policy and directing viewers to "make a voting plan" on IWillVote.com.[63] Earlier in the year, the Biden campaign similarly appealed to potential voters on the popular video game *Animal Crossing: New Horizons* for the Nintendo Switch. In the life-simulation game, the Biden campaign released yard signs players could display in front of their virtual house and a complete Biden HQ location where players could visit a virtual field office, learn about the candidate, and be encouraged to vote in real life.[64]

Snapchat, an emerging social media app with 249 million daily active users, embraced political advertisements in 2020, and the major-party candidates were quick to test the waters of this new platform.[65] The Biden campaign spent just over $3 million on Snapchat ads and the Trump campaign allocated $240,000 to ads on the new platform. Biden used the geotargeting feature of Snapchat to target battleground states with get-out-the-vote messages tailored with each user's name and instructing them to make a plan to vote early, an attack on President Trump's environmental policy containing images of wildfires in California, and several ads featuring video excerpts of the Biden's acceptance speech at the Democratic National Convention.

As previously mentioned, in addition to promoting the candidates' messages, online spending has the dual purpose of raising money, and, although his digital fundraising was slow off the line, the Biden campaign went on to break fundraising records.[66] Remarkably, *The New York Times'* Shane Goldmacher and Rachel Shorey called the campaign "perhaps the greatest magnet for online money in American political history."[67] The campaign raised three-quarters of a billion dollars in August and September ($364.5 million and $383 million, respectively), with approximately half of that coming from online.[68] Biden and his associated committees saw donations from nearly 5.9 million donors, while Trump received contributions from 3.7 million donors.[69] In the end, Biden had 45 aides dedicated to online fundraising and a once-unimaginable cash advantage over Trump, which allowed Biden to outspend the president on television ads.

Five key events propelled Biden's general election digital fundraising with large spikes in donations: Biden's victories in the South Carolina and on Super Tuesday primaries, the demonstrations following the police killing of George Floyd, the choice of Senator Kamala Harris as his running mate, his acceptance speech at the Democratic National Convention, and the first presidential debate.[70] In the 48 hours after the selection of Harris, more than $48 million poured in, roughly 80 percent from online.[71] The night of and day after the first debate, the Biden campaign raised $31.5 million.[72]

MISINFORMATION AND SOCIAL AND DIGITAL MEDIA

Misinformation, false claims and narratives, and conspiracies saturated social and digital platforms in 2020. *The New York Times'* Charlie Warzel described the typical American's Facebook feeds as "a dizzying mix of mundane middle-class American life and high-octane propaganda."[73] In 2020, nearly one-fifth (17 percent) of engagement among the top 100 news sources on social media came from sources that independent experts judged as generally unreliable.[74] Joe Ondrak, a senior researcher at Logically, a group set up to counter misinformation, said: "From 2016 onwards, the political state of play has changed—disinformation narratives are how you play elections. This was always going to be the election of conspiracy theories."[75]

U.S. intelligence agencies found that much of the information that sought to influence the 2016 election originated from Russia. "In 2020, so far no significant foreign influence campaigns have been uncovered. Instead, Americans themselves spread misinformation and at huge scale," wrote Murphy and Venkataramakrishnan.[76] For example, conspiracy theories and misinformation were rampant on social media in the final weeks of the campaign. The research firm Zignal tallied 21.3 million mentions of Hunter Biden on social media, 4.5 million mentions of alleged corruption from Big Tech, 2.7 million mentions of Anthony Bobulinski, 1.7 million mentions of the Bidens and Ukraine, and 1 million mentioned of supposed voter fraud from October 13 to November 1, 2020.[77] Relatedly, the media literacy organization NewsGuard identified 40 Facebook pages that they called "super-spreaders" of election-related misinformation. These pages all shared false information about voting or the election to their audiences of at least 100,000 followers.[78]

The various social media platforms took steps to manage this misinformation. Twitter, for example, banned ads that supported specific candidates. Massoglia and Evers-Hillstrom explained: "The platform is expected to still allow groups to run ads related to issues of national significance, but not ads that advocate for a candidate or bill."[79] Congruently, Facebook implemented several policies designed to prevent misuse of its platform during the election such as not allowing advertising that leads to voter suppression or prematurely declaring that a candidate has won the election.[80] To promote transparency, Facebook also created an advertising library that shows all political spending and archives all ads. Further, Levy, Rodriguez, and Graham asserted: "While Facebook has become the dominant advertising platform for political campaigns, the company faces intense criticism from lawmakers, regulators and even investors for enabling the spread of false information and for letting political groups take advantage of the same types of targeting tools used by corporate advertisers."[81]

During the 2020 campaign, both Twitter and Facebook started enforcing their Terms of Service and Community Guidelines more often and placed sanctions and/or warning labels on content posted by politicians. Edelman explained: "Twitter got the ball rolling in May when it began applying fact-checking and warning labels to Trump tweets that violated its policies."[82] Further, "under pressure from a growing advertising boycott, Facebook announced it would begin implementing a similar policy. Snapchat has also recently declared it would stop promoting the Trump campaign's channel."[83] Reddit closed a Trump subreddit with 800,000 members because its members had broken Reddit's rules against allowing targeted harassment and hate speech. Twitch also banned a Trump channel because of "hateful content."[84]

One of the first incidents on Election Day that forced social media companies to enforce its community policies toward Trump occurred as election results were coming in and all indications were that the election outcome would be close, thus leading Trump to tweet, "We are up BIG, but they are trying to STEAL the Election. We will never let them do it. Votes cannot be cast after the Polls are closed!" Twitter flagged this late-night tweet with a label noting his claims were in dispute and prevented users from sharing and commenting on the tweet. Specifically, Twitter placed the following label on Trump's tweet: "Learn about US 2020 election security efforts" with a link to more information.[85] Twitter had started placing these labels on Trump's tweets in May during the campaign. With the same post, Facebook also added a label stating that "no winner of the presidential election had been projected," and the following label was used on other Trump Facebook posts: "as expected, election results will take longer this year."[86] Unlike Twitter, Facebook did not prevent comments and sharing from its users.

The enforcement of service terms and community guidelines continued to be an issue after the election. Twitter flagged many of President Trump's tweets about the final election results as unsubstantiated claims. Conger explained: "Twitter's labeling of Mr. Trump's tweets meant that people needed to click through their warnings to see the posts, making each one harder to share. In the past, those actions by Twitter have helped slow the overall spread of false or potentially misleading tweets."[87]

Shortly after the election, Facebook even banned certain hashtags such as #sharpiegate and #stopthesteal promoted by Trump and his associates. Perez and Hatmaker explained: "Instead of taking users to search results for the hashtag in question, Facebook presents a page where it explains that posts with the hashtag are being 'temporarily hidden.' This message also explains that 'some content in those posts goes against our Community Standards,' and offers to direct users to its guidelines under a 'Learn More' link."[88] As noted, Twitter also limited Trump's conspiracy theories about the election.

"On Twitter, many of Trump's recent tweets promoting unfounded election conspiracies have been hidden from view and placed behind a misinformation warning. Those hidden tweets also have likes, retweets, and comments restricted in order to limit their ability to spread in a viral way."[89]

Ultimately, the success of this content moderation was limited. For example, in June 2020, when Twitter and Snapchat removed Trump campaign political ads and posts for alleged policy violations relating to "organized hate," the app was used to continue the messaging in those ads and posts. In addition to using the Trump app to get the campaign's message straight to its supporters without being concerned about violating a social media platform's policies, the campaign used alternative platforms such as Parler.[90]

Content moderation might even be counterproductive in some instances. Renee DiResta, Technical Research Manager at the Stanford Internet Observatory, explained how content and behavior moderation has serious downstream implications and may create a feedback loop for users already paranoid about the control exerted by the platforms:

> That moderation, particularly when sloppily executed, is perceived as censorship by those affected, and the content or accounts taken down are recast as forbidden knowledge. The claim of censorship is turned into a mass-aggrievement narrative, deployed as a cudgel by politicians who use it cynically to rally their base, and various demi-media outlets and grifters attempt to leverage it for profit. Ordinary people, meanwhile, are pushed deeper into echo chambers.[91]

Accordingly, regulating speech on digital platforms and social media companies became a policy issue in the 2020 campaign and will likely remain a topic of interest for the Biden administration and the 117th Congress convening in 2021.

CONCLUSION

After the 2016 presidential election that propelled Donald Trump into the White House with allegations of Russian social media interference that may have influenced the election's outcome, big tech companies viewed political use of social media somewhat differently by 2020. For example, to prevent as much misinformation as possible during the 2020 campaign, Facebook created the Election Operations Center to monitor in *real-time* any potential abuses that might influence the democratic process.[92] Just weeks prior to the election, ABC News's Catherine Sanz and Catherine Thorbecke reported:

> The company said that so far it has removed more than 120,000 pieces of content from Facebook and Instagram in the U.S. for violating voter-interference

policies it has set, and displayed warnings on more than 150 pieces of content. Moreover, the company said it removed 30 networks engaged in coordinated inauthentic behavior targeting the U.S.[93]

Approximately three months before the election, Facebook also initiated a campaign encouraging its users to vote in the 2020 election. As previously mentioned, Twitter banned all political advertising from the platform a year prior to the election. With the same goal as Facebook's Election Operation's Center, Twitter created the "2020 US Election Hub."[94] Equally, YouTube updated its Community Guidelines in order to better oversee election-related content on its platform. YouTube explained: "These policies prohibit hate speech, harassment, and deceptive practices, including content that aims to mislead people about voting or videos that are technically manipulated or doctored in a way that misleads users (beyond clips taken out of context) and may pose a serious risk of egregious harm."[95]

Social media experienced a heightened sense of importance during the 2020 election because of the pandemic's requirement that society social distance prevent the spread of the deadly COVID-19 virus. Politicians could not *physically* go to the voters to communicate with them via traditional stump speeches, so politicians went *virtually* to the voters with all the technological capabilities that the digital and social media platforms allowed. Comparing the 2020 election to the 2016 election, NPR's Miles Parks asserted: "Americans' usage of social media has only increased—and drastically so, as a result of the pandemic. More people are online right now than at any point in human history."[96] The pandemic afforded Americans an extraordinary amount of time sequestered in their homes with more time than normal to spend online.

Facebook CEO Mark Zuckerberg asserted: "We know that people especially rely on social apps in times of crisis and in times when we can't be together in person. And, right now, we are experiencing both of those all around the world at the same time. So we're seeing major increases and use of our services."[97] Zuckerberg reported more than 3 billion people had used Facebook properties (Facebook, Messenger, Instagram, and WhatsApp).[98] Miles Parks, of *National Public Radio*, postulated that the drastically increased usage of social media would enhance and exacerbate polarization and misinformation during the 2020 election, and that was indeed the situation.[99] At congressional hearings before and after the election, both politicians and technology CEOs agreed that problems exist intensifying discussion and debate of whether regulating the digital and social media is warranted.

All of these issues and concerns surrounding social media's role in political campaigns will continue to be discussed and analyzed to seek solutions to the problems discussed before the next presidential election in 2024. It is important that big tech CEOs and politicians find solutions because social media and politics are now an entrenched aspect of American politics. *The Washington Post*'s Craig Timberg and Elizabeth Dwoskin illustrate the role social media play in politics for even a candidate who lost an election: "Trump would leave office with a singularly powerful online megaphone—at least 88 million followers on Twitter, 31 million on Facebook and 23 million on Instagram—that will give him a unique ability to communicate his thoughts to legions of supporters accustomed to hearing from him more than three-dozen times a day."[100] The health of our nation's democracy depends upon finding reasonable and effective solutions to eliminating misinformation, polarization, hate speech, and deceptive practices on social media leading up to Election Day.

Chapter 6

Media Coverage and the Practice of Journalism in the 2020 Presidential Campaign

Robert E. Denton Jr.

The media, in all its forms and platforms, remain one of the primary ways citizens learn about politics in general. During elections, the news media, more specifically, influence the political attitudes, knowledge, and voting behaviors of citizens. Coverage of campaigns and elections shape not only electoral choices but also public trust in democratic norms, values, and the electoral process itself. Naturally, the decisions news media make in covering elections have a direct impact upon the electoral process and outcomes. As Ezra Klein argues, "The news media isn't just an actor in politics. It's arguably the most powerful actor in politics."[1] Thus, in essence, the news media are the filter and lenses that shape citizen understanding of politics, political campaigns, and voting decisions.

Since the 2016 presidential election, President Trump certainly had a major impact on the news media. In the words of Ben Smith, Trump "succeeded in making the old media great again, in part through his obsession with it."[2] Cable news outlets and legacy media became profitable despite the continuing shift to new media technologies and platforms. Trump filled a vacuum providing daily, even hourly headlines resulting in what Ethan Zuckerman calls "agenda compression."[3] Barack Obama's name appeared in one in ten news stories published by major news outlets during his presidency compared to Trump's name appearing in one in four stories.[4] According to Zuckerman, in 2020 only the coronavirus received more media attention than Trump.

In July of 2020, Martha Sullivan of the *Washington Post* offered advice on how the media should cover the presidential campaign to avoid the mistakes of the 2016 presidential election. Rather ironically, the first piece of advice was to focus on voting rights and election integrity. "Without a valid, publicly accepted vote, anything can happen. This should be front and center for journalists. There is no bigger story."[5] Yet, as will be noted, the media's approach to this issue generated debate, especially postelection. Second, Sullivan suggested the news media should present the results of polls with more context and explanation. However, once again, collectively the polls were off. In the final days of the campaign, national media outlets were touting polls with large margins of error arguing for a certain and easy Biden victory. Another suggestion was for the media to stop "falling" for Trump's distractions. By and large, the media heeded this piece of advice generally avoiding issues raised by the Trump campaign on Joe Biden and Kamala Harris. More to the point, Sullivan suggested for this cycle, the media should not participate in another "but her emails situation." As an example, in this analogy, the media clearly avoided the federal investigation of Hunter Biden and business dealings with mainland China with possible connections with father Joe Biden. Finally, Sullivan suggests a better understanding of the influence and impact of social media, specifically Facebook. Indeed, Facebook and other social media served as a gatekeeper of information and self-appointed arbiter of truth. For others, Facebook was a major source of content bias and even censorship.

This chapter provides an overview of some of the issues and characterizations of how primarily the news media covered the 2020 presidential campaign. I surveyed news articles and opinion pieces focused on how the media covered the election. I do not argue for the validity of any of the issues or characterizations of coverage. Rather, major observations and concerns raised by the media themselves are identified. As you can imagine, there are rather stark differences of coverage between mainstream media and partisan outlets, from cable media organizations and social media platforms. And what citizens see and hear influences what they think, believe, and act. The media, broadly defined, are partners in the growing division and polarization of America.

In order to understand the issues raised by media coverage, it is important to recognize the transformation of the practice of journalism, especially in the last two decades.

THE TRANSFORMATION OF THE PRACTICE
OF JOURNALISM IN AMERICA

The practice of journalism has certainly changed since the revolution and founding of the nation.[6] Over the years, American news media transformed from partisan press to professional, objective, fact-based journalism into now for some critics a biased and liberal press.[7] It was in the 1960s that American journalism began leaning to the ideological left followed by issue-oriented activism by journalists resulting today in a partisan press. For Jim Kuypers, the difference in today's partisan press from those of the Jacksonian era is that today journalists "operate behind a veil of objectivity. They present opinion under the guise of an objective journalism."[8]

Michael Delli Carpini argues that today's media regime consists of "a mix of legacy, partisan, and online actors and media institutions, this regime has blurred distinctions between fact and opinion, news and entertainment, information producers and consumers, and mass mediated and interpersonal communication."[9]

In the 1950s, conservatives felt they were under represented in the major newsrooms in America. Conservatives launched the publications of *National Review* and *Human Events* in an attempt to bring some balance. Some scholars credit Vice President Spiro Agnew in a speech in Des Moines, Iowa, in 1969 where he forcefully declared that a "small and unelected elite" had a profound power of influencing American public opinion without any checks or regard to fairness. Ronald Reagan routinely noted his differences with the perceived bias of the press during his presidency. The Media Research Center was formed in 1987 with the purpose of demonstrating media bias and subsequently expose patterns of slanted and ideological coverage of the news. In 1996, Rush Limbaugh and Fox News Channel hit the airwaves. Every subsequent Republican president has publicly noted the inherent bias of the mainstream and then the majority of cable media.[10]

In the 1970s, most households had only six or seven channels to choose from for entertainment and news. In rural and remote areas, households were down to two or three channel options of networks. However, by 2010, over 90 percent of homes had access to cable or satellite television routinely providing over 130 channels.[11] The conventional wisdom at the time was that the cable news channels and options would provide even more access to all types of news, information, and viewpoints. However, over the years, as Kevin Arceneaux and Martin Johnson observe, "cable news outlets have become purveyors of pitched, partisan discourse."[12]

Actually, according to Ezra Klein, the Internet has exasperated the problems even more. The Internet promised to provide much more information, viewpoints, and access. But it has become clear that in general we have not become more politically informed. "Political journalism is a business that serves people interested in political news and that tries to create more people interested in political news. And to be interested in politics is, for most people, to choose a side. . . . In today's media sphere, where the explosion of choices has made it possible to get the political media you really want, it's expressed itself in polarized media that attaches to political identity, conflict, and celebrity."[13]

Historically, the Standard Model of Professional Journalism "includes the disciplines of accuracy, disinterestedness in reporting, independence from the people and organizations reported upon or affected by the report, a mode of presentation sometimes called objective or neutral, and the clear labeling of what is fact and what is opinion."[14] The gold standard was "objective report-ing," a process of gathering facts and information fairly and then represent them as they exist. However, over the years increasingly the notion of objec-tivity in reporting requires providing multiple points of view on issues and presentations.[15] Today, as noted above, the transition in reporting has become one of advocacy and activism. For example, Pulitzer Prize–winning journal-ist Wesley Lowery openly rejects the notion of objective reporting. For him, objectivity is simply a myth.[16] "Objective journalism and all journalism is built on a pyramid of subjective decisions. . . . I think that our identities make us better journalists and I think that's really important."[17] In effect, journalists bring their life experiences to every story and coverage of events.

Seth Lewis and his colleagues find Lowery's perspective problematic. "The relevance of journalism—in its main-stream, neutral, evidence-based form—is in danger in no small part because identity politics have weaponized what news we watch. Historically, our theories of media—especially around media consumption—have been based on characteristics of information. . . . With ideological media machines in overdrive, however, journalism and political communication scholars have come to realize that the world is no longer defined by information, but by identities."[18] In essence, the lenses of identity and activism diminish the relevance and trust in contemporary journalism.

Thus, for years the primary objective of news was to inform the public. Within the last couple of decades, the objective of news has apparently become to persuade viewers to specific issue positions and political or ideological attitudes. Mathew Levendusky defines partisan media as presenting facts in such a way to support a specific conclusion. Stories are framed and slanted towards particular political agendas. "News is not an end in and of itself, but rather, the news is a vehicle to advancing a particular point of view."[19] Stud-ies have shown that indeed, partisan news can influence attitudes and even voter choice.[20] Thus, partisan media leads to the bolstering and reinforcement of preexisting beliefs, attitudes, and values. Kevin Arceneaux and Martin Johnson argue that not only does partisan media reinforce existing views, but they actually motivate viewers to maintain the existing views, becoming even more resistant to counter-information or viewpoints.[21] The resulting inclina-tion of news viewers to select corresponding partisan channels may well create a public that views the world from their own point of view resulting in more polarized and extreme political attitudes.[22] In addition, Levendusky speculates that because partisan media is so critical of "the opposition," consumers come to have less respect for the opposition and become less willing to compromise. Thus, members of the opposition are untrustworthy and merit ridicule.[23] Arceneaux and Johnson conclude that cable news and opinion show gave rise to an "increasingly polarized presentation of political information and in-your-face, vituperative commentary."[24]

The presidential election of 2016 generated a new phrase: "fake news." According to Diana Owen, one of the hallmarks of the 2016 campaign was "the amount of misinformation, misleading stories, and boldface lies that were propagated."[25] James Ceasar and colleagues define fake news as "deliberately falsified or distorted online stories that go viral within political communities of the left and right."[26] Key for them are the notions that fake news is deliberately created falsehoods, targeted for online consumption, and then transmitted by other individuals, groups, and media outlets.

As noted, the preponderance of misinformation originated on social media platforms. Items "liked," "shared," and "retweeted" generated the "fake news" phenomena.[27] Highly partisan websites published questionable material of speculation, rumors, and innuendos. Websites would release fabricated, half-truth, speculative, and sensational stories that would sometimes be reported by cable and other journalists. Many of the sites, such as *Infowars, The Rightest,* or *National Report*, were designed to look like legitimate news sites or political blogs.[28] In 2020, liberal donors poured millions of dollars into operations like Courier, which was a network of eight websites with a staff of twenty-five. They created articles and videos favoring Democrat candidates and unfavorable content aimed at the opponent. Courier spent $1.4 million on Facebook ads. It is important to note that because Courier was set up as a media organization, it did not have to disclose donors nor follow election law guidelines being protected by the First Amendment.[29] Conservative activists ran similar sites like the Star News group in the states of Tennessee, Virginia, and Minnesota.[30] Alex Thompson views such media outlets "more akin to a PAC than a newsroom."[31] Sharyl Attkisson is alarmed by the vastness and number of "quasi news outlets doing what they call reporting are really no more than political operatives or corporate interests disguised as reporters who have no intention of providing accurate information."[32]

These websites received money based upon "hits"; thus the more sensational the stories, the more "hits" for the sites. The stories and material were "true" enough to appeal to the readers fitting their ideological and political preferences. The so-called "fake news" reached millions of people during the campaigns. And the "fake news" was reposted and mentioned on legitimate sites such as Facebook or Snapchat.

The consumption of social media is very different than traditional or legacy media. Social media encourages a "minute by minute" coverage of campaigns. Social media sources also exaggerate the sensational, the unusual, and the wacky relative to more traditional coverage of issues and events. Consequently, social media coverage seldom encourages the in-depth coverage and analysis of traditional media. Likewise, Ceaser and his colleagues argue today's new media environment creates echo chambers with outlets catering to narrow and specific political parties, ideologies, or issue perspectives. Facebook has algorithms that provide news stories that complement the political views of the reader.[33] Political discussions and exposure are with sources of "like mind." Thus, individual beliefs, values, prejudices are reinforced, seldom challenged. Thus, they argue this environment allowed for the growth of "fake news."

Amy Mitchell and colleagues of the Pew Research Center found that those who obtain political news primarily from social media tend to be less likely to "closely follow major news stories" and are less knowledgeable about the topics.[34] Ironically, 62 percent of Americans think it is more difficult to be well informed because of too many sources and outlets for information. Some of the reasons given include being overwhelmed, confusion from the mix of news with nonnews/information on the web, and the increased number of outlets reporting the news.[35]

Finally, it appears that news organizations have become more open and comfortable with expressing biases. Rich Lowry, editor of *National Review*, wrote after the 2016 election that "going forward news organizations may become less apologetic about those biases. It could be a step to a British-style journalism that's a little more partisan and wears its biases on its sleeve."[36]

From an operational perspective, Klein argues that to fully understand the transformation of the practice of journalism, one must understand how the changing financial and audience forces shape the media and subsequently the presentation of news. "In an age of choice, political journalism is a business that serves people interested in political news and that tries to create more people interested in political news. And to be interested in politics is, for most people, to choose a side."[37] With choice, people select news sources they "like," that reflects their beliefs, attitudes, values, and world views. The only way news outlets can gain an audience and hence increase revenue is to provide content that mirrors the audience. More choice actually means more targeted and narrow audiences. Which came first, tribalism and polarization of media content or public and politics?

Some of the features and characteristics of the transformation of the practice of journalism became issues of how the media covered the 2020 presidential election. What is very clear, the source of news coverage of campaigns certainly shaped a multitude of perspectives and issues surrounding the campaign. Views of the electoral process very much depended upon which "window" you were watching the election unfold.

SOURCES OF POLITICAL INFORMATION

Not surprising, there were stark differences between Democrats and Republicans in sources for political and election news. Republicans and independents who lean Republican rely on a smaller group of sources than Democrats and independents who lean Democrat. The preferred sources of campaign news on a weekly basis for Republicans include 60 percent from Fox News, 30 percent ABC News, 28 percent NBC News, and 26 percent CBS News. In contrast, only 14 percent regularly sought information from MSNBC, 11 percent NPR, 9 percent *The New York Times*, and 8 percent *The Washington Post*. Thus, Fox News was clearly the overwhelming choice for Republicans and those Independents who lean Republican.

The distribution of sources among Democrats and Independents who lean Democrat was much larger. Not surprising, 53 percent went to CNN on a weekly basis, 40 percent NBC News, 37 percent ABC News, 33 percent CBS News, 33 percent MSNBC, 30 percent NPR, 31 percent *The New York Times*, 26 percent *Washington Post*, and 22 percent PBS. Even the *Wall Street Journal* pulled in 15 percent. Interestingly, a sizable percentage of members of both parties regularly went to primary sources of the opposition party. Twenty-four percent of Republicans and leaners checked in with CNN on at least a weekly basis and 23 percent of Democrats with Fox News.[38]

According to the Pew Research Center, 18 percent of adults used social media for political and election news compared to 25 percent turned to news websites and apps, 16 percent for cable news and local television.[39] Pew Research Center also found that those who relied most on social media were younger, less likely white and possessed lower levels of education than those who used other platforms. In addition, just 8 percent of those who said they were following the campaign "very closely" got their news from social media compared to 37 percent from television and 33 percent from print sources. Not only did 26 percent of adults reveal they get news from YouTube, but 72 percent indicated YouTube was an "important" source for keeping up with news.[40]

The impact of our sources of information influences our beliefs, attitudes and values as well as electoral behavior. It is rather common knowledge among digital media folks that visuals accompanying a story impacts understanding and interpretation. Visuals and graphics focus attention on the elements of a narrative. Thus, although covering the same story, the use of different visuals can influence very different interpretations of a story. A study by Kalev Leetaru, Senior Fellow at George Washington University Center for Cyber & Homeland Security, found that the degrees of similarities across the networks in story coverage has varied the most during the Trump administration and especially during the first two quarters of 2020. "Since Donald Trump's election, the tone of news coverage has become darker and the media has fractured, with parallel universes that extend even to the pronouns each outlet uses."[41] The three major networks (NBC, CBS, ABC) were closely parallel in coverage from 2010 through Barack Obama's reelection in 2012. Upon the election of Trump, the networks became less and less similar.

Thus, as Leetaru asserts, the study reminds "us just how different the view can be depending on what station we tuned into."

ISSUES AND CHARACTERIZATIONS OF MEDIA COVERAGE OF THE 2020 PRESIDENTIAL CAMPAIGN

The transformation of the practice of American journalism, the clear partisanship of sources of campaign and election news as well as the growing dependence upon social media have transformed not only elections but also how the public views and understands the candidates, issues and entire electoral process. Those writing about how the media covered the 2020 presidential election within and outside the industry raised several issues, concerns and characterizations of media performance. It is important to note that I am not favoring or endorsing one perspective over another. In each case, there are multiple perspectives and arguments to be made about the validity of influence upon voter behavior. Space does not allow the full fleshing out of the various issues, concerns and characterizations. Rather, the purpose here is to primarily identify the major topics raised about the news media and the 2020 presidential election.

Lack of Trust in News Media

Sadly, for decades, public trust of the media continues to decline. Yet, the vast majority of Americans understand the importance of the news media in the functioning of a healthy democracy. According to Gallup polling, over 80 percent of Americans think the news media is "critical" (49 percent) or "very important" (35 percent) to democracy. Ninety-two percent think it is important for the media to provide "accurate and fair news reports," and the same percentage believe that the news media should keep Americans informed about public affairs. And 85 percent view one of the major roles of the news media is to hold leaders and politicians accountable for their actions.[42]

A report by the Knight Foundation in 2020 examining trust and media noted, "With each passing benchmark study, the American people render deeper and increasingly polarized judgments about the news media and how well it is fulfilling its role in our democracy."[43] In 1972 Gallup first polled American sentiment about trust of the media and yearly since 1997. During the 1970s the range of trust was between 68 percent and 72 percent. In the 1980s and 1990s there was a decline of trust but still remained over 50 percent. However, in 2004 trust in the media dipped to 44 percent. With the exception of 2005, trust in the media has not risen above 47 percent.[44] In fall of 2020, just 9 percent of Americans had "a great deal of trust" in the news media and 31 percent "a fair amount." Twenty-seven percent expressed "no very much trust" with 33 percent "none at all." The latter percentage is a record high, a five-point increase since 2019.[45] Perhaps most alarming is a total of 41 percent of Americans think the media is "unfriendly to" and even "an enemy of" the American citizenry.[46]

Also noticeable is the partisan difference in views of trust and the media in general. Gallup finds Republicans express "more negative sentiments on every aspect of media performance compared to Democrats and Independents."[47] The partisan divide was most noticeable in 2016. Republicans' trust hit a record low of just 32 percent and has not recovered. In contrast, Democrats' trust has drastically increased over the last four years to record highs for any party in the last twenty years. In fall of 2020, Democrats trust in media a "great deal" or "fair" was 73 percent and just 10 percent for Republicans. Independents' trust was at 36 percent.[48] Finally, younger Americans are significantly less trustful of media than middle aged and older Americans. "Very" or "somewhat" favorable views of media for those under 30 was just 19 percent.[49]

The continued general and partisan decline in trust in the media jeopardizes foundational principles of functioning democracy. As we know, it is our reliance upon the news media to inform the citizenry in order to collectively make decisions.

Bias

There is simply no denying that media bias exists. The economic pressures of media organizations to build audiences in new competitive environments forces them to design content that impacts coverage decisions. Likewise, the partisan and ideological slant of self-selected audiences by definition reflects some degree of content bias. The question is what is the impact upon voter behavior and the practice of democracy.

Americans are certainly well aware of media bias and actually increasingly think the news media are responsible for the political division in the country. According to Gallup, in fall of 2020, 49 percent of Americans see "a great deal" and 37 percent "a fair amount" of political bias in news coverage. Even 56 percent of U.S. adults even see "a fair amount" of bias in their own selected news sources.[50] Ironically, according to the Knight Foundation, 69 percent of Americans are concerned about the news bias *other people* are getting compared to just 29 percent of the bias to which they may be exposed. And 73 percent of Americans acknowledge that bias in reporting of news that is supposed to be objective "a major problem."[51] In fact, 61 percent of Democrats and 77 percent of Republicans view media bias or reporting from a specific point of view "a major problem." Finally, a significant number, 54 percent, believe that reporters intentionally misrepresent facts and information and 28 percent even say reporters actually make up facts altogether.[52] Thus, the vast majority of Americans not only recognize media bias but also view it as problematic.

Over the course of the presidential election, there were those in the industry who left news organizations in light of concerns of bias. MSNBC producer Ariana Pekary left because the network was totally focused on ratings instead of quality and balance of news coverage. "The longer I was at MSNBC, the more I saw such choices—it's practically baked in to the editorial process—and those decisions affect news content every day."[53] Noted magazine writer, Andrew Sullivan, left *New York* magazine because of not only the loss of diversity of opinion represented but also the editorial intentional slant of content.[54] Bari Weiss, in a public resignation from *The New York Times*, wrote that a new consensus has emerged in the press, but perhaps especially at this paper: "that truth isn't a process of collective discovery, but an orthodoxy already known to an enlightened few whose job is to inform everyone else. . . . Stories are chosen and told in a way to satisfy the narrowest of audiences, rather than to allow a curious public to read about the world and then draw their own conclusions."[55]

There were substantial allegations that social media platforms suppressed some partisan sites in favor of highlighting mainstream media outlets. Facebook, for example, altered their algorithms to repress "hyperpartisan pages" promoting visibility and pushing big, mainstream media such as CNN, *The New York Times* and NPR, to name a few.[56] According to Dr. Robert Epstein, a research psychologist, Google's search results during the weeks and months before the election were "strongly biased in favor of Democrats. . . . The bias was being shown to pretty much every demographic. . . . Conservatives got more liberal bias in their search results than liberals."[57] There are other issues with social media that will be discussed later.

In addition to recognizing bias, most Americans think the media tends to favor one side. According to Pew Research Center, 80 percent of Americans say news outlets tend to favor one side when reporting news on political and social issues.[58] As noted earlier, Republicans have long complained of the liberal bias in the mainstream news media organizations. Ninety percent of Republicans think news coverage favors one side compared to 70 percent of Democrats.[59]

Numerous surveys and self-reporting of journalists' ideological views and party affiliations lends left and favor Democrats fourteen to one.[60] I think a certain worldview or political orientation would be true for most professions. It is reasonable to assume, for example, that police officers and business people would lean more conservative than teachers or social workers. However,

Ezra Klein makes the argument that the demographic and generational change itself will impact the newsrooms. Millennials are now the largest generation, and their views are much more liberal than earlier generations. Thus, as they dominate the workplace, specifically newsrooms, their beliefs, attitudes and values will naturally impact news coverage.[61]

The reality is that with the transformation and proliferation of news media outlets, there are a wide range of biases. The question becomes: Should there be journalistic standards or expectations of news coverage? The implications are rather straightforward, one receives very different views and facts depending on which news sources are viewed. And Americans know this to be true. Pew Research Center found that 89 percent of Trump voters and 84 percent of Biden voters recognize that the news sources viewed influence the tone and content of presentations that will widely differ.[62]

Press Censorship

Somewhat related to media bias are the allegations of press censorship. Throughout the campaign (and the Trump presidency) there were many essays and stories about how the media would simply not report or avoid certain stories that might run counter or challenge certain beliefs or perspectives. In the words of Victor Davis Hanson of RealClearPolitics, "the real warping of the news is not just a matter of slanting coverage, but deliberately not covering the news at all."[63] At the time he noticed the absence of coverage of the "stunning" breakthroughs in Middle East diplomacy, the strategic decline of Iran, the successes against terrorist groups to include Hezbollah, bombing of ISIS into dissolution, NATO members meeting financial obligations, to name only a few.

There are numerous examples, but perhaps the most discussed and noted among some observers were the lack of full coverage of the spring and summer unrest and riots. It was alleged that networks played down the extent of violence, damage and visuals of burning, looting and destruction that took place in Seattle, Portland, Chicago, etc. In Portland, rioters threw frozen water bottles, cans of beans and rocks at officers. They shined high-powered lasers at police eyes and in buildings. Setting fires was routine, as was tossing Molotov cocktails. One weekend in Portland, twenty officers were injured. The characterization of "peaceful protests" became the mantra of CNN, Reuters, and ABC News. For Victor Joecks, "the rampant violence isn't a small part of the story. It is the story—just not one the mainstream media want to talk about."[64] During the mass destruction of downtown Chicago, MSNBC and CNN did not include reports of looting and burning of stores and private property, thirteen officers hurt, or damage of more than $60 million. CNN dedicated only two minutes and 36 seconds to the subject.[65]

As another example, CNN removed the word "violent" from the on-screen display while reporting on the riots in Kenosha, Wisconsin.[66]

There were several controversies surrounding various reporters and editors resulting in termination over counter reporting. *The New York Times* solicited and published an essay by Senator Tom Cotton that suggested the military should be deployed to restore order in the streets of the cities of rioting. Internal staff revolt of the publication of the opinion essay resulted in James Bennet, editor of the opinion section of the newspaper, resigning and the reassignment of Jim Dao, the deputy editor. The same week the editor of the *Philadelphia Inquirer* op-ed section, Stan Wischowski, resigned after publishing an article titled "Buildings Matter, Too." In a statement, the paper said Wischowski "leaves behind some decades-old, deep seated and vitally important issues around diversity, equity and inclusion, issues that were not of his creation but that will likely benefit from a fresh approach."[67]

Very controversial throughout the campaign was social media's attempt to diminish the spreading of "misinformation." As noted earlier, it seems reasonable to argue attempts to "bury" conservative and Republican leaning posts to artificially raise visibility of mainstream media is a form of censorship. However, once again, there were claims of unparallel attempts to label and censor based on very subjective and broad criteria. Actions ranged from taking down accounts and networks to closely targeting content of postings. Facebook created an elections operational center consisting of a team that would monitor political posts and note those that abuse the "democratic process." For example, Facebook removed content that explained the need for identification or driving license in order to vote. The rationale? Such information might encourage people to not vote. They removed posts with "militarized language" such as "army" or "battle." A week before the election, Facebook banned all new political ads regardless of content.[68] In May 2020 Twitter started flagging tweets that they decided contained misleading content. Towards the end of the campaign virtually all tweets by Trump were tagged or hidden from view. Many such tweets contained concerns about mail-in voting and the potential for abuse. Such tagged or hidden tweets could not be retweeted or accept replies. Twitter and Facebook censored Trump's media accounts and those of his campaign 65 times. None for Biden or his campaign.[69] YouTube's policy was to remove content that violated its Community Guidelines. "These policies prohibit hate speech, harassment, and deceptive practices, including content that aims to mislead people about voting or videos that are technically manipulated or doctored in a way that misleads users (beyond clips taken out of context) and may pose a serious risk of egregious harm."[70] In each case, Republicans and conservative outlets claimed abusive and subjective targeting of posts resulting in general censorship of material. For Mollie Ziegler, Facebook and Twitter openly meddled in the 2020 election "by censoring political opponents, suppressing their supporters, limiting the distribution of articles and arguments in their favor, and other draconian efforts."[71]

Critics claim the most egregious censorship or ignoring an important story that could have impacted the election was that Hunter Biden, son of Joe Biden. It was alleged that he had received help from his dad as vice president with dealings in China. Postelection it become known that Hunter Biden had been under investigation by the Justice Department since 2018 related to tax issues, money laundering, and more recently, as of this writing, FBI investigation of Chinese business dealings. David Harsanyi, columnist for the *New York Post* and *National Review*, acknowledges that he is not convinced that full and detailed media coverage of the Biden investigations would have changed the outcome of the election. However, he is "convinced that journalists thought the case mattered—and for this reason avoided it. They simply abdicated their professional responsibilities to help Democrats win because many don't take their craft seriously anymore. That, we will continue to see, is a potential disaster for the nation."[72] Frank Miele, contributor to RealClearPolitics, thinks, "The ability to bury the Hunter Biden story throughout the 2020 presidential campaign ranks as one of the greatest victories in the history of propaganda."[73] The *New York Post* blamed the lack of coverage as part of "media collusion" and intentionally tried to suppress the story.[74] Most media outlets dismissed the story as "Russian Misinformation" or, as NPR did, publicly refused to waste time covering stories that are not real.[75] Twitter and Facebook suppressed the distribution of arguments and materials about the allegations surrounding Hunter Biden. As noted legal scholar Jonathan Turley observed, the major media and social media companies "imposed a virtual blackout on the allegations. It didn't matter that thousands of emails were available for review or that the Bidens did not directly address the material. . . . After all, an allegation is a scandal only if it is damaging. No coverage, no damage, no scandal."[76]

Even associating the notion of censorship with the practice of journalism is alarming. Even the allegations of deliberate bias are problematic. A postelection study by the Media Research Center is interesting. Clearly the Center is a major and loud critic of the media in general. The study asked voters about eight actual news stories, "important topics that our ongoing analysis had shown the liberal news media had failed to cover properly."[77] Three of the topics were negative stories on the Biden-Harris ticket and five were positive stories about the Trump administration and accomplishments. In a survey, they found 17 percent of people who cast their vote for Biden "would have changed their vote if they had been aware of one or more of these important stories." Among the nearly two thousand voters surveyed in the seven key swing states, 82 percent of those voting for Biden did not know of at least one of the total eight stories.

Press Hostility

Of course, there are countless allegations that the media collectively were simply anti-Trump from the beginning of his administration. Indeed, within twenty minutes of Trump's inaugural, *The Washington Post* wrote that a push for impeachment had begun.[78] Frank Miele of RealClearPolitics acknowledges that "needless to say, Donald Trump gets 'out of line' every day—he marches to the beat of his own drummer, as Thoreau said, and the press can't stand it. So, they engage in a near constant attack to destroy him and his presidency. . . . Their goal is to create the illusion that mainstream America hates Trump just as much as the media does. That requires amplifying any story that attacks Trump and ignoring those that benefit him. This has been going on for five years now. . . . Satan gets more respect."[79] But the hostility is not just for Trump; all surrogates, spokespeople and senior members of the administration were continually attacked, confronted, and interrogated in "smackdown" fashion. Paul Farhi noticed the increasing confrontational mode leading up to the election. "In the months leading up to the 2020 presidential election, the spokesman-and-surrogate smackdown has become a popular cable-news ritual. Once reluctant to brand transparently false statements as lies, or betray frustration with their interview subjects, even the most traditionally neutral anchorpeople now seem eager to join the fray. . . . It helps that Trump and his surrogates have provided so much raw material for aggressive TV interviewers to push back on for the past four years. But the volume of confrontational clips is a relatively new development in the media's relationship with this White House."[80]

Rich Noyes of the Media Research Center provides some content analysis of coverage of Trump that certainly appears very slanted. From March 4, when it became apparent that Joe Biden would be the Democrat nominee, until the end of May, Trump's coverage on the three major television networks was 94 percent negative. Of the 474 evaluative comments about Trump, 445 were negative. In terms of Biden, of the total of only 85 evaluative comments, 51 were negative or 61 percent.[81] Another example is with *The Washington Post*. Again, the Media Research Center reviewed the headlines relative to the government's response to the coronavirus between January 17 through April 25. The Center found 53 highly negative headlines compared to just two that were clearly positive.[82] Once again, during the two months of June and July 2020, the newscasts of ABC, CBS and NBC provided 668 evaluative statements about Trump with 95 percent negative and 67 percent positive for Biden.[83]

The general public recognized differences in coverage of Trump and Biden. Rasmussen found that 67 percent of likely voters thought the media was more interested in where Biden stood on issues than in creating controversies about him. In contrast, 41 percent thought the media were more interested in where Trump stood on issues. Even among Democrats, 53 percent thought they were more interested in where Trump stood on issues compared to 73 percent for Biden.[84] Over his five years in the political arena, President Trump has received the most minutes of news airtime, but also by far, the most negative evaluative coverage.

Use of "Faulty" Polls to Suppress Trump Vote

Within days after the election, the inaccuracy of polls nationally and across states became the focus of news stories and commentary. For months polls indicated a substantial lead for Biden nationally and within key battleground states. Some were reporting Democrat takeover of the Senate and possible a pickup of up to a dozen additional seats in the House. By Election Day, polls had Biden ahead between 10 and 17 points, indicating a major "Blue wave" and historic electoral college result. The Trump campaign said the reported polls were "fake news." In the aftermath of the election, noted pollster Frank Luntz characterized the entire polling industry as in a "systemic breakdown. . . . The political polling profession is done . . . it is devasting for my industry."[85] Just days before the election, *The Washington Post* had Biden ahead 17 points. According to Luntz, that poll was "not a mistake. That's not an error. That's polling malpractice. . . . And you have to go to tremendous lengths to be able to get something that wrong so close to the election. And there's a significant review by all of the media outlets of the work they were doing. The fact is the published pulling was so wrong, and not just for president but for House races and for the Senate races."[86]

Trust in polls declined after the 2016 presidential election. All major polls showed clear advantage to Hillary Clinton, although collectively most were within the margin of error. In 2020 polls were equally as bad. Quinnipiac had Biden up 5 points in Florida, where Trump won by 3 points, Monmouth University poll had Biden up 7 points in Pennsylvania to win by 1 point, ABC/*Washington Post* had Biden up 17 points in Wisconsin where he won by less than 1 point, and the final NBC/*Wall Street Journal* poll had Biden up 10 points nationally to ultimately win by less than 4 points.[87]

In addition to media outlets attempting to explain how polls could so widely miss the mark for a second election in a row, several journalists and outlets suggested an alternative (and more sinister) explanation. Mollie Ziegler suggests that "some polls have at times seemed to become a vehicle to express deep-seated media bias in favor of particular candidates—in the hopes that the polls might move public opinion rather than reflect it."[88] Virginia Allen says it's not about their methodologies; "maybe they're not bad at their job if their job is to try to shape public opinion rather than accurately measure it. I think we can draw no other conclusion based on the evidence we saw in 2016, and again in 2020."[89] Thus, there was suggestion that some of the polls were not designed to measure public opinion but to shape public opinion by the media companies that pay for them. Victor Hanson of RealClearPolitics argues that the majority of pollsters are "progressives" and have become "political operatives." "They see their task as ginning up political support for their candidates and demoralizing the opposition. Some are profiteering as internal pollsters for political campaigns and special interests." Worse, some reporting from conservative media outlets suggested that reporting of the polls suggesting winning support for Biden was one strategy to suppress Trump voters.

One thing I certainly did notice and publicly commented on, especially as the election neared, was the reporting of polls favoring Biden but well within the margin of error. And I have never witnessed such frequency of reporting of polls with margins of errors of 5 to 10 points.

Postelection Coverage of "Fraud" and Voting "Irregularities"

There were numerous concerns raised about voting across the nation and especially among several states. Generally, the concerns include:[90]

- Statistical anomalies in vote counts early on November 4
- Hundreds of affidavits reporting all types of irregularities and legal violations
- Statistically abnormal absentee vote counts with high percentages favoring Biden, some over 90 percent
- Thousands of missing votes found across several states days following the election
- Restrictions and limits of voting and vote count monitoring
- Numerous procedural issues and protocols such as matching signatures on mail-in ballots
- Historic low ballot rejection rates
- Missing votes
- Nonresident votes
- Votes counted twice, absentee and in-person
- Localities with over 100 percent voting
- States constitutional issues questioning authorities of changing

Articles and commentary focusing on coverage of the immediate postelection tended to focus on three facets of media coverage. As with all the other concerns, the distinctions were clear among the partisan media outlets. The first was rushing to judgment by calling the election over and for Biden when clearly several states were "too close to call." In addition to making early calls for Biden, Christopher Bedford accused the mainstream media of "holding calls on Republican wins like Florida for hours, and North Carolina for days, while recklessly rushing calls on states like Arizona for Team Blue."[91] An editorial by the *New York Sun* posed the question, "Why would the country be irreparably harmed by waiting for official results as prescribed by law?"[92]

Second, the dominant media focused on the allegation of "systemic fraud" declaring there was no evidence, such charges were baseless. The coverage became a battle over semantics. There certainly may not have been "nationwide systemic fraud," but there were certainly hundreds of "irregularities," some quite alarming. And sworn affidavits are indeed a form of evidence, perhaps weak or poor evidence, but some form of evidence nevertheless. At end of December 2020, John Lott, who works for the Department of Justice, published an interesting study titled "A Simple Test for the Extent of Vote Fraud with Absentee Ballots in the 2020 Presidential Election: Georgia and Pennsylvania Data" in Social Science Research Network.[93] SSRN, the world's largest open-access repository of academic and scholarly research across disciplines, is owned by Elsevier. Lott's analysis indicates between 70,000 and 79,000 "excess" votes in Georgia and Pennsylvania. In adding the analysis from the states of Arizona, Michigan, Nevada, and Wisconsin, the total amounts to 289,000 "excess votes." Lott concludes, "The precinct level estimates for Georgia and Pennsylvania indicate that vote fraud may account for Biden's win in both states. The voter turnout rate data also indicates that there are significant excess votes in Arizona, Michigan, Nevada, and Wisconsin as well."[94]

My straightforward point is, rather than exploring the strengths and weaknesses of the various state voting laws, regulations and protocols, statistical anomalies, issues related to mail-in ballots, absentee ballots, and perhaps the benefits of national expectations going forward, the partisan media (both sides) narrowly focused on an almost all or none perspective on the issue of election integrity. That is, either there was rampant voter fraud or none at all. Investigative journalism would have at least provided detailed information, research, analysis of affidavit allegations, consulting with voting experts, explore the history of voter fraud and explanations of voting concerns, etc.

Finally, on a daily basis there was reporting on the lawsuits brought by the Trump campaign and other groups challenging the election results in several states. Once again, there was a great divide in media coverage of the veracity of the lawsuits and reporting of the daily number of lawsuits dismissed by the courts. What was lacking was an understanding of the decisions of many of the lawsuits. Some were dismissed because of legal issues, technicalities or lack of standing never addressing the key arguments or questions raised. This was certainly true of the Supreme Court's dismissal of the Texas suit that 18 Republican state attorneys general and 126 House Republicans supported. The Court dismissed the lawsuit because "Texas has not demonstrated a judicially cognizable interest in the manner in which another state conducts its elections."[95]

CONCLUSION

Media coverage of the 2020 presidential campaign simply reflects the current media environment. The practice of contemporary journalism with new economic realities, along with the ever-evolving role of social media provide the context for coverage. Tribal and partisan journalism with the self-appointed censors of social media impacts who runs, who is elected and the nature of our democracy. It is easy to speak of reforms: return to the practice of "objectivity," "fact-based reporting," "sense of fairness," "accuracy," and "balance" of news presentations. Yet every outlet will fiercely defend their coverage and proclaim that indeed, their coverage embraced all of the above characteristics. But as noted earlier, Americans know better. As Joel Ferullo observes, "calling the major cable channels 'news outlets' is a misnomer: news is not opinion, nor is it commentary. But on cable, those things all blend together."[96] Sharyl Attkisson thinks that the news industry has helped to create a crisis of confidence in our American institutions. "By refusing to cover things fairly and accurately and making it clear that we're trying to tell people what to think, they tend to not believe anything."[97]

In theory, journalism is to provide "accurate" information and "facts" so that citizens can make "informed" decisions. For a democracy to thrive, must have access to true, accurate and adequate information. The notion of propaganda is a dishonest attempt to persuade people of a certain "reality" or "truth." Frank Miele put it this way: "Journalism starts with facts and allows people to reach their own conclusion. Propaganda starts with a conclusion and manipulates people into accepting it as fact. You can decide for yourself whether what we have today is journalism or propaganda."[98] And when it comes to social media and politics, well, the Constitution may guarantee freedom of speech but the major online gathering space for political expression certainly does not support that concept.

Thus, media is essential to our democracy. For Jim VandelHel there is a growing danger for our union. We are losing the "war" for "truth." "There is no bigger crisis for media, politics and society than the growing number of people who do not believe facts and verifiable figures. If we do not collectively solve this, we are all screwed."[99]

Edward R. Murrow, the famous pioneer of radio and television journalism and one of the most influential broadcasters in history, said, "We cannot make good news out of bad practice." And for journalism "to be persuasive we must be believable; to be believable we must be credible; to be credible we must be truthful." The real story of media coverage of the 2020 presidential election raises the questions of what is the nature and practice of news and did the coverage enhance our democracy and election processes?

As a footnote, there is growing speculation, that Trump actually may have contributed to the creation of a new type of journalist. Those who pushed back the most on Trump and those who defended him and targeted the media at large grew in stature, fame, and enhanced careers. As McKay Coppins observes, "The Trump era has been especially rewarding to a certain class of Washington reporter."[100] The White House beat provided worldwide exposure and to be the target of the president's tweets was golden. The higher profiles followed with thousands of Twitter followers, book deals, and cable news contract offers. As Coppins ponders, "As the story draws to an end, the reporters who got famous fighting with Trump are facing a question: What do we do now?" And I ponder, four years from now, what will be the assessment of media coverage of the 2024 presidential campaign?

Section II

STUDIES OF COMMUNICATION IN THE 2020 PRESIDENTIAL CAMPAIGN

Chapter 7

Political Branding in a Digital Age

The Role of Design- and Image-Based Messaging Strategies in the 2020 Presidential Campaign

Lisa M. Burns and Courtney Marchese

Presidential campaigns are visual spectacles—a series of image events created to sell a candidate to voters. Thanks to both television and the Internet, design aspects of campaigns have become increasingly important. How politicians visually present their brand can contribute significantly to their communication strategy. For example, the now-ubiquitous red MAGA hat successfully distilled Donald Trump's campaign messaging into a single piece of merchandise. But sometimes the "mantras and merchandise that might have worked in one election cycle fail in the next."[1] The 2020 race between President Donald Trump and former Vice President Joe Biden featured a battle between two different political brands. The contenders used the visual components of their brands to clearly differentiate themselves. In a race shaped by the COVID-19 pandemic, social media took center stage and masks, or lack thereof, emerged as a powerful symbol defining each campaign. This chapter analyzes how esthetics contributed to the branding efforts of the Trump and Biden campaigns in the 2020 presidential election by examining the visual messaging strategies represented in their design choices, social media imagery, and merchandising.

POLITICAL BRANDING

Branding is a staple of political campaigns. Having an effective logo, slogan, and colors is as old as campaigning itself. However, the "conceptualization of political candidates as brands has been sparsely discussed in academic literature," only emerging as a distinct research area in the 1990s.[2] But given campaigns' reliance on marketing and design techniques, it is an important lens through which to study political strategy.

Political brands offer a "short cut" to what a candidate is about through a combination of visual imagery and pithy messaging, helping voters to distinguish between political entities. Some of the key components of successful brands are creativity, a clear purpose, possessing emotional appeal, and the ability to target messaging to key demographics.[3] Communication strategist Dellvin Roshon Williams explains that political branding "tells the public not just who a political actor is, but shapes how a political actor is perceived" by manipulating symbols and concepts to tell a story.[4] He offers Trump's "Make America Great Again" as an example of a narrative that emotionally resonated with a key demographic of the American electorate, the white male working class, invoking a sense of nostalgia, inspiring hope, and eliciting a desire for change among those voters while being simultaneously anxiety provoking for others. According to Catherine Needham, successful political brands, like their commercial counterparts, have six attributes: they act as simplifiers highlighting a few key pieces of information about the candidate, they are unique and clearly differentiated from competitors, they reassure voters and minimize perceptions of risk, they are aspirational and offer an emotional link to a desired way of life, they symbolize the internal values of the candidate and offer voters reasons to choose them over others, and they are perceived as credible and able to deliver on their campaign promises.[5] Trump's "Make America Great Again" slogan has all six attributes, which is one of the reasons why it's among the most recognizable phrases in politics and pop culture today. Even though the slogan was a direct knockoff of Ronald Reagan's "Let's Make America Great Again," it is now an indelible part of the Trump brand.

Since the product being "sold" in political marketing is a person, brand personality is important. The concept of brand personality was initially designed as a way to anthropomorphize products, giving them human qualities including sincerity, excitement, competence, sophistication, and ruggedness to explain why consumers were attracted to certain brands.[6] Other characteristics of effective brand personality include capability, openness, and empathy.[7] In political branding, candidates seek to incorporate these traits into their public personas. This is accomplished through the use of value-laden words and images that are strategically disseminated through various communication channels. Candidates "configure their identities to appeal to their target publics and the general public, and as such to encourage identification of citizens with their personas."[8]

Trump and Biden have distinctive brand personalities. Trump's brand can be summed up as BIG, BOLD, and DEFIANT. The capital letters are intentional, mimicking Trump's tweets and typeface. He positions himself as an "outlaw who doesn't have time for politeness or political correctness,"[9] projecting a type of rugged sincerity and an extreme confidence in his capabilities.

Andrea Schneiker describes Trump's brand as a "superhero anti-politician celebrity."[10] In stark contrast to Trump, Biden's brand is calm, casual, and cool. He's familiar, likeable, and trustworthy, which conveys competence, sincerity, openness, and empathy. Market research company Ipsos conducted a study in mid-October 2020 of the Trump and Biden brands by applying tools they use to assess the performance of commercial brands. They found more intensity and supporter loyalty for the Trump brand, whereas Biden's supporters were more anti-Trump than pro-Biden. When asked, "What pops into your mind when you think of Joe Biden or Donald Trump?" participants didn't have many clear and unique associations with Biden. While "great (potential) president/person" was the number one response, "old" was a close second followed by "cares about the people/kind." However, participants had very intense positive and negative reactions to Trump. "Great president/ person" was also the top response for Trump, but "arrogant/rude" and "bad president/person" received the second and third most mentions. When looking at what drives brand preference, participants offered detailed reasons why they were attracted to or repelled by Trump. Trump supporters viewed him as "bold, good for the economy, intelligent, and as someone who will respect law and order while fighting political correctness," all traits of the "superhero anti-politician celebrity." But others described him as corrupt, racist, reckless, bully, liar, arrogant, and narrow-minded, pushing them toward Biden. Meanwhile, Biden's positive attributes were a bit more general and included likeable, trustworthy, qualified, stands up for people, and respects the right to protest. His negatives—irresponsible, boring, and old—were more muted than the Trump responses. Ipsos researchers concluded that Brand Biden is a bit nondescript while Brand Trump is well-defined in both positive and negative ways. They predicted that the intensity would be a key factor in voter turnout, but it was all about supporting or rejecting Trump rather than an enthusiasm for Biden.[11]

Using these political branding concepts as a guide, what follows is an analysis of the design- and image-based messaging strategies employed in the branding of the 2020 presidential candidates.

DESIGN ASPECTS

Visual aspects of branding presidential candidates have long been one of the most accessible ways to convince voters to support them. Because of increased web presence and social media, the visual messaging of a campaign has become a more complex system that also presents more potential opportunities. While the Democratic primaries offered a smorgasbord of fresh colors and logos, the presidential race ultimately boiled down to patriotic palettes.

As the incumbent, Trump's campaign made minimal changes to their branding from the 2016 to 2020 elections. However, Biden's branding saw more evolution from his initial announcement that he was running for president to Election Day. The original Biden logo designed by Aimee Brodbeck of the creative agency Mekanism featured three red stripes stretching outward to replace the letter E in his first and last name. The typeface (Brother 1816 by TipoType) was selected for its similarities to Gotham, the successful type used for Obama's branding. Brodbeck says that both the E treatment and the typeface choice were an intentional homage to Obama's O logo, designed by Sol Sender. The logo is intended to convey unity.[12]

Early response to the logo indicated a collective underwhelm, especially compared to the nontraditional color palettes of the democratic primaries. Biden's red, white, and blue felt decidedly conventional and bland up against Senator Elizabeth Warren's "liberty green," Senator Kirsten Gillibrand's bright pink, and former Representative Beto O'Rourke's black and white. When Biden's eventual deputy design director Carahna Magwood inherited the brand, she felt like it was patriotic in a very traditional sense but "did not represent all of America."[13] As a first step, Magwood modernized the color palette by bringing in variations of reds and blues to give more depth to the brand guidelines.

The real turning point for Biden's esthetic came with the opportunity of reintroducing him when Senator Kamala Harris joined the ticket as vice presidential nominee. In preparation for the announcement, Robyn Kanner joined the campaign as a creative adviser and encouraged the team to capture Biden's unique voice. While many view logos as the touchstone of a campaign, it is the messaging surrounding the logo that's crucial. The logo itself is both a technical and an emotional problem to solve. Kanner focused on Biden's speaking cadence, movements, and speech patterns, as well as what Biden's voters sound and look like. To mimic Biden's speech of strong action words combined with gentle prepositions, Kanner ultimately chose two typefaces in part for their connection to truth, in consultation with famed typographer Jonathan Hoeffler. Inspired by the actions words, Kanner chose Decimal, a sans serif inspired by vintage watch lettering "as true as time." As the secondary type, the serif type Mercury was used, which "held the truth of the written word" for its usage in publications like *The Atlantic*.[14]

At the virtual 2020 AIGA National Conference, Kanner described the process of designing the Biden-Harris brand as being more about the Democratic ticket than the candidate. The visuals required balanced footing for president and vice president, with the campaign acutely aware that 2020 was not an Obama-esque moment and was never meant to be. Rather than focus on a memorable mark like the Obama O or Hillary's H, the idea was to push Biden and Harris as household names rather than the overly polished corporate-style branding of past Democratic candidates. The original logo needed to be evolved and not altogether ditched because it already had equity and a base. A complete redesign risked implying that those who always loved Biden were somehow "wrong." Authenticity and semiotics are needed to win.[15]

Another significant visual component that evolved throughout the campaign was the use of gradients rather than sharp lines and solid colors. The creative team intended the gradients to bring life to the brand and counter the feeling of the isolation born from the country's pandemic and divisiveness. When gradients are used well, they have a natural warmth to them, feeding a need in 2020 for things that looked and sounded uplifting. Gradients making their way into politics mirrors commercial branding trends in technology and entertainment contexts like Spotify, Instagram, and the Miami Heat, to name a few. Many of these visual references have positive associations and broad familiarity that was welcome in a presidential brand. As Hunter Schwarz describes, by the closing weeks of the 2020 race, "reds and blues blended into pink and purple hues, especially on @votejoe, a secondary campaign Instagram account that ditched the strict campaign style guide for 'a look that was more VMAs than DNC.'"[16]

While many of the campaign's visuals used on Facebook and Instagram were relatively traditional, the creative team also created hundreds of pro-Biden and pro-voting gifs to complement the colorful and experimental posts by the @votejoe account. Joe Biden's official accounts showcased a more traditional gradient application, but ultimately the brand proved flexible enough to be traditional and progressive. Schwarz notes that Biden's visual system "sold a candidate who simultaneously promised a return to normalcy of the past but with a bold, progressive agenda designed for the future."[17] The Biden brand's evolution allowed his message to reach a diverse coalition of voters because of the vast yet coherent visual strategy that allowed for spontaneity and fun.

In contrast to Biden's campaign, the Trump team did little in the way of evolving. Rather than creating any brand design strategy, they relied heavily on Trump himself as the brand. Many have speculated about which the typeface is used on the "MAKE AMERICA GREAT AGAIN" hat, but that could be because there are a few variations in circulation. For Trump, typefaces do not matter as long as they are in all capital letters. Jadalia Britto of Colgate Palmolive notes that "instead of taking the opportunity to highlight what defines his campaign, 'the logo communicates and depicts Trump's strong personality in his name rather than his ideology as a candidate.'"[18] While it is not surprising that an incumbent would stick closely to the branding that won the first time, the choice to use patriotic red, white, and blue is interesting because Trump has positioned himself as the "antipolitician" and a champion against a "rigged system." Although visual esthetics are often necessary, they are only one of many tools used in designing. Ultimately, the design is a user experience shaped by how people feel, and that notion should shape what combination of copy, flow, colors, shapes, and typefaces are used.[19] What Trump lacks in a thoughtful visual system he makes up for in copy, which is one of the most critical components to holding a design together. While Biden's speech pattern combines action words and gentle prepositions, Trump mostly ends sentences with a keyword playing into the "serial position effect" of human psychology, which impacts recall accuracy. He also plays into the "illusory truth effect" by repeating the same words over and over, further emphasized by persistent all-capital letter usage.[20]

A *Boston Globe* study showed that Trump speaks at a fourth-grade level (compared with most Obama speeches geared to an eighth-grade level), avoiding long words and using short sentences. Some see this as proof that he is an idiot, while others see it as deliberate and calculated. Tony Aubé argues that the way Trump talks takes advantage of humans' limited attention, creating a positive bias toward easier things to understand. His message inevitably reaches the most people possible, including those who may not speak English as a first language. The combination of effects from Trump's speech patterns effectively destabilizes the system through lies and diminishes the value of truth. Unfortunately, even when humans doubt a statement or tweet, the more we are exposed the more we *feel* like it is true even if it disagrees with our preexisting knowledge. It is in humans' nature to conserve mental energy and instead rely on heuristics, or mental shortcuts, to process messages quickly. Simple language repeated often plays right into Trump's ability to hook followers.[21]

There is no better evidence of Trump's simple language's success than the infamous red "MAKE AMERICA GREAT AGAIN" hat. As Young notes, "The DIY nature of the hat embodies the wares of a 'self-made man' and intentionally distances itself from well-established high-design brand systems like Obama or Hillary. Tasteful design becomes suspect . . . the trucker cap is as American as apple pie."[22] It is no fluke that Trump didn't bother with good design because he understands his audience. Just compare his decidedly "undesigned" hat with the sophistication of Trump hotel websites. Good design is expensive and easily associated with the polished corporate America that is so unfavorable to many.

Trump's unchanged strategy and wide-open playbook over the past four years made the response from the Biden campaign much easier. At the AIGA National Conference, Kanner recounted how many times responses were already prepared and were just a matter of timing to share them. Nothing was surprising from Trump, making jabs about hand sanitizer, tax return stickers, and fly swatters an easy, rapid response item for the campaign.[23] Like so many of Trump's personal and business endeavors, his presidential brand did not seem to have a plan for longevity.

Creating a clear design strategy to visually represent a candidate is the first major hurdle in establishing a political brand. How the campaigns choose to apply those design aspects across websites, social media, merchandise, and more is equally as important in having a consistent voice that voters can trust.

MULTICHANNEL BRAND INTEGRATION: CONSISTENCY IN ONLINE PRESENCE

Once a campaign develops a brand identity, those visual elements need to be integrated across platforms and used to support the candidate's messaging strategy. In today's digital age, candidates need to have a consistent, memorable brand to connect with voters online. Websites and social media platforms have become "increasingly important for the branding of political actors, and have brought new opportunities and new challenges to political branding practices."[24] Multichannel brand integration requires a robust strategy that is still relatively new to the campaign world. Barack Obama was the first nominee to successfully use social media to reach supporters in 2008. In 2016, Trump's campaign made Twitter and Facebook a central part of their strategy, using the platforms to communicate directly with voters and generate free media coverage through Trump's constant tweeting. His former digital media director Brad Parscale even claimed that social media "were the reason we won."[25] Today, people's first interactions directly with candidates are increasing through social media.[26] The COVID-19 pandemic accelerated this trend in 2020, forcing candidates to shift to primarily digital strategies given the limitations on traditional campaign events due to COVID-related restrictions. Social media platforms served as the main way to shape each candidate's brand, promote their message, connect with voters, and get out the vote. Facebook and Twitter remain two of the best social media platforms for campaigns because they reach the widest voter demographics. According to a Pew Research study, 44 percent of Americans learned about the 2016 presidential election from social media.[27] That figure jumped to 55 percent according to a November 2020 Pew report.[28] While Facebook and Twitter reach the largest audiences, the campaigns also used Instagram, YouTube, Snapchat, TikTok, and Reddit to target younger voters. Images and videos were shared across channels with the accompanying text modified on the basis of the platform and target demographic, reflecting the best practices of social media branding. Both campaigns employed over 100 people on their digital media teams.[29]

Previous campaigns have used social media to "construct a positive political image through visual images" by showing the candidate on the campaign trail and engaging with voters or by sharing personal or candid shots.[30] The same was true in 2020. But the images also highlighted how the pandemic came to dominate the campaign. The conventions needed to be reimagined. Stump campaigning had to be drastically modified. Even Trump, who clung to a "business as usual" strategy in an attempt to minimize the effects of the pandemic, had to shift his rallies from arenas to airplane hangars, significantly decreasing crowd sizes. Not surprisingly, masks became a symbol imbued with meaning for both campaigns. The Biden campaign embraced masks and social distancing, making it a cornerstone of their messaging. Meanwhile, the Trump campaign largely avoided masks, with the president particularly adamant about not wearing one in public. As one article noted, the candidates were "taking diametrically opposite approaches to campaigning during a pandemic—and the differences amount to more than political theater. The candidates are effectively staking out different visions for the country."[31] Thus, the pandemic response became one of the primary visual distinguishers between the candidates that permeated their image-based branding strategies on social media.

Social media continued to be central to Trump's campaign strategy in 2020. As of Election Day, Trump had more than 87 million Twitter followers, 30.5 million followers and over 36 million likes on Facebook, and 24.5 million Instagram followers. He also had 5.2 million social media mentions from June through early November according to social listening research firm Awario.[32] True to his personal brand, Trump's social media imagery emphasized crowd sizes, patriotic symbolism, and his celebrity status. Based on visuals alone, it would be almost impossible to tell that the campaign was happening in the midst of a deadly global pandemic.

Since Instagram is an image-based platform, it provides the most comprehensive look at each candidate's visual messaging strategy. Most of the images and videos also appeared on their other platforms, so they are representative of the campaigns' overall social strategies. Starting with the thumbnails on Trump's Instagram, there was a clear color story. Everything was red, white, and blue. The majority of images featured President Trump, American flags, and crowds of supporters at Trump rallies, with many being a combination of the three. Very few posts contained any graphics or text. American flags were frequently featured in the background. Trump always wore a red or blue tie, white shirt, and dark navy blue suit and overcoat. Sometimes he donned a red MAGA hat at rallies. Red dominated the crowd images with supporters wearing red MAGA hats and other Trump swag in shades of red, white, and blue. The crowd images are strikingly uniform by design. Red MAGA hats, TRUMP PENCE 2020 T-shirts, signs with the slogans "MAKE AMERICA GREAT AGAIN" and "PROMISES KEPT," and even MAGA face masks were distributed for free at rallies by campaign staffers to create a cohesive look. The only deviations from the color palette were the occasional hot pink "Women FOR TRUMP" signs at events in areas where Trump was trying to woo what he called the "suburban housewife" vote and the seafoam blue of Air Force One, which often served as part of the backdrop at Trump's hanger rallies.

Based on Trump's Instagram feed, you would not know there was a pandemic with the exception of the sporadic MAGA masks worn by some supporters. The wide-angle crowd shots emphasized the size of Trump's rallies with people standing shoulder-to-shoulder, not six feet apart. Trump crowed about the rally sizes, saying he believed the crowds were bigger than in 2016 while making fun of Biden's socially distanced events like his drive-in rallies, claiming they drew "a tiny, tiny crowd."[33] He also routinely mocked Biden for wearing a mask, saying "Did you ever see a man who likes a mask as much as him?" eliciting laughs and cheers from his largely unmasked audiences.[34] However, the campaign was required to distribute masks in some states as a condition of holding a public event. They capitalized on it by passing out branded MAGA masks. But mask-wearing was not widely enforced, as seen in photos and videos from rallies. It seemed the only people encouraged to wear masks were those seated behind the stage who would be clearly visible on camera, offering Trump a backdrop of MAGA masks to go with the typical campaign signs, Trump T-shirts, and MAGA hats. But even those images frequently show people without masks.

This is not surprising given Trump's stance on masks. There were just three photos of Trump in a mask on Instagram. The first was a black and white image from July 20 with a caption stating, "Many people say that it is Patriotic to wear a face mask when you can't socially distance. There is nobody more Patriotic than me, your favorite President!" The CDC recommended Americans wear masks in early April, but at the time Trump said it was voluntary and he was "choosing not to do it."[35] The July 20 photo was posted about a week after the CDC issued yet another call for people to wear masks following a spike in cases.[36] It was one of the few times Trump wore a mask in public. The other two images were both posted on October 5, the day Trump left Walter Reed Medical Center after being treated for COVID-19. The first shot was taken when Trump's motorcade drove around the hospital to thank supporters gathered outside. It showed Trump in the SUV's window wearing a plain navy mask and giving two thumbs up. The second was a video from Trump's choreographed return from Walter Reed. He's wearing a white mask as he gets off Marine One. After ascending to the White House balcony, he defiantly took off his mask and shoved it in his pocket. The staged image event was quickly turned into a campaign ad, further politicizing the topic of mask wearing and downplaying the seriousness of the pandemic. Trump released several videos in the following days telling people "don't let it dominate you" and "don't be afraid of" COVID. After receiving an experimental treatment not widely available to the public, he bragged about feeling "amazing" and even claimed he may "be immune."

All of the imagery on Trump's social media supported his "superhero anti-politician celebrity" brand. When the *Boston Herald*'s front page declared him "SUPERTRUMP" in comic book typeface, the Trump team shared the image—one of the few items to feature text in his Instagram feed. The bold red, white, and blue hues, the MAGA hats, the American flags, and the packed rallies were recognizable components of Trump's political brand. His large public events were held in defiance of public health recommendations, much to the delight of his supporters, and may have led to increased cases in some parts of the country.[37] He "fought" and "beat" COVID, demonstrating his ruggedness. He claimed a new level of expertise by going "to the real school" and learning about the disease by having it instead of from "books." Trump's comments showed little empathy for other Americans who contracted COVID, including the over 200,000 who had died.[38] But the images projected a strong, confident leader who did not see the pandemic as a major threat. In fact, he barely acknowledged its existence. This messaging resonated with Trump's base but may have cost him the election.

Biden's team had some catching up to do when it came to his use of social media: "During the Democratic primary, competitors like [Bernie] Sanders, Elizabeth Warren and Pete Buttigieg built sophisticated digital-outreach efforts; Biden emerged as the nominee despite having just a skeletal digital operation. Quarantined at home in the early days of the pandemic, he struggled at first to adjust to the Internet campaign, releasing a series of tepid videos to muted response." Realizing a change was needed going into the general election, the campaign quadrupled the digital team's size to 100 by hiring staffers from rival primary campaigns and online outlets like *BuzzFeed*.[39]

As of Election Day, Biden had 13.5 million Twitter followers, 3.783 million followers and 3.381 million likes on Facebook, and 5.9 million followers on Instagram. Research firm Awario recorded 2.2 million social media mentions for Biden from June through early November.[40] These numbers paled in comparison to Trump's well-established social media operation even after the Biden campaign expanded its social reach by adding Kamala Harris' followers (13.5 million on Instagram, 12.8 million on Twitter, and 3.8 million on Facebook) to the fold. In order to compensate for a smaller social media operation, the Biden team turned to celebrities and influencers, tapping into their followings to reach both a larger audience and specific voting demographics.[41] This network of supporters allowed the campaign to adopt a mostly positive messaging strategy, leaving negative attacks to surrogates, and positioning Biden as the antithesis of Trump in both personality and policy stances. According to digital director Rob Flaherty, their goal was to promote Biden's message through "feel-good" imagery designed to "highlight the candidate's warmth" and practical graphics focused on his plans. Flaherty talked about running a campaign to "restore the soul of the Internet" that mirrored Biden's pledge to "restore the soul of the nation."[42] Again, this was a stark contrast to Trump's messaging and a way to capitalize on anti-Trump sentiment.

Biden's Instagram featured a wider variety of content than Trump's including graphics, candid shots from the campaign trail, and images of everything from Biden-Harris bread to their logo in mehndi body art submitted by supporters. There was also more video content, much of it featuring Biden's supporters and surrogates rather than just the candidate, which was Trump's style. This included reaction videos (a video style popular on YouTube and TikTok) of average voters like moms, veterans, and teachers responding negatively to Trump statements; testimonials from supporters talking about the issues that matter to them; policy videos narrated by former primary challengers like Elizabeth Warren and Julián Castro; and clips of Biden chatting with both regular people and famous supporters including President Obama, Dwayne "The Rock" Johnson, Cardi B, Jennifer Lopez, Alex Rodriguez, and Tom Hanks. By making voters and issues the focus of his feed, Biden was able to project competence, openness, and empathy. While Trump's celebrity was central to his brand, Biden seemed to embrace the #SettleForBiden trend and allowed others, including running mate Kamala Harris, to take center stage and highlight yet another way he was different from Trump.

Based on the thumbnails, there is clearly more color and creativity in the Biden feed. As noted earlier, the Biden team used various gradients adding depth and dimension beyond the standard flat blue representative of the Democratic party. They also mixed it up at times with greens and blues, which were often used on graphics related to voting and flipping states. Even with the policy-related content and calls to get out the vote, the feed looked more organic and genuine. Although Trump may be the "antipolitician," his feeds featured traditional campaign imagery. In contrast, Biden's social media looked more like that of an average user with its photos of babies and baked goods, kids, and cars. Of course, this was the result of careful curation by the Biden digital team. By being less prescriptive and more spontaneous, using less strict corporate-like branding and more loose overarching guidelines, Biden was able to reach a constituency that Hillary was never able to tap in 2016.

The most striking difference between the Trump and Biden visual messaging relates to the pandemic. Biden fully supported social distancing and masks as recommended by public health officials. He severely curtailed travel, opting instead for virtual events. When he returned to the campaign trail, he held small events in accordance with local restrictions and developed the drive-in rally as a way for larger crowds to safely gather.[43] Having fewer campaign event images is likely one reason why Biden's social platforms featured more videos and graphics. Meanwhile, face masks became a powerful symbol representing Biden's response to the pandemic. While Trump rejected masks and made fun of Biden for wearing them, Biden countered by making masks central to his campaign. There are over fifty images of Biden in a mask dating back to mid-August compared to the three of Trump. One is a short clip from October 5 juxtaposing Trump forcefully removing his mask on the White House balcony after his release from the hospital with Biden putting his mask on with a graphic saying "MASKS SAVE LIVES." There's also a GIF of Biden saying, "Be a patriot. Wear a mask." A number of other photos feature people in masks including Biden's wife Jill, VP pick Harris, and those attending Biden campaign events. There are also several videos from medical professionals, frontline workers, and individuals who lost family members proclaiming their support for Biden's pandemic response and condemning Trump's handling of the COVID crisis.

Even though Biden's imagery included frequent references to the pandemic, it did not detract from the overall message of hope and positivity. The "feel-good," personal vibe of the Biden social strategy could be considered dull compared to Trump's overbearing style. But that is by design in more ways than one. "Good digital programs are really boring," says Democratic digital organizer Amanda Litman. "It is very authentically Joe Biden. It is stable. It is solid. It is a little boring. But it gets the job done."[44] Biden's imagery reinforced his brand personality as someone who is likeable, trustworthy, and sincere. He also exhibited competence and empathy in response to the pandemic, a message that many voters found reassuring.

Overall, the candidates' visual imagery on social media contrasted Biden's calm and cool demeanor with Trump's brash and bold style: "If Biden's digital content often has the feel of a friendly grandpa telling a story that goes on slightly too long, Trump's is all about outrage. His team blankets Facebook with ads that leverage fury to sell swag—Trump T-shirts! Trump hats! Trump wineglasses!—and harvest the data. This strategy has made the President a digital Goliath."[45] These branding strategies carried over to the candidates' merchandise.

SELLING THE BRAND: CAMPAIGN MERCHANDISE

Campaign paraphernalia is nothing new. Over the years, candidates' names, likenesses, and slogans have been printed on everything from the traditional buttons, posters, hats, and shirts to matchboxes, dishes, jewelry, paper dresses, pajamas, and even a chamber pot.[46] Campaign merchandising, commonly called "merch," has long been a key component of candidate branding for a few reasons. First, it allows campaigns to spread their message by using their supporters as walking advertisements while letting backers show their allegiance by doing their part to promote the candidate. Merch also helps supporters recognize each other, helping to foster a group identity similar to sports fans who wear their teams' apparel or put stickers on their cars.[47] Meanwhile, merch can showcase candidates' creative and quirky sides, injecting a bit of fun into the political process and helping to make candidates seem more relatable. Merch also lives on after the campaign ends, becoming a lasting artifact of the election. Displays of campaign memorabilia can be found in presidential museums and collectors pay top dollar for rare campaign mementos. Finally, since 2007, merch has counted as a campaign contribution, providing candidates with another fundraising vehicle to sustain their campaign coffers.[48] According to *Politico*, "Political professionals said merchandising is increasingly becoming an important way to court small donors. People get something in return for their money, making it attractive to those who don't ordinarily give to campaigns."[49] This final section focuses on how the candidates' brands were represented in their merchandise.

The most prolific online store belonged to President Trump, who made effective use of merch in his 2016 run and continued to capitalize on his brand's popularity with his base in the 2020 race. As of Election Day, there were 242 items for sale in the "Official Trump Store" linked to the campaign website. Most of the products were the standard campaign fare: shirts, signs, buttons, glasses, and stickers. But there were also toys, a jigsaw puzzle, playing cards, plastic straws, gold cufflinks, and Christmas ornaments. In terms of design, the campaign rarely diverted from its red, white, blue, or camo color scheme or its use of basic typeface, which gave its merch a sense of continuity.

But this also resulted in a lot of repetitiveness throughout the store. For example, all of the adult shirt designs were the same with the exception of the "Women FOR TRUMP" and "Maga MAMA" tees aimed at women. While there were 102 tops available, there were only 52 designs. The same was true for face coverings. Even though the Trump campaign did not publicly promote face masks, they had eighteen for sale. But there were only three design options: the large font "TRUMP" or "MAGA" that filled the width of the mask or gaiter and a mask with a small "Trump Pence 2020" logo available in camo, hot pink, and the standard red, white, and blue. Then there were the hats. The store had 40 hats for sale, but fifteen of them were the famous "MAKE AMERICA GREAT AGAIN" baseball caps. Most were variations of red, white, blue, and camo. There were specific versions for Greek, Polish, and Israeli supporters and two "Boaters for Trump" options—campaign demographics that are not often singled out. The slogan is so ubiquitous that two hats just said "MAGA." Yet there was only one "KEEP AMERICA GREAT" hat and two "TRUMP PENCE 2020" caps (in slightly different camo patterns) for sale. The campaign clearly relied on the strong brand loyalty and emotional appeal of its initial slogan. The MAGA hats are the most recognizable symbol of Trump's political brand and part of their allure is their simplicity. Designer Lindsey Ballant told CNN that the "undesigned" hats "didn't represent what one thinks of when you think of traditional politics in terms of visual messaging, and that's essentially what Trump was as well."[50] Thus, the sameness and plainness of the merch may have been a strategic decision to keep the messaging clear.

One of the few places where the campaign switched up its style was in merch designed for target demographics. But they did so by using colors stereotypically linked to gender, race, and ethnicity. For example, the "Women FOR TRUMP" and "Maga MAMA" merch featured pink somewhere in the design. The "Black Voices FOR TRUMP" merch was black and white. The "IRISH AMERICANS FOR TRUMP" logo was emerald green with a four-leaf clover and was available on tees and pint glasses. Other ethnic group merch employed flag colors, like red and white for the Polish American tees and blue and white in the Greek and Israeli MAGA hats. Similarly, the "Latinos FOR TRUMP" logo was red and green on a white tee, the colors of the Mexican flag, which is not representative of all Latinx's heritage. Trump's merch aimed at other key demos was also very literal. For example, one "Veterans for Trump" shirt was olive green and the other had the slogan printed in a dog tag, the "Cops for Trump" merch included the Blue Lives Matter flag, and the Pride shirts featured rainbow colors. Despite the stereotypes, the Trump camp deserves credit for featuring a diverse group of models on their site, including several persons of color.

Some of the more creative Trump merch showcased familiar catchphrases and capitalized on key campaign moments. Popular crowd chants from Trump's rallies were turned into shirts and stickers including "Build the Wall," "Four More Years," and "Fill That Seat," which became a Republication rallying cry following the death of Supreme Court Justice Ruth Bader Ginsberg. Other phrases fit Trump's "defiance as lifestyle" brand, like "If you don't like Trump then you probably won't like me" and "Trump Ain't a Mistake Snowflake!"[51] Most products focused on Trump, but there were a few exceptions. Trump's team turned Biden's "#YouAin'tBlack" gaffe into a T-shirt with Biden prominently credited for the comment. Then, after Biden called the Latinx community diverse, "unlike" the Black community, a second version of the shirt had "Black" crossed out with a thick red line and "Diverse" printed above. The website caption stated, "First we were told we 'AIN'T BLACK.' Now we aren't diverse. Who knows what he will say next?"[52] A similar design was used on shirts and stickers saying "DEFUND THE POLICE" in black and blue with "DEFUND" scratched out multiple times and "DEFEND!" printed in handwritten block letters above, which was a response to the Black Lives Matter protests following the death of George Floyd. Meanwhile, the site continued to sell a "BABY LIVES MAT-TER" onesie, originally designed for the January 2020 March for Life, in the wake of the social unrest. The most interesting product was a white hat with "Woke" in black letters. It is not clear whether the hat was a joke or if the campaign was not clear on the meaning of the term.

The store also featured an interesting mix of novelty gifts. Over the years, Trump has not shied away from putting his name on everything from hotels and resorts to steaks, wine, and bottled water.[53] Some of the kitschier items included Trump swimsuits, wrapping paper featuring Trump in a Santa hat, a wooden train set with the "TRUMP PENCE" logo, a coloring book with Trump as a superhero, red Solo-style cups, and a "KEEP AMERICA GREAT" red hat collectable Christmas ornament, one of the site's priciest items at $60. Among the most popular products were the reusable plastic straws etched with "I Heart TRUMP." They launched in 2019 via an email with the subject like "Making straws great again." The online ad copy said, "Liberal paper straws don't work. STAND WITH PRESIDENT TRUMP and buy your pack of recyclable straws today."[54] The first batch sold out in hours, with initial sales estimated at half a million dollars.[55] Trump's merch is so successful because Trump knows his brand and is willing to capitalize on it.[56] His campaign communications director Tim Murtaugh told the *New York Times*, "President Trump is a master of communication and brand-ing, and his campaign merchandise is emblematic of that."[57] From a visual messaging standpoint, the merch successfully represented Trump's brand. But, based strictly on design elements, Trump's merch was a fairly standard campaign swag.

Biden's campaign store offerings were pretty basic in the primaries, espe-cially compared to the creativity of other Democratic contenders, but the campaign upped its merch game once Biden clinched his party's nomination. One publication noted, "Joe Biden's campaign has mastered the art of mak-ing memorable merch."[58] As of Election Day, there were 107 items for sale in the official "Team Joe Store" on the campaign's website ranging from the standard shirts, signs, mugs, tote bags, buttons, and bumper stickers to pet collars, bucket hats, baby onesies, face masks, and hand sanitizer with Biden's COVID-19 plan printed on the label. There were also 126 free digi-tal downloads including 14 types of merch for *Animal Crossing* characters, from yard signs to Biden-Harris sweaters and T-shirts, capitalizing on the pandemic popularity of the Nintendo game.

During the primary, most of the merch said either "Biden President" or "JOE 2020," using a standard red, white, and blue color scheme and emphasizing the three-line red "E" design. The "CUP O' JOE" mug was an early best seller. *GQ* said, "like Biden the candidate, this mug is distinguished from its many competitors—for now—by the grandpa energy in the pun."[59] But campaign's decision to feature the aviator sunglasses as part of Biden's persona had some journalists scratching their heads. One article pointed out, "One other odd design choice was thinking Biden's aviator-style sunglasses preference is enough of a trademark."[60] Another reporter observed that "several items punch up the former VP's older guy coolness by putting his love of aviators front-and-center. Don't get me wrong: I'm a fan of the sunglasses—but personal style isn't my number one concern when it comes to a Commander-in-Chief."[61] Yet the campaign continued to feature the aviators on T-shirts, socks, mugs, and buttons. Even Biden's *Animal Crossing* character sports his signature shades.

The campaign started to move beyond basic after adding Kamala Harris to the ticket. First, they updated the standard stock by adding the new "BIDEN HARRIS" logo, with the three-line "E" now appearing in Biden's last name, to every type of merch. Several products were created just for Harris, including "Kamala" pins, stickers, and T-shirts with black backgrounds and her signature in white. Her niece Meena Harris and artist Cleo Wade designed a T-shirt with a photo of a young Harris and the words "The First But Not The Last." You could also buy stickers with "KAMALA" in pink and green, her Alpha Kappa Alpha sorority colors. These were some of the first items to deviate from the red, white, and blue color palette. Following the viral story about Harris' love of Chuck Taylors, T-shirts featuring her Converse and Biden's aviators went on sale. Around the same time, the campaign added more issue-based merch. They highlighted the pandemic response with their "BIDEN HARRIS" logo face mask and stickers saying "Wear a Mask," a healthcare-themed button collection featured the phrases "Obamacare is a BFD" and "Protect Our Healthcare," and a reusable water bottle emblazoned with "Secure a Clean Energy Future."

The campaign got even more creative in September when they dropped a capsule collection created by 19 American-based fashion designers from diverse backgrounds. The merch team may have been inspired by Bernie Sanders and Elizabeth Warren, who featured similar creative collaborations in their campaign stores. The "Believe in Better" collection featured the typical campaign swag—tops, hats, totes, buttons, and bandanas—but there were no limits placed on the designers' creativity, resulting in a collection as diverse as its creators. The new merch garnered a lot of media buzz, with one article noting, "The all-star fashion line-up gives the campaign license to release merch that feels genuinely, well, cool. As nice as the standard Biden-Harris logo is, that standard-bearer navy T-shirt probably isn't getting a lot of mileage outside of campaign events or a morning jog. And it also aligns Biden and Harris with creative, young, exciting people."[62] All items were under $60 with proceeds going directly to the campaign. One article described the collection as "'Vermont college student,' with lots of tie-dye and rainbows."[63] The vibe was similar to Pete Buttigieg's primary merch, which was praised for its athleisure wear appeal. Many of the designers included messaging that targeted the diverse demographic the campaign hoped to reach. Joe Perez's "World Stage" tie-dye was designed to look like a concert tee, but instead of tour dates, the back featured international issues Biden would tackle including the climate crisis, supporting refugees, and repairing U.S. alliances. Monique Péan, whose fashion focuses on sustainability, created a linen face mask featuring one word, "Unity." Jason Wu's black sweatshirt said, "Rebuild with Love." Prabal Gurung's message was "Future Stronger in Color" with "Color" in rainbow hues. Aurora James, the founder of Brother Vellies, created a sweatshirt in fall colors (soft brown, orange, and gold) with the slogan "We Make the Difference: Black Women for Biden/Harris 2020" that was inspired by election merch from earlier decades, including the campaigns of Shirley Chisholm and Jesse Jackson. Like her fellow designers, James hoped voters would see the meaning in the merch, "This is not just a collection of items, it's an offering, a blend of our collective hope, passion, and belief in a world that can look a lot brighter than it is today. This sweatshirt is one small way I can energize people to get out there and vote for this ticket, especially Black women as I feel their impact on this election is going to be felt the most."[64] Many of the items in the capsule collection sold out, becoming a lucrative revenue source for the campaign. They also possessed all of the qualities of strong branding: creativity, a clear purpose, emotional appeal, and the ability to target messaging to key demographics.

The Biden team really stepped up their game by capitalizing on several campaign moments, turning them into merch almost immediately. The first followed the *New York Times*' September 27 story that Trump paid just $750 in federal income taxes in 2016. After seeing people's reactions online, Biden's campaign released buttons, stickers, and shirts that said, "I Paid More in Taxes than Donald Trump."[65] Then, during the first presidential debate, as Trump continued to interrupt, an exasperated Biden said, "Will you shut up, man?" His merch team was quick to respond: "Online, Biden's line has already been plucked as a Democratic rallying cry from last night. And because it's 2020, it's also been made into a T-shirt. It wasn't long after asking Trump to shut up that the merch machine started whirring—it's as if Biden was speaking directly into a screen-printing device. And now the former VP's comeback is suddenly the hottest tee slogan in the world."[66] The shirts were available in the Team Joe store before the debate ended and sold out within 24 hours. The Biden team also pounced on the top viral moment of the vice presidential debate when a fly perched on Mike Pence's head. Shortly after Harris and Pence left the debate stage, a "Truth Over Flies" blue fly swatter was available for $10. In just a few hours, the limited run of 35,000 swatters was sold out. Zach McNamara, merchandise director for the Biden campaign, explained to CNN, "We saw the internet and our supporters sharing a viral moment online, so our digital team came together on the fly."[67] All punning aside, McNamara hoped that voters focused on the deeper message delivered by the lighthearted items: "Yes, the fly swatter thing is cute and of the moment, but what's printed on it—the allusion to truth over lies—I think it is a key reason why it resonated and why we sold so many because we consistently see that those products that feature those short, simple phrases are among our bestsellers always."[68] The Biden team found a lot of success once they allowed themselves the creative freedom to move beyond the basic logo and capitalize on the cultural zeitgeist.

While the items based on viral moments were successful in generating media coverage and driving traffic to the website, they were not the Biden campaign's most popular products. "BIDEN HARRIS" yard signs, one of the most traditional forms of merch, were the biggest sellers by far. Having a wide range of free downloads was also a smart way to engage supporters, particularly on digital platforms. The campaign designed 23 different social media banners. Along with the standard logo, several featured quotes supporting the Black Lives Matter movement while others went for clever quips like "Tweet Less, Listen More." Some of the banners were also featured on the candidates' pages, like the "Keep the Faith" script banner that Biden and Harris posted after Election Day. They also had 27 desktop wallpapers, 19 phone wallpapers, and 16 Zoom backgrounds featuring what felt like discarded slogans and designs including "#Joementum," "Hope," "Bring Back Kindness," "Democrats Unite," and "Our Moment, Our Mission" in a wide-ranging color palette. But, since the items were free, they did not distract from the overall brand cohesiveness. McNamara said the merch team's goal was to "strike the perfect balance between stressing the political gravity of this election and providing some much-needed comedic relief."[69]

For both candidates, the merchandise was a successful way to promote their brands beyond digital platforms. Supporters were able to show their allegiance while also helping to spread each campaign's message thanks to the ease of e-commerce. As one article noted, "If clothing is our primary mode of self-styling, a medium through which we present ourselves to the world, consciously or not, then merch is its logical endpoint—a way to literally wear our allegiances on our sleeves. If you're willing to rep a politician, you're definitely willing to vote for them."[70] Even after a campaign, these items have value as tangible artifacts that will be collected, studied, and displayed. While merch may not decide elections, it plays "a fascinating—and significant—part in the process."[71]

CONCLUSION

For presidential candidates, developing a political brand that will connect with voters has always been a key component of campaigning. But this is a major undertaking according to branding strategist Laura Ries: "Running for President of the United States means building a brand that at least 51 percent of the country is willing to buy on Election Day. Not an easy task in a country as large and diverse as America. Too narrow a focus and you won't get a majority vote. A narrow focus builds a brand, but a wide base wins the election. The task is huge."[72]

In the 2020 race, both candidates developed brands that clearly differentiated them from one another. Trump's narrow focus on his established political brand kept his messaging consistent, appealing to his loyal base and, in some cases, making them more fervent followers. His dogged commitment to his brand extended to his pandemic response. He continued to be the rugged individualist and antipolitician who ignored the advice of public health officials on things like masks and social distancing, which emboldened his supporters. But his myopic viewpoint on a number of issues, including COVID, alienated a substantial portion of the American electorate, creating an anti-Trump sentiment on which Biden was able to capitalize. Biden's brand may have been more nondescript, but that worked to his advantage, allowing his team to reach a wider base, including Independents and disaffected Trump supporters. Being trustworthy, kind, and empathetic may be boring compared to the excitement and brashness of Trump, but those traits resonated with many voters, especially during a pandemic and in an election that was largely a referendum on Trump.

The 2020 election highlighted the importance of design- and image-based messaging strategies in campaigns that are increasingly focused on digital engagement with voters. Add in a global pandemic that forced campaigns to go virtual and visual messaging became vital. With typical stump campaigning curtailed due to COVID, social media moved from an ancillary messaging tool to a primary platform for campaign communication, while merchandise was a way for voters to express their loyalties as well as a critical source for campaign fundraising. More than ever, a consistent, memorable brand across all mediums was essential in promoting the candidate, telling a story, and connecting with potential voters. Trump continued to personify his "superhero anti-politician celebrity" brand by being the central focus and then surrounding himself with patriotic imagery and cheering supporters in red

MAGA hats who gathered despite a raging pandemic. In terms of his visual branding, Trump was the more conventional political candidate. The patriotic color palette, the campaign rally photos, and images of Trump in front of Air Force One or at the White House are typical election images of incumbent presidents. Biden adopted a common challenger strategy by putting Trump at the core of his campaign as well. Being the anti-Trump extended to his design choices and visual messaging. While Trump's imagery used traditional red, white, and blue, Biden used a modern gradient style that blended colors. The divisiveness and negative attacks that characterized Trump's social media and merch were countered with images and products promoting unity and positivity from the Biden team. And, in what became the most potent symbol of 2020, face masks came to represent presidential leadership in a time of crisis, serving as one of the clearest differentiators between the candidates.

The 2020 election was unique in many aspects. In particular, the pandemic pushed campaigns to focus more on digital strategies, showing them the value of visual branding in virtual spaces. While in-person campaigning will always be important, design- and image-based messaging strategies will continue to increase in significance as political branding adapts to the digital age.

Chapter 8

The Politics of Food in the 2020 Presidential Campaign

Emily J. H. Contois

From ill-fated Philly cheesesteaks and tamales to food worker labor rights and climate change legislation, food plays a significant role in American politics. Despite this, presidential candidates rarely highlight food policy on the campaign trail. News media instead give outsized attention to stories that focus on local specialties consumed in diners, fried food on a stick at the Iowa State Fair, and, of course, food-related mishaps. To be fair, these stories have significant entertainment value, earning clicks in a competitive attention economy. Such media attention has also resulted in award-winning food coverage; the multistory piece "Food and Loathing on the Campaign Trail" from the food website *Eater* earned a well-deserved 2020 James Beard Award nomination in the innovative storytelling category.[1] During the 2020 campaign, food also played a starring role in unexpected moments. A food emerged as the runaway social media star of the virtual Democratic National Convention when Rhode Island proudly, and conspicuously, promoted during the roll call their state dish: calamari.

Presidential candidates' food and beverage habits are put beneath a cultural microscope, voraciously reported by journalists, gobbled up by viewers, and bandied about on social media, but food and drink have been part of candidates' appeals to the voting public for much of U.S. history.[2] Writing in the *Historical Cooking Project*, Justin Irwin proposed that food and drinking have served three key roles in political campaigns: as "an enabler of activities" (that is, sustenance for the candidate and their staff, as well as opportunities to meet with voters), "a symbol of identity" (including a candidate's gender, class, race, and regionality), "and as an esthetic prop that can either bolster or undermine a candidate's public image," particularly through food gaffes.[3] Irwin is one of a relatively few academics who have researched campaign food politics, a gap that this chapter seeks to address.[4]

Methodologically, I employ discourse analysis and close reading to inter-pret a corpus of 2020 campaign news articles and social media posts, from the primaries through the November election. When demonstrative, I exam-ine historical examples from past presidential campaigns. I also examine relevant events involving Donald Trump from both the 2016 and 2020 cam-paigns. As these examples reinforce, food is always political—personally and structurally—but particularly so during presidential campaigns. This chapter ultimately illuminates why campaign food gaffes dominate the news cycle to the detriment of covering real food policy issues that have far graver impacts upon the lives, livelihoods, and health of everyday Americans.

HOW CANDIDATES PERFORM AUTHENTICITY THROUGH FOOD, EATING, DINERS, AND FAIRS

Food figures prominently in candidates' attempts to win over the electorate, particularly as they endeavor to assure voters that they are real, authentic, and trustworthy people—a proposition often at odds with the general public's perception of politicians.[5] This requires a layering of seemingly genuine sym-bols; as food writer Meghan McCarron asserts, "The conventions of authentic political eating require authentic restaurants serving authentic food."[6] These purportedly authentic food locations are also the spaces in which candidates enact "retail politics," which political writer Hugh Mulligan defined during the buildup to the 1980 New Hampshire primaries as "where the candidate must sell himself on the doorstep, in the supermarket, at the factory gate, atop a ski lift and, a relatively recent wrinkle, at endless coffee klatches."[7] As Michael Owen Jones writes, such politicking remains popular despite a lack of evidence that such tactics deliver results.[8] Nevertheless, campaigns tend to focus on two specific food spaces as key sites for retail politics to cultivate this sense of can-didate authenticity: diners (and other local restaurants) and the Iowa State Fair.

In the national imagination, the diner resonates as a strongly "American" symbol that communicates nostalgic notions of national belonging, homey comfort, and accessible, satisfying food.[9] Despite this supposedly universal meaning of the diner, it may be most meaningful to older, white, and working-class voters. This may be particularly true in the early primary states of New Hampshire and Iowa, where more than 90 percent of voters are white, and older voters exhibit higher rates of political participation. What's more, writer Doug Mack asserts that after the 2016 election, political food stories reframed the diner, characterizing it as a space primarily for Trump supporters rather than varied, community debate.[10]

Even as some restaurants (including some diners) have turned toward organic and farm-to-table trends, state fairs celebrate fried fantastical fare, as well as rampant abundance and convenience, values central to the American Dream myth. Journalists thus closely cover what and how candidates eat at the fair, as voters pay attention for clues that might reveal a candidate's "true" identity, especially before the Iowa caucuses, candidates' first real test of the presidential race.

Of the 2020 Democrat candidates, Pete Buttigieg ate big for the camera. An *Eater* photo essay covered everything he consumed at the fair, tallying in order: a root beer float, pork chop on a stick, a Gizmo sandwich (a Fair staple since 1947 of beef, sausage, tomato sauce, and melted mozzarella cheese), a BLT bacon ball sandwich, deep-fried Oreos with chocolate milk, and a red, white, and blue slushie.[11] Photos at the fair often captured Buttigieg in expressions by turns unflattering and funny, which he embraced. For such antics, *Eater* writer Gary He proclaimed Buttigieg's campaign eating "the stuff of electioneering legend."[12] As a millennial candidate, Buttigieg was also notable among the primary pack for food behaviors like taking photos of what he eats and sharing them on social media. Perhaps given such proclivities, he was also the most receptive of all the 2020 Democrat candidates to give full access to *Eater* to report on everything he ate.

Although notable as the U.S. first openly gay presidential candidate, Buttigieg was able to eat in such carefree ways in public and at the fair, in part, because of his gender. As another *Eater* piece on the Iowa State Fair put it, "there's no elegant way to eat a corn dog," a fact that can be more difficult for women candidates to navigate than male ones, given social expectations for "dainty" eating.[13] One can hope these expectations lessen at the fair, where typical dietary rules fly out the window. In such spirit, Kamala Harris, for example, gleefully ate a pork chop for the cameras.[14] But women candidates participating in the food antics of campaigning take a calculated risk when gnawing on fair food in public, as they work to appear both presidential and feminine. For example, during the 2016 campaign, Hillary Clinton visited Junior's, a well-known Brooklyn spot, for a photo op. When asked if she would be trying the cheesecake, she responded, "I learned early on not to eat in front of all of you."[15] Subsequent coverage spun this to her advantage but in problematic ways, praising her self-control for not eating the dessert, associating her with social expectations for female dieting and restraint.[16] Elizabeth Warren made a similar choice at the 2019 Iowa State Fair, holding a corndog throughout the entire event, but not eating it, clutching it even as she got in a car to leave.[17]

Despite the belief that food, ways of eating, and specific food spaces (like the diner and the state fair) can connote candidate authenticity, every food interaction on the campaign trail comes with the risk of getting it wrong. In considering campaign food gaffes, Irwin writes that these events "confirm something that the voting public already thought about the candidates in question: they're all just a bit out of touch."[18] This is important for at least three reasons. The first is the relative gap in wealth and lifestyle comforts between most political candidates and the electorate. Of the more than twenty-five people who at some point ran for president during the 2019 primaries, their median net worth was $2 million, ranging from billionaires Michael Bloomberg, Donald Trump, and Tom Steyer to a pack dominated by millionaires.[19] American politics continue to be enacted primarily by career politicians long removed from the everyday pressures faced by their constituents; they *are* in fact out of touch.

Second, the social distance between candidates and voters also demonstrates how the veneer of celebrity shapes the presidency and election campaigns.[20] Asserting that candidate campaign visits minimally affect voters' intentions, Thomas Wood writes that "attendance at candidate visits is a key way that Americans bring the glamour of a presidential campaign into their own lives."[21] Public relations teams scrupulously craft candidates' public images and personas so as to appeal to the widest voting base possible, not necessarily to represent the candidate's "true" self. Encounters over coffee or pie are meant to function as moments that peel back that carefully constructed presidential self to reveal the person underneath for voters to connect to, ask questions of, to believe in, and to vote for. Campaign eating contributes to the performance and perception of both celebrity and authenticity. And third, eating with voters at a local venue provides an opportunity for the candidate to prove their knowledge of, and commitment to, the entire nation, but earned one district, town, or city at a time. As such, candidates run national campaigns comprised of nearly innumerable local campaigns, ones in which food can signal acknowledgment of, and attention to, localized constituents. As a result, there seems to be much to gain from these local food and beverage campaign stops, to such an extent that candidates risk the gaffes that sometimes ensue.

Some campaign food gaffes have been of historical proportion, perhaps none more so than one committed by Gerald Ford. In 1976, Ford ran against Jimmy Carter for a second term, following his stint as president after Richard Nixon's resignation. At a campaign stop in San Antonio, Texas, Ford bit into a tamale without first removing the corn husk.[22] Lila Cockrell, then the mayor of San Antonio, reflected on the event after Ford's death in 2006, saying, "I think he just picked up the plate because if someone had given him the plate, the tamales would not have had the shucks . . . The president didn't know any better. It was obvious he didn't get a briefing on the eating of tamales."[23] For Cockrell, this food gaffe reinforced who Ford was in a positive way: "What people forget is that President Ford was a big, lovable, kind of ordinary guy. Whatever he did was so human."[24]

But others remember, and judge, the event differently. Veteran CBS News correspondent Bob Schieffer recalls that Ford nearly choked, commenting, "No one remembered anything else about that day."[25] Of Ford's mistake, Mike Huckabee, a 2016 Republican presidential candidate and former governor of Arkansas, remarked that Ford lost Texas in the election because of this food gaffe: "Carter won Texas and Carter won the presidency, and it may have been a tamale that did it."[26] Huckabee assessed the risks of candidates eating in public, saying, "If you're too dainty that'll hurt you and if you're a pig that'll hurt you . . . you have to find the sweet spot. . . . Everything you do can and will be used against you."[27] Similarly, He wrote in *Eater*, "For most candidates, every single bite in front of a camera is a tight-rope walk over a pool of molten nacho cheese."[28] Indeed the press and the public have repeatedly proven ready to pounce whenever a candidate commits a perceived food faux pas. When John Kerry ordered Swiss cheese on a Philly cheesesteak when running for president in 2004, journalists immediately marked him as elitist and out of step with local norms. They also painted him as effeminate when he asked reporters to not photograph him eating the messy sandwich and then took small bites.

The history of food gaffes thus raises interesting questions as to how candidates might navigate these tensions more effectively. While campaigns have typically depended upon staff research to prep a candidate to perform with localized customization at every campaign stop, much might be gained from a more honest and transparent approach. How might a candidate willing to ask questions, to learn, and to truly listen play a role in crafting a revitalized image and role of the American president? As more women and people of color run for, and achieve, the office, the performance of all-knowing white masculinity may prove less convincing to an electorate that also grows more diverse by the day.

HOW FOOD'S SYMBOLIC MEANING CONSTRUCTS IDENTITY FOR CANDIDATES AND VOTERS

Beyond performances of authenticity, the press and electorate also analyze a candidate's food consumption for how it communicates, represents, and symbolizes identity, in at least two ways. On the one hand, food communicates specific elements of a candidate's identity, such as their gender, race and ethnicity, social class and status, age, and regionality. On the other hand, candidates also use food to connect with the electorate via voters' identities. On the 2020 campaign trail, one beverage (beer) and four foods—fried avocado, hotdish, fried chicken, and beans—demonstrated how food powerfully

communicates notions of identity, and how candidates maneuver these connections as part of their presidential campaigns.

Beer

Although 2020 presidential candidates Trump and Biden are both teetotal-
ers, beer functions symbolically in political campaigns to cultivate a sense of
class-based populism and authenticity for a candidate. A candidate's choice
of beer type and brand can be seen as emblematic of their social class, often
dichotomously divided into elites and everyday folks. One's choice of beer
can also belie regional identity and a sense of "good taste." One's chosen
drink can also work in the opposite direction. For example, while campaigning during the 1972 election, Democrat nominee George McGovern's running
mate, Sargent Shriver, visited a local bar near a steel mill in Youngstown,
Ohio. While locals ordered beers—Pabst, Schlitz, or Budweiser—Shriver
called out, "Make mine a Courvoisier!" With a food gaffe so notable that the
Washington Post included it in his 2011 obituary, Shriver spoiled any effort
to cultivate casual, social connection with working-class voters when he
ordered French cognac rather than beer.[29]

Given its social meaning, a number of candidates in the 2020 pack of
Democrat presidential hopefuls spoke of beer, and drinking it, in an attempt
to connect with voters.[30] Indeed, beer drinking has proved pivotal in previous elections. Pundits argued that voters elected George W. Bush in part
because he was the candidate with whom they would want to have a beer.[31]
Elizabeth Warren seemed to build on this approach as part of her campaign.
She interrupted an early Instagram livestream broadcast, saying, "Hold on a
sec, I'm gonna get me a beer." Social media filled with debates about whether
Warren's use of "me" proved authentically folksy, given her Oklahoma
upbringing, or incongruent with her professional status, but the populism of
beer still rang true.[32] Indeed, later on in Warren's campaign, her contributors were given the chance to grab a drink with her. The campaign email
read: "Elizabeth and Bruce like to kick back and catch up over a couple of
beers. But if you win, you can order whatever drink you'd like—hot, cold,
caffeinated, decaf, sweetened, unsweetened, sparkling, still, anything (the
world is yours)."[33] "The beer test" also approximates candidates' perceived
likeability. Given how voters and pundits exhibit bias when assessing women
candidates' likeability compared to men, Warren's campaign beer promotion
attempted to ameliorate such effects. It had measured success, as likeability
continued to be a concern of commentators.[34]

Beer also served to characterize other 2020 candidates. For example, when
Eater followed Pete Buttigieg on the campaign trail, the author noted that
from a selection of hard seltzer, red wine, and a bottle of Bulleit bourbon,

"Buttigieg stuck to IPAs—like his politics, a beer style that is progressive but ultimately safe."[35] Here, beer type symbolized Buttigieg's overall politics and growing critiques of the candidate himself. Alternatively, *Civil Eats* gave Colorado's John Hickenlooper's connections to beer historical resonance as they acknowledged him as "the first brewer to become a governor since Samuel Adams led Massachusetts in 1792."[36] Nevertheless, Hickenlooper rarely mentioned beer or food on the campaign trail.

Beer also figures into how political analysts categorize candidates and their typical approaches, which link alcohol with the place, style, and political affiliation. "Beer-track" Democrats refer to moderates from the middle of the country, such as Amy Klobuchar.[37] The "wine track" is comprised of "coastal liberals," such as Kamala Harris and to some extent Elizabeth Warren, Bernie Sanders, and Cory Booker. Lastly, the "craft-beer track" of candidates represents the middle of the country but appeal more strongly to college-educated voters, as candidates Beto O'Rourke and Pete Buttigieg did, at least for a time.

Alcohol also communicated social anxiety at a key moment in the 2020 election. Pete Buttigieg's campaign persona took a hit during the December 2019 Democrat debate when Elizabeth Warren critiqued Buttigieg for attending a private fundraiser in a Napa Valley wine cave with billionaire owners.[38] Despite the fact that Buttigieg's personal wealth was reported as the lowest of all the 2020 candidates at $100,000, his fundraising—symbolized at that moment by the elitism and exclusivity of a Napa wine cave—came to be viewed as socially corrupt, especially as candidates and pundits alike discussed the need for campaign finance reform.[39]

In these various ways, beer on the campaign trail symbolizes and operationalizes notions of social class, elitism, and populism, at the same that it navigates dynamics of regionality, gender, and likeability.

Fried Avocado

New Jersey senator Cory Booker and Hawai'i representative Tulsi Gabbard were the nation's first vocally vegan presidential candidates. Pundits and voters variably perceived the candidates' veganism as either politically progressive and aligned with climate change policy or effeminate, elitist, too cosmopolitan, and fearfully prescriptive, particularly among working-class and conservative voters.[40] For example, a Fox News article title decreed, "Iowa Voters Have Beef with Non-Meat Eaters Booker, Gabbard at Iowa State Fair," while opinion pieces asserted perspectives like "Why I vote 'hell, no!' on a vegan president."[41] As these headlines reveal, these candidates' veganism stood out at key moments in the campaign, including at the Iowa State Fair, famous for its meat. Iowa's pork industry generates dozens of billions in sales per year, making visits to spots like the Iowa Pork Producer Association Tent to flip meat behind the grill a requisite stop for candidates at the fair, regardless of their own dietary lifestyle.[42]

With regard to their personal consumption at the fair, Booker and Gabbard both ate at the Veggie Table, which has provided for the last 38 years vegetarian fair treats like fried zucchini, pickles, cauliflower, and mushrooms—and new in 2019, fried avocados, which Gabbard ordered. Iowa State Fair food coverage on Gabbard focused on how the fried avocados were vegetarian, but not vegan since the batter contained milk. Multiple news stories quoted the Veggie Table's owner, Ruth McCoy, saying "I'm sorry we contaminated her."[43] Such a focus framed Gabbard as an overly persnickety eater, a common antagonistic framing of vegans.[44] At the same time, Gabbard might have contributed to such framing herself. When asked by the *New York Times* about her favorite comfort food while campaigning, she responded vegan cupcakes, saying they were "probably a real threat on the trail."[45] Her choice of words framed comfort food and desserts in the diet culture terms of good and bad, virtuous and dangerous, perhaps situating her within voters' minds as a candidate preoccupied with strict food rules.[46]

Alternatively, Booker ate fried peanut butter and jelly sandwich on a stick and said, "Can we settle the Democratic primary by how many of these you can eat? I think I could take the field."[47] Booker's comments about eating fair food competitively perhaps attempted to frame his veganism as not limiting his participation in the fair's gustatory antics, which are essentially a part of the primary process. It also served to combat any perceptions of his veganism as effeminate.[48] Like Tulsi, however, when asked about his favorite comfort food, Booker said, "lots of veggies."[49] Some voters might perceive his response as admirably healthy or faithful to his lifestyle and beliefs, but given the connotations of comfort food most typical among Iowa voters as pleasurably fattening and carbohydrate-rich, his response might have alienated voters.[50]

Although veganism and refraining from meat-eating played a relatively minor role for the vegan candidates, meat provided the first blip of rancor after Joe Biden announced Kamala Harris as his running mate. At the "Farmers and Ranchers for Trump" event in Iowa in August 2020, Vice President Mike Pence mentioned Harris' comments at a 2019 CNN climate change panel, where she addressed the role of personal diets and meat consumption in climate change. Her comments earned little attention at the time. To arouse booing from his audience, however, Pence said, "We're not going to let Joe Biden and Kamala Harris cut America's meat."[51] While such a comment intended to appeal to ranchers whose livelihoods depend upon meat production and consumption, Pence went further. He made an almost vulgar taunt toward Biden and Harris, saying directly to the camera, "I've got red meat for you," which drew laughter from the crowd.

In these various ways, meat and nonmeat-eating veganism operated within the 2020 presidential campaign to communicate notions of gender, health, and dietary rules, with partisan consequences.

Hotdish

Amy Klobuchar's campaign navigated the dynamics of both gender and regional affiliation through a comfort food unique to her state of Minnesota: hotdish. With roots back to at least World War I, hotdish recipes typically include a protein (often meat), vegetables, and a binder (most often canned creamed soup), topped with cheese and a crunchy starch, like tater tots. Food TV star Andrew Zimmern, who cooked hotdish with Klobuchar in a virtual campaign event, asserts that the dish "represents the three pillars of the Midwest: thrift, hospitality, and farm history."[52] To connect with voters in early primary states, New Hampshire and Iowa, Amy Klobuchar's campaign hosted Hotdish potluck parties, where they served the homecooked comfort food. A Facebook invitation to one such event linked the dish to the candidate herself, asserting, "Hotdish is a great unifier—just like Amy."[53] The campaign even printed recipe cards for "Amy's Hotdish," which won the inaugural hotdish competition that Al Franken started in 2011, involving all members of the Minnesota legislature.[54]

In all aspects of campaigning, women candidates walk an impossible line when it comes to gender performance and public perception, especially since the United States has yet to elect a woman president. If women candidates appear too feminine, voters perceive them as unfit to serve, but if they appear too masculine, voters view them as failed women.[55] Legal researcher Joan Williams calls this "gender judo," such as when women "do a masculine thing (which establishes their competence) in a feminine way (to defuse backlash)."[56] While Warren's strategy with beer also leaned on the gendered cultural meaning of food and beverages, it did not risk appearing overly feminine. Given the conventional connotations of home cooking as feminine, Klobuchar took a novel campaign risk by linking her strategy to recipes, cooking, and a homey, regional specialty like hotdish.[57]

Cooking and its gendered connotations have played a thorny role in past elections for women candidates. For example, Geraldine Ferraro ran as Walter Mondale's VP in the 1984 presidential election, as the first woman on a major-party ticket. At the time, there were only two women serving in the Senate and only one woman as governor. During a campaign event in Mississippi, state Agriculture Commissioner Jim Buck Ross called Ferraro "young lady" and asked her if she could bake a blueberry muffin. After laughing, she responded, "I sure can. Can *you*?" to which Ross replied, "Down here in Mississippi, the men don't cook."[58] Press widely covered the exchange at the time.[59] It appears in nearly every story reflecting on Ferraro's contributions to American politics. Mondale even addressed it in his remarks at Ferraro's funeral in 2011, citing them as part of the "struggle and adversity" she faced in politics, where she was "patronized in a way not experienced by her male counterparts."[60]

While first lady, Hillary Clinton similarly faced scrutiny around cooking when the press reported her comments about "staying home" and "baking cookies." Rather than invoking cooking as a test to her femininity and an insult regarding her political ability, as in Ferraro's case, Clinton's remarks were interpreted as not feminine enough. Perhaps seeking to cast herself as politically competent *and* suitably feminine in the eyes of voters, Kamala Harris mentioned cooking Sunday dinner in her first speech as the 2020 Democrat vice presidential nominee, while also foregrounding her role as a mother and nurturer.

In such ways, women candidates continue to navigate voter perceptions of both gender and electability through food and cooking, as Klobuchar did with a dose of Midwestern charm.

Fried Chicken

In the *New York Times*, Ashley Parker wrote in the months leading up to the 2016 election that Donald Trump was "hoping to become the nation's fast food president," as she described both his diet and campaign as "improvised, undisciplined, rushed and self-indulgent."[61] Alternatively, Kellyanne Conway asserted that Trump's eating "goes with his authenticity."[62] Others discuss how the president's fast-food affinity endorses values of speed, efficiency, cleanliness.[63] Folklorist Michael Owen Jones concludes that Trump seems to like fast food for how it tastes. He posits that Trump's comfort food consumption "could be linked to psychosocial needs in someone like Trump who is said to possess extreme narcissistic traits."[64] Trump himself somewhat addresses the incongruence of his wealth and food preferences himself, saying, "I always say that we're blue-collar Americans who've been very blessed by success."[65] No matter how one analyzes it, Trump's fast-food diet is yet another way that he departs from presidential precedent, especially as he not only publicly and frequently eats McDonald's Quarter pounders, Big Macs, and Filet-O-Fish sandwiches himself but also has served them to guests at White House dinners.[66]

In 2016, Trump posted a photo to Twitter with different fast-food fare: a bucket of Kentucky Fried Chicken, positioned atop a copy of the *Wall Street Journal*. In the photo, Trump sits in a plush cream-colored seat on "his private plane with gold-plate seatbelt buckles."[67] On the table in front of him rests what appears to be a fried wing on a plate covered with napkins. He grins with his chin jutted forward to the camera, which is positioned at an odd angle, too high above him. He holds a knife and fork in hand, committing what many fried chicken enthusiasts consider a faux pas, ire Trump had previously incited when he ate pizza with a knife and fork with 2008 Republican vice-president nominee Sarah Palin.[68] Trump's tweet with the KFC photo read, "Great afternoon in Ohio & a great evening in Pennsylvania—departing now. See you tomorrow Virginia!"[69] Despite the state callouts in his tweet, Trump did not employ the typical campaign maneuver of eating local specialties as a way for national candidates to connect with local voters. Instead, he ate the food of a "nonplace," what anthropologist Marc Auge describes as generic, transitory places that people pass through without conferring any intimate sense of identity or connection.[70] While some eaters feel strong cultural ties to KFC—for example, as a Christmas tradition in Japan—the fast food brand overall lacks a strong connection to a sense of place despite "Kentucky" in its name, as is the case with most national fast food brands.[71] Trump's fast food choices complicate voter perceptions of his class status, as they pose a departure from campaign food photo ops that typically seek to capitalize upon local resonance.

Fried chicken also tells powerful stories about race and racism, particularly for African-American voters. In her foundational book, *Building Houses out of Chicken Legs: Black Women, Food, and Power*, Psyche Williams-Forson critiques the reduction of Black foodways to fried chicken at the same time that she documents how Black women have for centuries resisted racial fried chicken stereotypes and reclaimed the dish in powerful ways.[72] Fried chicken frequently appears on the menu at Soul Food restaurants and is a dish of historical, complex, and rich significance for African Americans, particularly in the South.[73]

In such ways, fried chicken, and Soul Food more broadly, often plays a role in how candidates, particularly white ones, seek to reach African-American voters, which can come across as pandering, stereotyping, or worse. 2020 Democratic hopeful Kristen Gillibrand gained media attention when she met with twenty Black leaders at Kiki's Chicken and Waffles in South Carolina, a critical early primary state, for a small business roundtable. Journalist Jasmine Wright tweeted about Gillibrand's visit. While other tweets in her thread (including one documenting Gillibrand's comments on the health disparities Black women face) earned at most hundreds of likes, her final tweet aroused more than three thousand likes, retweets, and responses: "Eventually the food is served & Gillibrand starts to eat her fried chicken with a fork. She looks around, sees other people eating with their hands and says, 'Um Kiki, do we use our fingers or forks for the chicken?' Kiki said to use her fingers, and use her fingers she did."[74] Some responses on Twitter and in the press dismissed this fried chicken and fork exchange, while others viewed Gillibrand's confused faux pas as emblematic of faults in her candidacy.

Eating fried chicken on the campaign trail also incited media discussion for a Black candidate. In February 2019, Kamala Harris, who identifies as a Black woman, met with Rev. Al Sharpton at Sylvia's, a well-regarded Soul Food restaurant in Harlem. He ordered bananas and toast. She ordered chicken and waffles. A tweet by New York–based political reporter Dave Evans incited a Twitter storm after he wrote, "Chicken & waffles. Seriously? For Kamala D. Harris & toast & bananas for [Sharpton]." Responses variably assessed his tweet as sexist, for scrutinizing what a woman candidate ate, and racist, for questioning Harris' Blackness and critiquing her order as somehow pandering to African-American voters.[75]

In such ways, eating fried chicken on the campaign trail, whether from KFC or a renowned Soul Food restaurant, comprises a complex food moment through which candidates have performed their social class, race, and gender in their attempts to connect with voters.

Beans

Canned beans also provided a flash point of identity-based controversy, especially as Donald Trump campaigned for reelection. On July 9, 2020, Robert Unanue, CEO of Goya Foods—the largest Latino-owned food company in the United States—visited the White House as part of the "White House Hispanic Prosperity Initiative." While there, he praised Trump, saying, "We are truly blessed to have a leader like President Donald Trump, who is a builder."[76] Political and cultural critics alike responded negatively to Unanue's praise, especially given Trump's past anti-Latino policies and positions. They pointed to his xenophobic comments and views (including characterizing immigrants from Mexico as "rapists" and "bringing drugs") to his 2016 campaign promise to build a border wall between the United States and Mexico.[77] Although no longer a presidential hopeful at the time, Julián Castro was one of the first to call for a boycott against the company, tweeting, "Goya Foods has been a staple of so many Latino households for generations. Now their CEO, Bob Unanue, is praising a president who villainizes and maliciously attacks Latinos for political gain. Americans should think twice before buying their products."[78] In response, the following day, Trump tweeted, "I LOVE @GoyaFoods!"—marking the beginnings of a food-based political conflict.[79]

Some people cleared their kitchens of Goya products and joined the boycott, while Trump loyalists piled their shopping carts high as part of a reactionary buycott. In this vein, Senator Ted Cruz tweeted, "Goya is a staple of Cuban food. My grandparents ate Goya black beans twice a day for nearly 90 years. And now the Left is trying to cancel Hispanic culture and silence free speech. #BuyGoya."[80] Ivanka Trump tweeted a photo of herself posed in the style of a midcentury advertisement with a can of Goya black beans, along with the company tagline, "If it's Goya, it has to be good," in both English and Spanish.[81] Donald Trump's Instagram account also shared a photo in which he posed with Goya products lined up on his desk in the Oval Office as he smiled and gave a thumbs up with each hand.[82] This image and message played out against Trump's previous, and tenuous, history of courting Latinx voters through food. In 2016 he tweeted: "Happy #CincoDemayo! The best taco bowls are made in Trump Tower Grill. I love Hispanics!" Like many of Trump's tweets and much of his bluster, this tweet primarily promoted himself and his empire, even as it made a misguided attempt to win over Latinx voters.

As the *New York Times* covered the aftermath, their reporters wrote, "In a polarized country, at a polarized time, the buying of beans had become a political act."[83] Scholar Fabio Parasecoli goes further, writing, "Food is inevitably political, and the food of immigrants is even more so, as it gets drawn into debates about who belongs and who doesn't. Politicians don't hesitate to leverage these tensions, even if that means dealing with accusations of pandering, populism, appropriation, and cultural insensitivity."[84] This may play an even larger role in future elections, particularly given the significant racial and ethnic diversity of younger, Gen Z voters.[85]

Everyday Eating on the Campaign Trail

During a presidential campaign, candidates and their staff often embark on bus tours of battleground states with multiple stops, leaving little time to eat at all. It can take focused planning to ensure well-rounded and healthful meals and snacks. Gary He covered Andrew Yang's campaign trail diet in *Eater*, deeming him "a supreme snacklord," as a way to humorously ingratiate him to voters who might have known nothing about the candidate beyond his campaign promise of a universal basic income.[86] Beyond snacks, staffers tell stories of procuring most meals at national chains closest to the campaign route. Domino's, McDonald's, Jimmy John's, and Dairy Queen make for meals eaten "while the bus wheels are in motion."[87] These restaurants operate on the principles of "McDonaldization," identified by sociologist George Ritzer—predictability, efficiency, calculability, and control—which he asserted have been adopted throughout society with deleterious effects.[88] It is unsurprising that campaign food would depend upon such principles on practical terms, but they also reveal an important collision of values between the overall aims and pragmatic logistics of presidential campaigns. Aspects of McDonaldization privilege quantity over quality, minimize time and seek influence in much the same way that presidential campaigning now depends more than ever upon the data analytics of social media microtargeted advertising rather than in-person interactions.

What the candidate and their staff eat also documents a perceived endorsement, or not, of multiculturalism. For example, *The Guardian* published an analysis of each campaign's food spending—which totaled $1.9 million through December 31, 2019—categorizing the results by cuisine nationality.[89] More than half of that total ($1 million) was spent on catering typically categorized as "American," such as national chains like Panera Bread and Dunkin' Donuts. Campaigns also spent $900,000 in the following categories, in descending order: Mexican (a third of which came from the Warren campaign), pizza, pubs, or breweries, Soul Food, Chinese, BBQ, Italian, steakhouses, Japanese, Mediterranean, Korean, Thai, Indian, and Filipino. Perhaps emblematic of their campaign platforms, the Warren and Sanders campaigns demonstrated the most diversity in their choices. In his analysis of eating and politicking, Michael Owen Jones made a similar claim of Hillary Clinton's 2016 cuisine preferences, characterizing them as "diverse, often global, and frequently local, regional, and/or ethnic American."[90]

The Bloomberg campaign proved a notable exception, spending the most on Japanese food, including nearly $17,000 at one sushi restaurant over a period of six weeks. Similar to Bloomberg's significant investment in television ad buys, the campaign spent lavishly on food for staff and at various campaign events as well.[91] In his far-reaching food sociology study, Krishnendu Ray documents the division between expensive Japanese sushi and American consumer expectations for quick and cheap "ethnic" cuisine, such as the Chinese, Korean, Thai, Indian, and Filipino restaurants included in *The Guardian*'s analysis.[92] In such ways, a great deal of the food purchased and eaten for campaign sustenance endorses the tenants of McDonaldization, with an array of potential consequences.

HOW FOOD POLICY SHAPES POLITICAL CAMPAIGNS, AND HOW IT OUGHT TO

Although food gaffes and fried food on a stick garner far more media attention, all candidates have food policy agendas, despite the fact that they are rarely mentioned in debates or discussed on the campaign trail. Food studies scholar Fabio Parasecoli explains this inattention as he writes, "The separation between our roles as consumers and citizens is still prevalent and widely accepted."[93] In this way, many voters may not see or understand the connections between presidential campaigns, policy, a highly networked global food system, and their everyday lives.

Another limiting factor is that candidates typically frame food policy as a primarily rural issue that affects American farmers and livestock producers, along with the lobbies and organizations that represent their interests. For example, in October 2008, author Michael Pollan penned "An Open Letter to the Next Farmer in Chief" in the *New York Times*.[94] He called upon candidates Barack Obama and John McCain to prioritize food policy, but within a primarily agricultural framework, despite food policy's much broader influence.

The 2020 campaign revealed relatively little about Joe Biden's personal foodways—beyond his love of ice cream and Jill Biden's quip that "he's pretty much a basic eater" who loves peanut butter and jelly sandwiches and angel hair pasta with red sauce—but he emphasized food and farming in his policies.[95] As is typical, his plan mostly focused on revitalizing rural economies.[96] Policies included trade policy reform, microloan programs for beginning farmers, investment in land grant universities' agricultural research programs, financed environmental stewardship toward net-zero emissions, and strengthening antitrust enforcement, including for seeds. Other policies sought to foster regional food systems to create supply chains from small and midsized farms to state and federal institutions, such as schools, hospitals, and the Defense Department. Although many farmers and rural voters still supported Trump, his trade policy decisions in many ways hurt the agricultural industry and rural communities. For example, agricultural exports from the United States to China declined from $15.8 billion in 2017 to $5.9 billion in 2018, remaining depressed in 2019 as well.[97] Trump policies limiting immigration and undocumented migrant workers also influenced farm jobs and worker rights.[98]

A candidate's food policy agenda belies their commitments to more than just farmers and rural communities, however. It affects policies related to the environment—including EPA protections of land, water, and air, which the Trump administration significantly curtailed, rolling back more than 70 actions.[99] Furthermore, given the global connectivity of our systems of food, media, and politics, U.S. food policy affects all eaters everywhere, involving healthcare, hunger, safety, education, and so much more.

From May 2019 through Super Tuesday 2020, the food website *Civil Eats* tracked the various Democratic and Republican candidates' policy positions and public statements on food and farming.[100] *Civil Eats* framed food as a notable and central focus for only three candidates—Tim Ryan, Tulsi Gabbard, and Marianne Williamson—none of whom garnered significant voter or pundit interest. Ohio representative and author of a 2015 book *The Real Food Revolution: Healthy Eating, Green Groceries, and the Return of the American Family Farm*, Ryan hoped to run as "the food candidate," with an agenda that centered food policy focused on health and wellness. Gabbard focused on food security (especially since her home state of Hawai'i imports

85–90 percent of its food), agricultural policy to reduce antibiotic use and promote organics, and consumer-facing issues, such as GMO labeling, which Bernie Sanders also supported. Lastly, Williamson framed food policy as an issue of personal health and well-being, in keeping with her career as a self-help book author.

While less central to their policy positions, other candidates presented positions that would have affected Americans far beyond rural areas. Bernie Sanders and Julián Castro both endorsed a free, universal school lunch program (which Bill De Blasio passed in 2017 for New York City schools), which would ensure nutritious meals for all children across the country. Elizabeth Warren introduced the College Student Hunger Act of 2019, which would extend SNAP eligibility to low-income college students, startling proportions of whom experience food insecurity.[101] While Pence ridiculed Harris's comments about reducing personal meat consumption as part of climate change policy efforts, ten of the leading Democrat candidates took part in the same climate town hall hosted by CNN.[102] In addition, both Beto O'Rourke and Pete Buttigieg mentioned their support for farmer carbon-sequestering programs in the first Democrat debate.

Of the Democrat candidate pack, Bernie Sanders, Elizabeth Warren, and Cory Booker focused on agriculture not as a rural issue, but as an industry in need of regulation to fight corporate consolidation. During the first Democrat debate, Booker mentioned his New Jersey bill, the Food and Agribusiness Merger Moratorium and Antitrust Review Act of 2018, which sought to address the rampant consolidation in the food system by freezing mergers of a large farm, food, and grocery companies. Such consolidation has resulted in a food system where "the four largest pork packers, beef packers, soybean crushers, and wet corn processors have captured ever-larger shares of the supply chain, now controlling 71 to 86 percent of their respective markets," market control that negatively affects smaller food producers and consumers alike.[103]

As part of the 2020 campaign, a number of Democrat candidates also took a stand on labor issues and worker rights—in the fields, but also throughout the food industry. Pete Buttigieg, Joe Biden, and Elizabeth Warren each stood with striking workers at the grocery chain Stop and Shop. Kamala Harris earned the endorsement of the United Farm Workers union and of Dolores Huerta (who co-founded the union with César Chávez and Larry Itlion) for her farm worker policy, such as requiring overtime pay and promoting immigrants' rights, including a path toward citizenship. Julián Castro's platform included unique labor and education policy initiatives, such as harvest-time stipends to reduce children being taken out of school to earn extra money and a college scholarship program for farmworkers' children. Food and labor politics also made a brief appearance during the 2020 Nevada Democratic

Caucus, where the Culinary Workers Union represented more than 60,000 workers across the state. Discussions with members revealed healthcare, wages, and defeating Donald Trump as members' key priorities.[104]

Given the short shrift candidates usually give food policy, COVID-19 notably prioritized issues of food security, safety, and access. The pandemic forced restaurants to close and lay off workers, interrupted supply chains (at times leaving grocery store shelves bare), and caused meatpacking plants to erupt as disease hotbeds.[105] Given how ample meat consumption constitutes ideas of American abundance and affluence, Trump ordered meatpacking plants to continue functioning despite increasing disease rates and deaths among plant workers, drawing criticism.[106] In May 2020, Joe Biden participated in a virtual town hall with chef and activist José Andrés to address food security issues, adding to the mounting criticism of Trump's handling of the pandemic.[107] Biden also critiqued Trump for including in his 2021 budget cuts to the SNAP program, all the more needed during the economic recession caused by the pandemic. In keeping with his campaign slogan, Biden called food service workers "the soul of America," as they were "taking changes on their lives to make sure that we . . . have the ability to eat, the ability to be able to continue to survive."[108]

As these examples show, the 2020 presidential campaign revealed how far-reaching food policy issues are and how they ought to be more central to both candidates' messaging and how media cover food on the campaign trail.

CONCLUSION

Americans voted in November 2020, electing former vice president Joe Biden as the U.S. forty-sixth president. Despite a primary season in which food played all the typical roles in the candidate's campaigns, very real issues are on the table when it comes to food. They should play a key role in the recovery from the COVID-19 pandemic. They should impact how journalists cover food in future campaigns—not just the gustatory mishaps and fair food fodder that earn clicks but the food policy issues affecting the American people and the world at large.

THE 2020 PRESIDENTIAL ELECTION

Chapter 9

Campaign Finance and Its Impact on the 2020 Presidential Campaign

Cayce Myers

The 2020 election will be remembered largely because of its closeness in votes, the postcampaign litigation, and the inaccurate polling that predicted a Democratic landslide in both the presidential race and down-ballot races. However, behind all of these big issues of 2020 is the role of campaign finance. Both parties spent millions of dollars on campaigns, and their fundraising efforts were highly sophisticated, targeted operations that utilized digital and social media to garner larger and small donations. What has resulted are multibillion dollar presidential contests and congressional races that have resulted in hundreds of millions of dollars being spent to impact control of the House of Representatives and Senate. In fact, it was reported that the campaign spending in all presidential and congressional races nearly doubled that in 2016 for a total of $14 billion.[1]

It seems that in U.S. politics today we have reached a new norm of the billion-dollar campaign, or, in the case of congressional elections the multimillion-dollar campaign. How did this happen? Part of the reason is that campaign finance laws have permitted the growth of large donations through the growth of super-PACs. However, the other reason campaign finance has grown is the growth of technology. Small donor contributions have made a big difference in U.S. political campaigning. Organizations such as ActBlue, a Democratic candidate and progressive cause fundraising group established in 2004, use online donation tools to build a base of small grassroots fundraising.[2] This has been a highly successful approach, with ActBlue posting a running tally of donation dollars since 2004, which at the time of this writing exceeded $8 billion.[3] These types of online fundraising efforts assist in large-scale fundraising using small-donor contributions. Moreover, this type of digital campaign fundraising allows for the aggregation of data of contributors that can be valuable to campaign fundraising efforts. Technology has created the new reality of big data within campaign contributions, which is an effective tool for maximizing donations in U.S. elections.[4]

However, as the 2020 election demonstrates, money has its limits. While there is a certain level of financing required to enter presidential and congressional races, cash in accounts does not equate to victory. Many good finances campaigns that outspent their opponents ended up losing their races—e.g. Amy McGrath in the Kentucky Senate race, Sara Gideon in Maine's Senate race, and Jaime Harrison in South Carolina's Senate race all raised millions against their Republican opponents and still lost (by considerable margins).[5] Interestingly, billionaire Mike Bloomberg spent over $100 million of his own money in Florida, Ohio, and Texas to promote Democrat Joe Biden, only to have Trump handily win those states.[6] This type of result shows that candidate quality, the impact of tough primaries, candidate messaging, and a candidate's party ID matter to voters. Nowhere is this more evident in the highly unsuccessful primary campaign of Mike Bloomberg, who spent in excess of $1 billion on his less-than-100-day campaign to end up winning only fifty-nine delegates. These examples show that money in politics has its limits, and perhaps this is why campaign finance reform as a political movement has declined in the past election cycles.

However, money still matters in American elections. Presidential elections have become more competitive as the country has become more polarized politically. However, in 2020, what occurred is what looks to be a political realignment in national politics. States such as Michigan, Georgia, North Carolina, Minnesota, Wisconsin, Arizona, and Pennsylvania are competitive for Republicans and Democrats. That means that Electoral College math requires candidates to campaign longer and more frequently in states that were once solidly red or blue. At the congressional level, there were many Republican gains in the House of Representatives, notably flipping several House districts in California to Republicans.[7] With a House and Senate majority being extremely close, congressional fundraising is going to be more important because razor-thin margins in House districts and Senate races require candidates to raise cash to be competitive. Nowhere is that clearer than the Senate runoffs in Georgia, which will determine the balance of power in the U.S. Senate and, as a result, the Biden administration's legislative agenda. Once the runoff was apparent on the heels of a Biden victory in the state, there was $135 million worth of advertisements purchased in the state with the Republican National Committee (RNC) pledging in December 2020 that it will spend $20 million in the runoff elections held on January 5, 2021.[8] This type of competitiveness seems to garner questions not so much about how much money is raised, but rather where the money is coming from. Congressional elections are no longer local elections or even state elections. Instead, the balance of congressional power makes purple states and districts truly national elections in terms of fundraising, spending, and media buying.

This chapter looks at these new realities of campaign finance within the context of the 2020 presidential election by examining the fundraising of the presidential candidates using Federal Election Commission data that is publicly available. Unlike 2016 where there was a false assumption that a midwestern blue wall would all but guarantee a Democratic victory, the 2020 election recognized, to some extent, the competitiveness of many states. However, the narrative of the 2020 election is that despite many campaigns spending a lot of money the election was close in many states and districts. This chapter examines the president's primary fundraising of both Democrats and President Trump and the postconvention campaign fundraising of both nominees. The chapter concludes with some thoughts about campaign finance in the future, the possibility and likelihood of campaign finance reform, and the ultimate role and importance of money in American politics in the twenty-first century.

CAMPAIGN FINANCE REGULATION:
A BRIEF OVERVIEW

Campaign finance has been a political issue in U.S. politics since the early twentieth century. The issue has centered around how much money affects political access, and how that access equates to political power. What has occurred in campaign finance law is a tension between the right to exercise political rights through campaign donations versus the excess of having too much political power because of campaign donations. In politics, money has typically been thought of as a form of political speech, and the issue with a curtailing political speech by limiting political donations is a controversial subject.[9]

The genesis of political campaign finance reform can be traced to the 1904 presidential election of Theodore Roosevelt. Ironically the issue then was similar to the current political debate over money in politics. Essentially the issue then, as it is now, was determining whether organizations that contribute a lot of money to a campaign have a disproportionate voice in American politics. The U.S. Congress has attempted to deal with this issue through a series of laws that have resulted in legal challenges throughout the twentieth century. The Tillman Act of 1907 and the Federal Corrupt Practices Act (FCPA) passed in 1910 were the first such attempt to regulate campaign finance and contributions.[10] Those laws were constitutionally challenged in the U.S. Supreme Court case *Newberry v. U.S.*, which struck down campaign finance limitations enacted under a 1911 amendment to the FCPA.[11]

Laws affecting campaign finance continued with the creation of the first PAC in 1943 with the Congress of Industrial Organizations (CIO). The CIO-PAC was the result of the Smith-Connelly Act in 1943, which provided an amendment to the FCPA that banned direct contributions from union treasury funds to political campaigns. The PAC was an outgrowth of getting around campaign laws that tried to make union contributions more restrictive for campaigns, and as a result, the PAC was created as a force in American politics. Later regulations sought to limit campaign contributions but were met with constitutional challenges that focused on the rights of individuals to use money as a form of political speech.[12]

The Federal Election Commission (FEC) was created in 1974 is an independent regulatory agency of the U.S. government. This creation of the FEC was the outgrowth of new federal legislation attempting to regulate campaign finance, the Federal Elections Campaign Act, which limited federal campaign contributions, mandated disclosures, creating public financing for presidential elections, capped individual expenditures, capped personal candidate expenditures, and established the FEC. However, the FEC's power was challenged by a group of plaintiffs, including New York Senator James L. Buckley of the Conservative Party of New York, on grounds that the FECA violated the First and Fifth Amendments of the U.S. Constitution.[13]

That case, *Buckley v. Valeo,* resulted in a lengthy U.S. Supreme Court decision that upheld and struck down several aspects of the FECA laws.[14] Specifically, the Court held that individual contribution caps were constitutional and reporting contributions were constitutional. However, the Court also held that capping independent expenditures for a campaign was unconstitutional.[15] Express advocacy is an important concept in *Buckley v. Valeo* because it is express advocacy practices that trigger campaign finance rules. *Buckley* is famous for footnote 52, which articulated what has become known as the "eight magic words" that constitute express advocacy: "vote for," "elect," "support," "cast your ballot for," "Smith for Congress," "vote against," "defeat," and "reject."[16] This restrictive definition of express advocacy led to many exceptions within campaign finance law, which ultimately gave rise to practices that circumvented FEC regulations.

Buckley v. Valeo was a case that defined campaign contributions in context with political speech, and it was the precedent established in *Buckley* that led to the basis of the decision in the 1978 case *First National Bank of Boston v. Belotti.*[17] In *Belotti,* the U.S. Supreme Court again considered a state law in Massachusetts that banned corporate contributions that would be used on ballot initiatives. The U.S. Supreme Court held that this ban on corporate money used on ballot initiatives was unconstitutional under the First Amendment. *Belotti* is an important case in part because it was the first in a series of cases that dealt with corporate money and power within elections.[18]

Other cases followed the defined corporate ability to spend money in elections. *FEC v. Massachusetts Citizens for Life* was a 1986 case that held that political corporations could not be banned from independent spending on campaigns and required to make political statements through PACs.[19] Later in 1990, the U.S. Supreme Court addressed campaign finance again in *Austin v. Michigan Chamber of Commerce.* In that decision, the Court would limit corporate abilities to spend in campaign holding that a Michigan law that banned corporations from using treasury funds for political campaign contributions was constitutional under the First and Fourteenth Amendments. This case would serve as a limit on corporate spending in campaigns for the next twenty years, but ultimately would substantively be reversed in the famed 2010 decision *Citizens United v. FEC.*[20]

The 1990s and early 2000s saw a rise in the interest of campaign finance as a political issue. This was in part due to the high-profile legislation sponsored by John McCain (R-AZ) and Russ Feingold (D-MN) in the U.S. Senate. McCain-Feingold, or, as it was officially known, the Bipartisan Campaign Reform Act of 2002 (BCRA), served as a high watermark for campaign finance reform.[21] It specifically addressed the issue of soft money or money donated to political parties instead of candidates.[22] McCain-Feingold started years earlier, with the two senators writing an op-ed in 1996 titled "A Better Way to Fix Campaign Financing" in *The Washington Post* calling for reform to U.S. campaign finance laws.[23] They specifically noted that there should be spending limits on campaigns and that as a result of self-financed campaigns of multimillionaires there has to be an even footing for American campaigns in terms of fundraising and spending.[24]

When the BCRA was finally passed it contained several new restrictions to campaign finance. However, this was unpopular with some, especially Senate Republican Mitch McConnell. This led to a legal challenge to the law based on First Amendment grounds, with the U.S. Supreme Court in *McConnell v. FEC* upholding parts of the restrictions of the BCRA.[25] The net result of this, however, was similar to the creation of PACs in the 1940s: it generated a new work around to soft money bans. This came in the form of 527s, called that because of section 26 U.S.C. §527. While technically 527s may have varying purposes, the common usage of 527s is issue advocacy groups unaffiliated with individual campaigns. They became more widely known during the 2004 contest between President George W. Bush and Senator John Kerry (D-MA) because of the Swift Boat Veterans for Truth, an anti-Kerry 527 that criticized Kerry's characterization of his role and the role of veterans during the Vietnam War.

By the late 2000s, the issue of corporate money in politics would be revisited again by the U.S. Supreme Court in *Citizens United v. FEC.*[26] In that case, the Court held that the free speech clause in the First Amendment

prohibited the government to restrict independent expenditures by corporations and nonprofits. The impact of this case was viewed by many as a win
for corporations with President Barack Obama criticizing the decision in his
2010 State of the Union Address.[27] The result of the decision of the *Citizens
United* decision was the proliferation of the super-PAC, a PAC that can raise
unlimited sums of money from corporations, unions, and individual donors
but is not legally allowed to coordinate with a candidate's campaign. Super-
PACs emerged at all levels of campaigns in the United States. Other limits
were removed from campaign finance as well, with the U.S. Supreme Court
holding in *McCutcheon v. FEC* that caps of aggregate amounts that an individual donor can make to a national party or federal candidate committees are
unconstitutional under the First Amendment.[28]

Since 2010 with the U.S. Supreme Court decision in *Citizens United v.
FEC*, the case that effectively paved the way for super-PACs, the biggest
political issue has been the increase in super-PAC money spent during elections, and the fear that super-PAC money equates to increased political power
for elites. Compounding the issue of outside spending is so-called "dark
money" groups, which are nonprofit groups such as 503(c) organizations,
that do not have to disclose who their donors are, but still can spend money
during an election. Dark money is sometimes flowed through nonprofit organizations as donations to super-PACs, which then spend the money during
an election. This issue with multiple donations between organizations and
PAC to PAC creates another ethical issue with so-called "gray money." This
type of donation creates a problem of tracking a source because so-called
"gray money" originates from another organization, which may not disclose
the identities of their original donors. The reality creates an issue to the
current political campaign finance system that mandates transparency from
super-PACs, but the introduction of smaller, obscure PAC donations to super-
PACs shows that the U.S. campaign finance system is more opaque than
perhaps realized.[29]

What resulted was campaign financing has become a political issue in
terms of disclosure and the identity of donors. President Barack Obama was
highly innovative in campaign fundraising during 2008. In fact, it marked the
last year that a presidential candidate of either party accepted public funding for their campaign. Republican candidate John McCain accepted public
funding of $84 million that paled in comparison to the amount Obama was
able to raise through an increasingly sophisticated network on online systems
that attracted small donors.[30] Obama was the first presidential candidate to
decline public funds since the program was created in 1976.[31] By 2016 both
candidates declined public funding, then at $292 million, because they could
outraise that amount.[32] The role of receiving campaign contributions from
wealthy donors, the presence of out-of-state donors in Senate and House

races, and the behavior of super-PACs (although legally there cannot be any coordination between campaigns and super-PACs) has become political fodder for candidates. Even in the Democratic Party, which has a fundraising advantage, the progressive candidates, specifically Senator Bernie Sanders (D-VT), have raised issues about fundraising and the role of money within campaigns. Sanders famously said he did not want a super-PAC in his quest for the 2020 Democratic nomination, and progressive Democrat Elizabeth Warren (D-MA) criticized opponents Mayor Pete Buttigieg and Joe Biden for accepting large donations from wealthy donors.[33]

The arc of campaign finance in the United States is that while laws have been used to restrict donations and provide some controls over campaign fundraising, the campaigns and candidates have found ways to continue to raise and spend more money with each election cycle. Money is an essential ingredient in campaign success, and while it does not always equate to victory, campaigns with cash have more options available to them. The law, in many ways, has not been able to prevent what has been the fear of campaign finance reformers since the early twentieth century; that campaigns increasingly receive money more from sources that are difficult to track. As a result, the 2020 presidential election would be the most expensive in American history.

PRIMARY FUNDRAISING: DEMOCRATS

The 2020 Democratic Primary began with a large field of candidates that included a variety of officeholders, included several U.S. Senators, a U.S. Representative, and former Cabinet members. However, it also included figures outside of the political realm, including businessman Andrew Yang and former New York City mayor and billionaire Michael Bloomberg. The Democratic Primary displayed an intense intraparty fight between moderate and progressive wings of the party. By the end of the primary, the two remaining candidates represented these groups, with former Vice President Joe Biden representing the moderates of the party and U.S. Senator Bernie Sanders (I-VT) representing the progressives. In fact, there was media speculation that the tightness and fierceness of the Democratic primary would result in a brokered convention, the first since 1952 with Adlai Stevenson's nomination, because of the tensions between the progressive and moderate wings of the party.[34] This, of course, did not come to fruition, with Joe Biden receiving the nomination. He chose U.S. Senator Kamala Harris (D-CA), perhaps in an attempt to bridge the divide between moderate and progressive wings of the party. Harris's appearance on the ticket was a historical first, as she is an African-American and Asian-American woman on a major-party presidential ticket.

The tensions between the progressive and moderate wings of the Democratic Party did present some challenges in the primary. In fact, where donations came from became a political talking point in the primary. The reason is that fundraising by some Democratic candidates included donations from wealthy individuals, and one candidate, Michael Bloomberg, was a multi-billionaire candidate who was largely self-financed. This created an optical problem for Democrats who were campaigning as the candidates for working Americans or as progressive. In fact, during the primary debates, Senator Elizabeth Warren challenged Mayor Pete Buttigieg's campaign fundraising events that included holding an event in the wine cave with wealthy California donors. She said that wealthy donors like those in Buttigieg's wine cave fundraiser should not be able to choose the next president. Even the cost of the wine served became a political issue. Warren alleged the fundraiser featured $900 bottles of wine. The participants said that the most expensive wine produced at the winery was $350 per bottle. Warren contrasted this cost per bottle amount to her own average contributions, which she said was $32.[35] Warren also fiercely challenged Michael Bloomberg in his debate appearance challenging him on his personal behavior as a businessman.[36] Bernie Sanders similarly criticized the use of super-PACs during the race, stating that he was not interested in having a super-PAC.[37]

This created a new election issue of fundraising issues as it related to specific candidates. The amounts of individual contributions were of the issue with candidates touting the small amounts given by multiple donors as evidence that they were a candidate fueled by grassroots support rather than corporate backing. Other candidates used their opponents' use of campaign contributions and interaction with corporate interests as evidence of their lack of progressive values that would turn off the progressive voters. This strategy was one that was rooted in appealing to the liberal or progressive voters in the Democratic primary. However, those who received these donations pointed to the practicality of money in politics. Buttigieg and other Democrats noted that receiving the backing of wealthy donors stated that campaign contributions were essential for winning a general election against President Donald Trump.[38] Moreover, they warned of the issues that ideological purity could create for a Democratic candidate in a general election where the typical voter is thought to be more moderate.[39] Interestingly, Andrew Yang, a wealthy businessman, tied campaign fundraising to his guaranteed income plan. During a primary debate, he said he would give away $120,000 to ten families at random as a means to show how his guaranteed base income plan would work.[40]

Despite the campaign rhetoric of the Democratic candidates, the issue of fundraising was the basis of determining the strength, and longevity, of their primary campaigns. Table 9.1 shows individual contributions to the top five

Table 9.1. Individual Contributions to Democratic Primary Candidates January–June 2020*

Month	Biden	Sanders	Warren	Bloomberg
January	$8.88 million	$25 million	$10.4 million	$130,919
February	$18 million	$47.5 million	$29.4 million	$474,915
March	$46.6 million	$32.7 million	$4.9 million*	$61,187*
April	$43.5 million	$1.2 million*	—	$0
May	$36.9 million	$0	—	$288
June	$63.2 million	$0	—	$1,245
July	$48.2 million	$14	$25,298**	$143

   * Indicates the month candidate suspended campaign.
  ** In April 2020–June 2020, Warren had no monthly reports, as she switched to a quarterly report, which was filed in as her July quarterly report covering 4/1/2020 through 6/30/2020.
 *** These figures include itemized and unitemized total contributions from persons/individuals other than political committees. These figures do not include party committee, other committees, or candidate contributions. "Presidential Committee Reports Biden for President," Federal Election Commission, accessed January 2, 2021, https://www.fec.gov/data/reports/presidential/?is_amended=false&data_type=processed&committee_id=C00703975&cycle=2020; "Presidential Committee Reports Bernie 2020," Federal Election Commission," accessed January 2, 2021, https://www.fec.gov/data/reports/presidential/?is_amended=false&data_type=processed&committee_id=C00577130&committee_id=C00696948&cycle=2020; "Presidential Committee Reports Warren for President, Inc.," Federal Election Commission, accessed January 2, 2021, https://www.fec.gov/data/reports/presidential/?is_amended=false&data_type=processed&committee_id=C00693234&cycle=2020; "Presidential Committee Reports Mike Bloomberg 2020, Inc.," Federal Election Commission, accessed January 2, 2021, https://www.fec.gov/data/reports/presidential/?is_amended=false&data_type=processed&committee_id=C00728154&cycle=2020. Note that all of the data from these sites incorporates the candidate's February, March, April, May, June, July, and August 2020 Monthly Filings.

Democratic candidates from January to July 2020. Looking at the top four delegate winners, Biden, Sanders, Warren, and Bloomberg, it is clear that consistent campaign fundraising was important to stay in the Democratic primary contest. Interestingly, Sanders started out with over double the individual contributions of Biden in January 2020. Even Elizabeth Warren outraised Biden among individual contributions in January, February, and March. However, Biden was the odds-on favorite to win the Democratic primary, as many perceived him to be the most likely candidate to beat President Trump. Warren and Sanders continued strong fundraising until April 2020. Warren suspended her campaign in March and Sanders and April, which cleared the way for an inevitable nomination of Biden.[41] Interestingly, Biden's running mate, Senator Kamala Harris, was not as strong a fundraiser as Warren or Sanders. She suspended her campaign in December 2019, with the FEC records showing she had raised only $37.3 million in individual contributions from October 1, 2019 through December 31, 2019.[42]

Some 2020 Democratic primary delegates spent large sums of money only to receive a few delegates. For example, Buttigieg was a huge fundraiser during the Democratic primary spending $94.9 million in operating expenditures to received only received twenty-one pledged delegates before the convention.[43] Similarly, Michael Bloomberg spent over $1 billion on his primary campaign, largely self-funded, only to receive 49 delegates prior to the convention. His individual candidate contributions through October 31, 2020, totaled over $1 billion compared to only $914,487 raised through individual contributions.[44]

Table 9.1 illustrates that while campaign fundraising is an important ingredient to a primary campaign it does not guarantee success. What campaign cash does allow, however, is the longevity of the campaign. Several Democratic primary candidates dropped out because of an anemic campaign fundraising that resulting in them running out of money. However, again this Democratic primary also shows the limits of self-funding. Campaigns that rely on self-funding have longevity so long as the candidate wants to spend his or her own money. However, self-funded candidates have a difficult time winning the election, perhaps due to public sentiment, but it may also indicate a lack of grassroots support that results in individual donations. Interestingly, Bloomberg won only one primary contest, American Samoa, and ended up spending roughly $18 million per delegate.[45]

Table 9.2 shows the Democratic primary candidates' total operating expenditures compared with the delegates won going into the Democratic Convention in August. Operating expenditures are money spent by a campaign for campaign activities and related campaign costs.

However, the real takeaway is that the rivalry contributions from January through March by his more progressive opponents Sanders and Warren. This demonstrates that within the modern Democratic Party a progressive

Table 9.2. Democratic Primary Candidates Operating Expenditures versus Delegates Won***

Candidate	Operating Expenditures**	Pledged Delegates Won*
Biden	$223.8 million	2687
Sanders	$209.6 million	1073
Warren	$128.7 million	63
Bloomberg	$1.1 billion	59

* Lauren Leatherby and Sarah Almukhtar, "Democratic Delegate Count and Primary Election Results 2020," *The New York Times*, last updated September 14, 2020, https://www.nytimes.com/interactive/2020/us/elections/delegate-count-primary-results.html. These five candidates represented the top 4 holders of delegates going into the Democratic Convention.

** The campaign expenditures were through the following dates for the candidates: Biden (August 31, 2020), Sanders (November 30, 2020), Warren (September 30, 2020), and Bloomberg (November 30, 2020). Note that the FEC provided an operating expenditure for all candidates not receiving the nomination. Biden's operating expenditures were calculated from his August 2020 monthly filing, which covered operating expenditures cycle to date of July, 31, 2020.

*** "Reports of Receipts and Disbursements Biden for President," Federal Election Commission, accessed January 2, 2021, https://docquery.fec.gov/cgi-bin/forms/C00703975/1434676/; "Financial Summary Bernie 2020," Federal Election Commission, https://www.fec.gov/data/committee/C00696948/?cycle=2020; "Financial Summary Warren for President Inc.," Federal Election Commission, accessed January 2, 2021, https://www.fec.gov/data/candidate/P00009621/?cycle=2020&election_full=true; "Financial Summary Mike Bloomberg 2020 Inc.," Federal Election Commission, accessed January 2, 2021, https://www.fec.gov/data/candidate/P00014530/?cycle=2020&election_full=true.

candidate is viable in the primaries and can raise the necessary money needed to successfully mount a presidential primary campaign.

PRIMARY FUNDRAISING: REPUBLICANS

Incumbency has long been said to be a major advantage in presidential politics. In fact, from 1952 with the election of President Eisenhower through 2020 only two incumbent presidents have lost reelection, Democrat Jimmy Carter in 1980 and Republican George H.W. Bush in 1992. One major advantage of incumbency is campaign fundraising. Strong primary challenges typically are costly and create a weakened nominee. An incumbent who goes relatively unchallenged for the nomination typically has an advantage of the organization and consequently fundraising.

Table 9.3 illustrates the relative strength of President Trump's fundraising from January through July 2020.

President Trump faced a nominal primary challenge from former Massachusetts Governor William Weld, the former Republican Governor of Massachusetts and 2016 Libertarian nominee for vice president, who raised only $1.79 million from individual contributions, and had a little over $2 million in operating expenditures.[46] He suspended his campaign on

Table 9.3.   Individual Contributions to Donald Trump January–June 2020*

Month	Individual Contributions to Trump
January	$6.3 million
February	$8.59 million
March	$6.49 million
April	$10.8 million
May	$14.1 million
June	$29.7 million
July	$32 million

* "Report of Receipts and Disbursements, February Monthly 2020 Amendment 1, Donald J. Trump for President, Inc.," Federal Election Commission, accessed January 2, 2021, https://docquery.fec.gov/cgi-bin/forms/C00580100/1403600/; "Report of Receipts and Disbursements, March Monthly 2020 Amendment 1, Donald J. Trump for President, Inc.," Federal Election Commission, accessed January 2, https://docquery.fec.gov/cgi-bin/forms/C00580100/1405125/; "Report of Receipts and Disbursements, April Monthly 2020 Amendment 1, Donald J. Trump for President, Inc.," Federal Election Commission, accessed January 2, 2021 https://docquery.fec.gov/cgi-bin/forms/C00580100/1412555/; "Report of Receipts and Disbursements, May Monthly Amendment 1, Donald J. Trump for President, Inc.," Federal Election Commission, accessed January 2, 2021, https://docquery.fec.gov/cgi-bin/forms/C00580100/1428849/; "Report of Receipts and Disbursements, June Monthly 2020 Amendment 1, Donald J. Trump for President, Inc.," Federal Election Commission, accessed January 2, 2021 https://docquery.fec.gov/cgi-bin/forms/C00580100/1414193/; "Report of Receipts and Disbursements, July Monthly 2020, Amendment 2, Donald J. Trump for President, Inc.," Federal Election Commission, accessed January 2, 2021 https://docquery.fec.gov/cgi-bin/forms/C00580100/1440916/; "Report of Receipts and Disbursements, August Monthly 2020 Amendment 1, Donald J. Trump for President, Inc.," Federal Election Commission, accessed January 2, 2021, https://docquery.fec.gov/cgi-bin/forms/C00580100/1471578/.

March 18, 2020. President Trump's nominal competition allowed him to win the Republican presidential primaries handily in 2020. In fact, Trump's support from Republican voters was so strong in the primaries as he received larger amounts of votes than what is typical for an incumbent president. For example, Trump received over 31,000 votes in the Iowa Caucus, besting Democrat Barack Obama's record of 25,000 votes in 2012. This was attributed to the Trump campaign's get-out-the-vote efforts that fueled massive turnout.[47] These efforts and fundraising placed President Trump in a strong incumbent position in terms of both cash and organization going into the general election.

POSTCONVENTION CAMPAIGN FUNDRAISING

The 2020 presidential election was unlike any other in American history because of the restraints of COVID-19. What emerged was a campaign strategy that limited personal appearances and conventions that featured single speakers that were televised in lieu of large conventions. The presidential rallies were different with Joe Biden electing to do many digital events and Donald Trump having to pare down his large rallies to smaller venues outdoors. Even the presidential debates were different with smaller attendees. The debates were also complicated by President Trump contracting COVID-19 in early October after the first debate. After the White House announced Trump's COVID-19 diagnoses, there was disagreement about the format of the second debate on October 15. Originally designed to be a town hall format, the debate was going to be changed to a virtual setting. The Trump campaign criticized this change and refused to participate. Ultimately the debate scheduled for October 15 was canceled.[48]

Despite these COVID challenges, fundraising in the presidential race continued at a robust rate. Table 9.4 shows that both Biden and Trump continued to take in millions in individual contributions from August through the general election.

Biden clearly had an individual fundraising advantage over Trump in all reporting periods.

Individual contributions, specifically small donations, were very important to both campaigns. In the 2020 presidential election, individuals donated over $1.95 billion in aggregate, and small donations, those $200 and under, topped over $1.6 billion.[49] That is compared with large donations, those donations that were over $2,000 were $356 million.[50] To be fair, that is still a large sum, but small donors constituted three times the donations of large donors. Part of this success of small-donor contributions is online systems that reach out to small donors. As shown in Table 9.5, Joe Biden was the clear beneficiary of

Table 9.4.   Trump and Biden Total Individual Contributions August 1–November 23, 2020*

Month	Biden	Trump
August	$159.8 million	$45.9 million
September	$163.5 million	$68.3 million
Pre-General*	$70 million	$43.5 million
Post-General**	$103.2 million	$142.8 million

* Pre-General is from October 1–October 14, 2020. Note there is no October figures because they are included in Pre and Post-General Disclosures.

** Post-General is from October 15–November 23, 2020.

*** "Reports of Receipts and Disbursements, September Monthly 2020, Biden for President," Federal Election Commission, accessed January 2, 2021, https://docquery.fec.gov/cgi-bin/forms/C00703975/1440320/; "Reports of Receipts and Disbursements, October Monthly 2020, Biden for President," Federal Election Commission, accessed January 2, 2021, https://docquery.fec.gov/cgi-bin/forms/C00703975/1458940/; "Reports of Receipts and Disbursements, Pre-General 2020, Biden for President," Federal Election Commission, accessed January 2, 2021, https://docquery.fec.gov/cgi-bin/forms/C00703975/1463690/; "Reports of Receipts and Disbursements, Post-General 2020, Biden for President," Federal Election Commission, accessed January 2, 2021, https://docquery.fec.gov/cgi-bin/forms/C00703975/1481223/; "Reports of Receipts and Disbursements, September Monthly 2020 Amendment 1, Donald J. Trump for President," Federal Election Commission, accessed January 2, 2021, https://docquery.fec.gov/cgi-bin/forms/C00580100/1484015/; "Reports of Receipts and Disbursements, October Monthly 2020, Donald J. Trump for President," Federal Election Commission, accessed January 2, 2021, https://docquery.fec.gov/cgi-bin/forms/C00580100/1458436/; "Reports of Receipts and Disbursements, Pre-General, Donald J. Trump for President," Federal Election Commission, accessed January 2, 2021, https://docquery.fec.gov/cgi-bin/forms/C00580100/1463640/; "Reports of Receipts and Disbursements, Post General Amendment 1, Donald J. Trump for President," Federal Election Commission, accessed January 2, 2021, https://docquery.fec.gov/cgi-bin/forms/C00580100/1483220/.

Table 9.5.   Trump Biden Individual Donations by Size through November 23, 2020* *

Amount	Biden	Trump
$200 or less	$642.6 million	$475.3 million
$200.01–$499	$90.3 million	$88.3 million
$500–$999	$98.1 million	$56 million
$1000–$1999	$107.4 million	$47 million
$2000+	$178.8 million	$100.4 million

* These totals are given out to the $100,000 mark and are not rounded as listed by the Federal Election Commission through November 23, 2020.

** Note that figures were taken from the FEC website on December 4, 2020, the day after the last monthly filing deadline for presidential candidates. "Presidential Candidate Map Summaries 2020, Joe Biden," U.S. Federal Election Commission, accessed December 4, 2020, https://www.fec.gov/data/candidates/president/presidential-map/; "Presidential Candidate Map Summaries 2020, Donald Trump," U.S. Federal Election Commission, accessed December 4, 2020, https://www.fec.gov/data/candidates/president/presidential-map/.

small-donor contributions compared to Donald Trump, but he also outraised Trump in every single category of individual donation.

Compared to 2016, these individual contributions grew, especially among small donors. As shown in Table 9.6, Clinton and Trump's individual donation size was much smaller in 2016 compared to Biden and Trump in 2020.

What is clear in terms of individual donations is that Democratic candidates outperformed Republicans in 2016 and 2020 in all categories of

Table 9.6. Trump Clinton Individual Donations by Size through December 31, 2016* **

Amount	Clinton	Trump
$200 or less	$316.6 million	$126.6 million
$200.01–$499	$45.8 million	$28.5 million
$500–$999	$35.2 million	$16.4 million
$1000–$1999	$56 million	$13.3 million
$2000+	$174 million	$27.8 million

* Figures given to the $100,000 mark and are not rounded s listed by the Federal Elections Commission through December 31, 2016.

** Note that figures were taken from the FEC website on December 4, 2020, the day after the last monthly filing deadline for presidential candidates. "Presidential Candidate Map Summaries 2016, Hillary Clinton and Tim Kaine," U.S. Federal Election Commission, accessed December 4, 2020, https://www.fec.gov/data/candidates/president/presidential-map/; "Presidential Candidate Map Summaries 2016, Donald Trump and Mike Pence," U.S. Federal Election Commission, accessed December 4, 2020, https://www.fec.gov/data/candidates/president/presidential-map/.

Table 9.7. Trump Beginning and Ending Cash on Hand for Reporting Period August–November 23, 2020***

Month	Beginning	Close
August	$120.5 million	$121.09 million
September	$121.09 million	$63.1 million
Pre-General*	$63.1 million	$43.6 million
Post-General**	$43.6 million	$18.4 million

* Pre-General is from October 1 to October 14, 2020. Note that there are no October figures because they are included in Pre- and Post-General Disclosures.

** Post-General is from October 15 to November 23, 2020.

*** "Reports of Receipts and Disbursements, September Monthly 2020 Amendment 1, Donald J. Trump for President," Federal Election Commission, accessed January 2, 2021, https://docquery.fec.gov/cgi-bin/forms/C00580100/1484015/; "Reports of Receipts and Disbursements, October Monthly 2020, Donald J. Trump for President," Federal Election Commission, accessed January 2, 2021, https://docquery.fec.gov/cgi-bin/forms/C00580100/1458436/; "Reports of Receipts and Disbursements, Pre-General, Donald J. Trump for President," Federal Election Commission, accessed January 2, 2021, https://docquery.fec.gov/cgi-bin/forms/C00580100/1463640/; "Reports of Receipts and Disbursements, Post General Amendment 1, Donald J. Trump for President," Federal Election Commission, accessed January 2, 2021, https://docquery.fec.gov/cgi-bin/forms/C00580100/1483220/.

individual donations. However, there is evidence that Donald Trump made some inroads in closing that gap with his Democratic opponent. Cash on hand, or the amount of money a campaign has in its account, is a measurement of the strength of a campaign. As the primary fundraising showed, the lower the amount of fundraising the lower amount of cash on hand to spend for the campaign. Tables 9.7 and 9.8 show a comparison of Joe Biden and Donald Trump's cash on hand from August through the general election. As the fundraising numbers show, the cash on hand of each candidate shows that Biden had a clear cash advantage in the general election, especially in the latter days of the campaign.

Fundraising in 2020 also shows that there was a clear advantage for Biden in terms of operating expenditures, or the amount of money used by a campaign

Table 9.8. Biden Beginning and Ending Cash on Hand for Reporting Period August–November 23, 2020*

Month	Beginning	Close
August	$98.8 million	$180.6 million
September	$180.6 million	$177.2 million
Pre-General*	$177.2 million	$162 million
Post-General**	$162 million	$1.55 million

* Pre-General is from October 1 to October 14, 2020. Note there are no October figures because they are included in Pre- and Post-General Disclosures.

** Post-General is from October 15 to November 23, 2020.

*** "Reports of Receipts and Disbursements, September Monthly 2020, Biden for President," Federal Election Commission, accessed January 2, 2021, https://docquery.fec.gov/cgi-bin/forms/C00703975/1440320/; "Reports of Receipts and Disbursements, October Monthly 2020, Biden for President," Federal Election Commission, accessed January 2, 2021, https://docquery.fec.gov/cgi-bin/forms/C00703975/1458940/; "Reports of Receipts and Disbursements, Pre-General 2020, Biden for President," Federal Election Commission, accessed January 2, 2021, https://docquery.fec.gov/cgi-bin/forms/C00703975/1463690/; "Reports of Receipts and Disbursements, Post-General 2020, Biden for President," Federal Election Commission, accessed January 2, 2021, https://docquery.fec.gov/cgi-bin/forms/C00703975/1481223/.

Table 9.9. Trump and Biden Total Campaign Operating Expenditures*

Month	Biden	Trump
August	$128.8 million	$61.1 million
September	$281 million	$125.9 million
Pre-General*	$143.2 million	$63 million
Post-General**	$269.1 million	$198.6 million

* Pre-General is from October 1 to October 14, 2020. Note there is no October figures because they are included in Pre- and Post-General Disclosures

** Post-General is from October 15 to November 23, 2020.

*** "Reports of Receipts and Disbursements, September Monthly 2020, Biden for President," Federal Election Commission, accessed January 2, 2021, https://docquery.fec.gov/cgi-bin/forms/C00703975/1440320/; "Reports of Receipts and Disbursements, October Monthly 2020, Biden for President," Federal Election Commission, accessed January 2, 2021, https://docquery.fec.gov/cgi-bin/forms/C00703975/1458940/; "Reports of Receipts and Disbursements, Pre-General 2020, Biden for President," Federal Election Commission, accessed January 2, 2021, https://docquery.fec.gov/cgi-bin/forms/C00703975/1463690/; "Reports of Receipts and Disbursements, Post-General 2020, Biden for President," Federal Election Commission, accessed January 2, 2021, https://docquery.fec.gov/cgi-bin/forms/C00703975/1481223/; "Reports of Receipts and Disbursements, September Monthly 2020 Amendment 1, Donald J. Trump for President," Federal Election Commission, accessed January 2, 2021, https://docquery.fec.gov/cgi-bin/forms/C00580100/1484015/; "Reports of Receipts and Disbursements, October Monthly 2020, Donald J. Trump for President," Federal Election Commission, accessed January 2, 2021, https://docquery.fec.gov/cgi-bin/forms/C00580100/1458436/; "Reports of Receipts and Disbursements, Pre-General, Donald J. Trump for President," Federal Election Commission, accessed January 2, 2021, https://docquery.fec.gov/cgi-bin/forms/C00580100/1463640/; "Reports of Receipts and Disbursements, Post General Amendment 1, Donald J. Trump for President," Federal Election Commission, accessed January 2, 2021, https://docquery.fec.gov/cgi-bin/forms/C00580100/1483220/.

for its activities such as advertising and other campaign activities. Table 9.9 shows that Biden's campaign had much larger operating expenditures than Trump's beginning in August and continuing through the general election.

Looking at the general election campaign finance for both Biden and Trump shows that despite being a campaign year with limitations on campaign events, notably in-person rallies, the campaign fundraising continued at a high rate, outpacing 2016, which was at that time considered to be an expensive campaign. Democrats still had an advantage over Republicans, but, unlike 2016, it seems that there is a closing of the gap between both parties in fundraising, particularly at the small donor level.

CONCLUSION

American political campaigns are an expensive endeavor. The 2020 presidential election demonstrates that in spite of an unusual election year because of an international pandemic that presidential campaign costs continued to rise. However, this is expected. The campaign finance issues of 2020 showed that money in politics matters and that there is a threshold amount needed to stay competitive in presidential campaigns. Additionally, the campaign finance issues in the crowded Democratic primary show that there was a real competitiveness, at least in terms of fundraising, between moderate and progressive candidates. This may result in progressives in the Democratic Party continuing to make inroads into the party platform and may even result in more self-identified progressives earning a top spot on the national ticket.

So, what did 2020 show that was unique in American campaign finance? First, Democrats have an advantage in campaign fundraising. This has been the case for some time, and the analysis of the 2016 presidential campaign showed this phenomenon as well.[51] Second, a campaign year that was limited because of COVID-19 did not mean that fundraising was less important. Even Joe Biden, who ran a very limited in-person campaign, aggressively fundraised and had net operating expenditures than his opponent. Third, campaign fundraising is extremely important in a crowded primary. Those candidates with the most cash had the most staying power. Biden and Sanders continued in the primary because of their support.

What was the most important takeaway about campaign finance in the 2020 election? Three things. First, campaign finance as an issue is no longer the salient political issue it was in the late 1990s and early 2000s. Instead, campaign finance is used in a more nuanced political way. Pete Buttigieg's wine cave supporters proved to be a point his opponents could attack, but, despite the criticisms, all of the Democratic candidates, even the progressive Sanders, aggressively fundraised. Second, small donors matter a lot. The small-donor contributions to Biden and Trump were larger than those in 2016. They also equaled greater amounts than the largest $2,000+ donor group, as shown in Table 9.5. This is a direct consequence of a sophisticated online campaign fundraising operation. Donor dollars and data are a valuable commodity in American politics, and small donors demonstrate that their contributions are an essential part of campaign fundraising. Third, campaign dollars count to a certain extent, but message and politics matter most. The 2016 presidential election showed that more cash in campaign coffers does not equate to electoral success. The 2020 presidential campaign shows this as well. Biden, of course, was better financed and won the election. However, President Trump received over 74 million votes and 232 electoral votes. States including Florida, Georgia, Pennsylvania, Michigan, Wisconsin, Nevada, Arizona, and Minnesota were close races showing that outspending an opponent does not necessarily equate to victory.

The beginning of campaign finance law started because people feared the role of money in politics. The history of campaign finance regulations in the United States is a tension between the fear of too much money in politics and the importance of people being able to have a political voice through donations. That tension continues in American political races, but what is evident in 2020 is the money in politics remains essential.

Chapter 10

The 2020 General Election Vote in a Divided American Electorate

Kate Kenski and Henry C. Kenski

The 2020 general election took place amid a highly polarized American electorate during a global pandemic. Donald Trump's presidency contained little bridge-building. The incivility on social media perpetuated by candidate Trump during the preprimary season in 2015[1] foreshadowed his presidential Twitter activity. The general election showcased the partisan tensions that had been building. Ultimately, the election was won by Democrat and former Vice President Joe Biden in an Electoral College victory of 306 pledged votes to 232.[2] The victory, however, was not won overnight with congratulations from the opposition. Several swing states were in contention, and the mainstream media outlets did not call Biden as the winner until four days after Election Day.[3] As the 2020 year came to a close, Trump had not conceded his loss but rather claimed election fraud despite lack of evidence to support his contention.[4] This chapter examines key factors that helped Biden win.

The purpose of this chapter is to examine the presidential vote in 2020 with a focus on the public. We begin by discussing the overall political communication environment and then turn our attention to the rules of the game and the Electoral College. Next, we discuss the importance of party identification's relationship to the vote and provide an overview of how the candidates were perceived on favorability and temperament. Finally, we consider the demographic bases of the presidential vote, with special attention to the roles of gender and race-ethnicity in recent elections and the 2020 campaign. We begin first with observations on the overall political environment.

THE OVERALL POLITICAL
COMMUNICATION ENVIRONMENT

The 2020 presidential campaign took place in a complex information environment. Polarization between the parties loomed largely. Resentment over Trump's 2016 win had grown. Foreign and domestic agents circumvented news media's gatekeeping function by reaching people on social media with misinformation and disinformation. A global pandemic usurped the public's attention and affected the country's economic performance. And, civil unrest over racial injustice grew as videos displayed the killings of Blacks in different areas of the country.

Republican candidates dominated presidential elections from 1968 through 1988, the exception being Jimmy Carter's narrow victory in 1976. Democrat Bill Clinton won in 1992 and 1996. Republican George W. Bush won in 2000 and 2004. Democrat Barack Obama won in 2008 and 2012. While Republican Donald J. Trump won the 2016 presidential election with 304 electoral votes to Democrat Hillary Clinton's 227, he lost the popular vote by 2.1 percent.[5] With the exception of the first two weeks of his presidency, Trump's disapproval ratings were higher than his approval ratings, and his disapproval ratings were higher than 50 percent with the exception of two brief moments during his presidency.[6] Yet, his base of support was fairly consistent, resulting in a 2020 presidential race that was less about persuasion than it was about mobilization.

The overall U.S. political environment has become increasingly polarized since 1980.[7] This affective polarization resulted from people feeling animus toward the other side rather than feeling more positive about their own party.[8] The Republican win by George W. Bush in 2000 caused consternation because he won the electoral vote but lost the popular vote by approximately a half-percent.[9] Intense polarization continued through Bush's second term and during the Obama administration. As Obama finished his second term, he left a competitive political situation in which either major party could have won in 2016.

Both Trump and Biden were presidential candidates with high name recognition, and many voters had prior exposure to both candidates before the pandemic began and before Biden won the Democratic presidential nomination. In fact, almost two-thirds of the likely voters claimed they made up their minds when Trump was elected four years previously. Alexander Theodoridis contends that the 2020 presidential campaign represented a low watermark for persuasion effects. In a national poll, Theodoridis and his colleagues at the University of Massachusetts conducted between October 20 and 27, 2020, they discovered that few voters (1 percent) were undecided and that Biden had a decisive lead in the national trial heat poll with 53 percent of the vote compared to Trump's 44 percent.[10] When asked when these voters decided for whom to vote, "Sixty-one percent report having made up their minds when Donald Trump was elected four years ago."[11]

Democratic candidate and former Secretary of State Hillary Clinton won the popular vote in 2016, but Republican candidate Donald Trump, who had no previous elective experience, won the electoral vote. Trump's win was tainted with concerns that the Russian hackers and trolls helped elect Trump by shaping American opinion on social media and influencing the news media's focus on issues damaging to Clinton.[12] By 2019, over 7 in 10 Americans were using some type of social media,[13] and the potential for outside actors to shape the 2020 election remained. The concern over Russian influence was not a predominant theme during the 2020 presidential campaign, although some concerns over Russian interference were noted in news media and contended that Trump's misleading claims were being amplified by trolls.[14] FBI Director Christopher A. Wray told the House Homeland Security Committee that Russians were trying "to both sow divisiveness and discord, and I think the intelligence community has assessed this publicly, to primarily denigrate Vice President Biden in what the Russians see as a kind of an anti-Russian establishment."[15] In early October, "Twitter removed more than 1,600 accounts associated with influence efforts linked to Cuba, Russia, Saudi Arabia, and Thailand."[16]

Domestic misinformation and disinformation were also a concern. In May 2020, a 26-minute video called "Plandemic" went viral, claiming that a group of elites was using the coronavirus and potential vaccine to gain power and profit. This disinformation video was seen more than eight million times on YouTube, Facebook, Twitter, and Instagram.[17] Other conspiracy theories were peddled on social media. QAnon, a set of conspiracy theories, seeped into the mainstream. Writing for *The New York Times*, Kevin Roose explains that these theories "allege, falsely, that the world is run by a cabal of Satan-worshiping pedophiles who are plotting against Mr. Trump while operating a global child sex-trafficking ring."[18] It is difficult to know exactly how many people were affected by conspiracies on social media, but it is important to note that they were present in the information environment.

Three public policy issues stood out in the months leading up to the general election campaign: the novel coronavirus pandemic, the economy, and race relations/racism.[19] According to Gallup, when Americans were asked what they thought was "the most important facing the country today," 20 percent said coronavirus/disease, 19 percent said race relations/racism, 19 percent said the economy in June, 28 percent said coronavirus/disease, 10 percent said race relations/racism, and 10 percent said the economy in November. A related issue was 21 percent offering the government/poor leadership as the top problem in June and 22 percent reporting it as the top issue in November.

The novel coronavirus pandemic changed the political environment and turned the country's day-to-day routines upside down. On the evening of December 30, 2019, a cluster of pneumonia cases was reported in an urgent online notice issued by the Wuhan municipal health commission.[20] Less than two weeks later, on January 11, 2020, Chinese scientists published their genetic sequence of the novel virus, SARS-CoV-2. It was also the day that the first death in China was reported.[21] President Trump "announced that the US would bar entry to foreigners who had recently been in China, and urged Americans to avoid going there" on January 31, but he was slower to put travel bans in place from Europe and the United Kingdom.[22] The virus is pernicious, a vaccine was not readily available in 2020, and the virus' full effects were not understood. Contagious individuals could and did spread the virus for days before displaying symptoms, and some carriers were and are asymptomatic, making the virus difficult to contain.[23]

Over a year before Election Day, before the world was aware of the novel coronavirus, and over four months before the World Health Organization (WHO) declared the COVID-19 outbreak a global pandemic, Biden had tweeted that the United States was not prepared for a pandemic and that "Trump has rolled back progress President Obama and I made to strengthen global health security. We need leadership that builds public trust, focuses on real threats, and mobilizes the world to stop outbreaks before they reach our shores."[24] In early March, the United States, like other countries worldwide, was short on personal protective equipment (PPE) for frontline workers, which endangered them.[25] Between April and June 2020, Democrats and Republicans expressed different levels of concern about the seriousness of COVID-19. "This polarization was almost entirely driven by Republicans who were becoming less concerned about the virus or who had never been concerned."[26] The basic ways that the American public could participate in containing the virus (i.e. wearing face masks in public, avoiding large gatherings, and social distancing six feet or more from persons not sharing households) became polarized. On Election Day, the United States had its second-highest daily total of new coronavirus cases reported to date—91,530.[27] On November 4, Noah Higgins-Dunn reported, "There are now almost 9.4 million reported Covid-19 cases in the US and at least 232,635 deaths, according to Johns Hopkins."[28]

The health of the economy is a concern to many Americans and is often a major issue during presidential campaigns. The economy matters to parties and candidates in part because research suggests that being satisfied with the party and government at the time of voting affects a voter's decision to switch between incumbent and opposition parties.[29] If the economy is not doing well, that can reflect poorly on the incumbent party. If the economy is doing well, that can make it more difficult for the opposition to proclaim that a change in leadership is warranted.

One reason why the COVID-19 outbreak and its handling were a concern came down to how the pandemic affected the economy. Because of how quickly the virus spread, many businesses and workers in the service industry were affected by state and local shutdowns in March and April when many localities put in mandates or voluntary recommendations to limit business hours or sometimes close businesses down. Bipartisan congressional support resulted in the passing of the Coronavirus Aid, Relief, and Economic Security (CARES) Act and was signed by Trump on March 27, 2020, to provide relief to some Americans and businesses at the cost of $2 trillion.[30] Concerns arose over whether the health of the economy was being sacrificed for the health of individuals.[31] This dichotomy was arguably a false-choice dilemma, but it was one that seemed to resonate with the media and many members of the public with Republicans arguing that the economy needed to "reopen" and Democrats arguing that the science suggested the use of masks when in public and social distancing needed to take place. Without a strong directive from the federal government, each state did its own form of reopening.

While stocks fell in March, senior *Forbes* contributor Mike Patton wrote, "By September 2, stocks were a whopping 87.5% overvalued, the highest number ever, surpassing even the Tech Bubble in March 2000 when stocks were 49% overvalued."[32] Although some companies did quite well, Patton noted that "Unemployment spiked to its highest rate in the post WWII era, hitting 14.7% earlier this year. Although the rate has fallen for five consecutive months, it is still well above its February reading of 3.5%."[33]

A third issue loomed large in 2020—race relations/racism. Civil unrest appeared in many cities across the country because of a series of murders of black citizens either involving the police or calling into question the processes by which the police tracked down and arrested the alleged perpetrators. Before the COVID-19 situation was understood by many Americans, news media shed the spotlight on the murder of Ahmaud Arbery on February 23, 2020, in Glynn County, Georgia. Arbery, who was black, was jogging when he was confronted by two white men, Gregory and Travis McMichael. They claimed that Arbery looked like a suspect involved in alleged break-ins. The shooting was filmed by a third man. It took over two months before the men were arrested, and there may have been interference by public officials allowing police to arrest the perpetrators.[34] Less than a month later, on March 13, 2020, a black medical worker named Breonna Taylor was shot and killed by Louisville police who burst into her apartment during a raid.[35] In Minneapolis on May 25, 2020, an African American named George Floyd died while being handcuffed and pinned to the ground by a white police officer who had his knee on Floyd's throat. Floyd said, "I can't breath." "The encounter, captured on video, incited large protests against police brutality and systemic racism in Minneapolis and more than 150 American cities in the weeks and months that followed."[36]

The visible deaths of these African Americans and others set off nationwide protests. Some of the protesters called for "defunding the police," which was a slogan modified by some protesters who explained the proposal would involve a reallocation of resources from the police to social welfare workers and organizations in an effort to address some matters before involving police. The protests were a concern to Trump as demonstrated by his allocation of tweets that focused on unrest, law and order, and the threat of military use in the 15 days following Floyd's death in police custody. According to *USA Today*'s George Petras, one-fourth of Trump's 769 tweets and retweets in that 15-day period "were in reaction to Floyd's death, the angry protests for police reform that swept across more than 100 cities, and the movement to 'defund' metropolitan police departments."[37]

The major party conventions took place mainly through television owing to concerns about the COVID-19 outbreak. At the Democratic National Convention (August 17–20), the Democrats selected former Vice President Joseph Biden as their nominee. Biden emerged as the victor in a highly competitive field of Democratic candidates vying for the nomination. The following week (August 24–27), the Republicans selected Donald J. Trump who had little competition. Biden's campaign claimed that "Our best days still lie ahead," while Trump's campaign used the slogans "Keep America Great" and "Promises Made, Promises Kept."

THE RULES OF THE GAME: THE ELECTORAL COLLEGE AND THE POPULAR VOTE

Americans do not vote directly for president but instead cast their ballots for a slate of electors committed to a presidential ticket. Each state has a number of electoral votes equal to its representation in Congress. California, for example, has 53 representatives and two senators and therefore has 55 electoral votes. A small state like Wyoming has only one House member and two senators for three electoral votes. The District of Columbia (DC) has three electoral votes as a result of a constitutional amendment. There are 538 total electoral votes, and these votes in most states are counted on the basis of a "winner take all" rule meaning that the ticket winning the state's popular vote receives all of the state's electoral votes. Maine (four electoral votes) and Nebraska (five electoral votes) are the exceptions. Both states allocate two electoral votes to the ticket winning the state's popular vote and then give one electoral vote for each of the state's congressional districts. It takes a majority, or 270 electoral votes, to win the presidency. Prior to 2008, no candidate had captured a single electoral vote by winning a congressional district while losing a state until Obama carried a Nebraska congressional district while losing the state and earning one electoral vote in 2008. The norm is for all of a state's electoral votes to be awarded to one candidate.

In modern presidential elections, Democrats historically are consistently stronger in the East and the Pacific West, while Republicans have had an edge in the South, the Mountain West, and the rural Midwest. The larger Midwestern states are often competitive and historically battlegrounds for both party tickets. These Midwestern states again proved to be the battleground in 2020.

The political landscape in 2020 was such that 13 states were considered competitive or swing states plus the second congressional districts in Maine and Nebraska were also competitive. The battleground list included Arizona, Florida, Georgia, Iowa, Michigan, Minnesota, Nevada, New Hampshire, North Carolina, Ohio, Pennsylvania, Texas, and Wisconsin.[38] Many of these states have appeared on the most competitive list during the 2016 presidential campaign. Colorado and Virginia were considered competitive in 2016[39] but became blue-leaning states in 2020. That Arizona had shown signs of becoming a swing state in 2016[40] and became a toss-up state in 2020 and that Texas was in contention in 2020 were noteworthy and foreshadowed a crack in the Republican mobilization plan. Both states had been known as conservative states the past two decades, with Arizona offering John McCain as the 2008 Republican presidential nominee and Texas being home to two-term former president George W. Bush (2001–2008).

All states and their electoral votes are important, but battleground states are the most important because they are more influential in determining electoral outcomes and targeted the most heavily by the campaigns. Table 10.1 lists the 13 battleground states, plus Maine and Nebraska because of their battleground districts, their electoral vote counts, and the percentage of voters in each state that supported Biden and Trump. Of these 13 battleground states, Trump had won 10 of them in 2016. In 2020, Biden retained the three won by Clinton in 2016 (Minnesota, Nevada, and New Hampshire) and picked up five won by Trump in 2016 (Arizona, Georgia, Michigan, Pennsylvania, and Wisconsin). Trump retained five of the battleground states that he had won in 2016 (Florida, Iowa, North Carolina, Ohio, and Texas). As for Maine and Nebraska, Biden retained three electoral votes in Maine, which mirrored 2016's outcome, and Biden picked up one of Nebraska's five electoral votes, which was a net loss of one for Trump, who had won all five in 2016.

Of the 201 electoral votes available in the 13 battleground states plus Maine (CD2) and Nebraska (CD2), Biden won 94 of them and Trump won 107. Trump's battleground triumphs, however, came up short to win the

Table 10.1. Swing States 2020 Candidate Popular Vote Percentages

	Electoral Votes	Biden %	Trump %	Margin (Biden % minus Trump %)	Winner 2020	Winner 2016
AZ	11	49.22%	48.91%	0.31%	Biden	Trump
FL	29	47.76%	51.11%	−3.35%	Trump	Trump
GA	16	49.50%	49.26%	0.24%	Biden	Trump
IA	6	44.89%	53.09%	−8.20%	Trump	Trump
ME*	4	53.09%	44.02%	9.07%	Biden 3 to Trump 1	Clinton 3 to Trump 1
MI	16	50.55%	47.77%	2.78%	Biden	Trump
MN	10	52.40%	45.28%	7.11%	Biden	Clinton
NE*	5	39.17%	58.22%	−19.06%	Trump 4 to Biden1	Trump
NV	6	50.06%	47.67%	2.39%	Biden	Clinton
NH	4	52.71%	45.36%	7.35%	Biden	Clinton
NC	15	48.59%	49.93%	−1.35%	Trump	Trump
OH	18	45.16%	53.18%	−8.02%	Trump	Trump
PA	20	49.88%	48.70%	1.18%	Biden	Trump
TX	38	46.48%	52.06%	−5.58%	Trump	Trump
WI	10	49.45%	48.82%	0.63%	Biden	Trump

Note: State results for Main and Nebraska are presented, but it was their CD2 that were battlegrounds during the general election campaign.

Source: Dave Leip's Atlas of US Elections. Accessed December 29, 2020. https://uselectionatlas.org/RESULTS/.

election because he had a deficit in noncompetitive states. Trump went into Election Day with 125 fairly certain electoral votes to Biden's 212.

PARTY IDENTIFICATION AND
THE PRESIDENTIAL VOTE

Party identification is an important factor in voting. Researchers often treat party identification as a psychological concept that is measured by asking respondents if they think of themselves as a Democrat, Republican, Independent, or something else as it involves voter perception about their leanings at the present time. It should not be confused with party registration. Sometimes people register with one party but do not bother to change their registration or simply stay registered with the party to which their families historically have belonged. This is more of a problem in the South, where some older southerners think of themselves as Alabama Democrats or Mississippi Democrats and continue to identify as Democrats while voting Republican in presidential elections because the Democratic candidate may be viewed as too liberal. Party registration is, of course, important as well, as most voters feel affinity toward the party with whom they are registered, but it is important to acknowledge that there can be a difference between how one is registered and which party one feels affinity toward during a given election.

Because of the potency of party identification in predicting the vote, the two parties conduct massive registration drives in order to have an advantage over the other party. Gallup's poll showed that in October 2020, Democrats and Republican identification was at parity, with 31 percent of Americans identifying with each major party, while Independent party identifiers composed the plurality at 36 percent.[41] Most partisans vote for their party's candidate. Independents often split their support. The edge given by Independents to one party over another can make the difference in the outcome of an election.

The 2016 and 2020 data underscore how party identification shapes candidate support, as shown in Table 10.2. In 2016, Democrats were 36 percent of the voting electorate and voted 89 percent for Clinton and 8 percent for Trump. Republicans, who made up 33 percent of the voting electorate, were a near-mirror image, with 88 percent supporting Trump and 8 percent for Clinton. In 2020, even fewer partisans voted for the other side's candidate. Democrats made up 37 percent of the voting electorate in 2020, and 94 percent cast their ballot for Biden with 5 percent supporting Trump. Republicans composed 36 percent of the 2020 voting electorate, with 94 percent supporting Trump to 6 percent for Biden.

An examination of the battleground states shows that Democrats increased support for their party's candidate from 2016 to 2020. In only one state was the increase in Democratic support for the Democratic candidate countered and balanced by an increase in Democratic support for Trump (New Hampshire where Trump support among Democrats increased from 5 percent to 6 percent); in all other battleground states, Democrats' already weak support for Trump decreased further in 2020. On the Republican side, support for Trump increased from 2016 to 2020 in all battleground states, except Georgia and Maine, where Republican support remained the same. Republican support for the party's opposition candidate increased slightly in Florida, Georgia, Iowa, Maine, Minnesota, and New Hampshire, and remained steady in North Carolina and Ohio. The data suggest some overall modest gains in the partisan environment appeared to break slightly for Biden.

Biden's gains were demonstrable among Independents. In 2016, Independents favored Trump narrowly by a 46 to 42 percent margin. Biden flipped and expanded the Democratic candidate's 4 percent marginal deficit in 2016 to a 13 percent gain in 2020. As shown in Table 10.3, Trump's support from Independents decreased from 2016 to 2020 in all battleground states where exit poll data were available. It is important to note that in the nation overall,

Table 10.2.   Swing States: 2016 and 2020 National Exit Poll Profiles: Comparison of Democratic and Republican Voters (%)

Democrats	2016			2020		
	% of the vote	*Clinton*	*Trump*	*% of the vote*	*Biden*	*Trump*
Nat'l	36	89	8	37	94	5
AZ	28	89	7	26	96	3
FL	32	90	8	30	94	5
GA	34	94	5	34	96	4
IA	31	88	10	26	93	7
ME	31	90	8	28	94	5
MI	40	88	9	38	97	3
MN	37	87	10	35	95	4
NE	—	—	—	—	—	—
NV	36	90	8	35	95	5
NH	28	93	5	23	94	6
NC	35	90	8	34	97	3
OH	34	87	12	31	92	7
PA	42	87	11	40	92	7
TX	29	93	5	30	96	4
WI	35	91	7	32	96	4

Republicans	2016			2020		
	% of the vote	*Clinton*	*Trump*	*% of the vote*	*Biden*	*Trump*
Nat'l	33	8	88	36	6	94
AZ	32	7	88	35	9	90
FL	33	8	89	38	7	93
GA	36	4	94	38	6	94
IA	34	6	90	36	7	93
ME	30	7	89	31	9	89
MI	31	7	90	38	6	94
MN	35	7	86	34	8	91
NE	—	—	—	—	—	—
NV	28	8	88	35	5	94
NH	28	7	89	31	10	90
NC	31	4	94	37	4	96
OH	37	7	90	39	7	93
PA	39	9	89	41	8	91
TX	38	9	88	41	5	94
WI	34	6	90	37	7	93

Sources: Numbers retrieved December 28, 2020 from *https://www.cnn.com/election/2016/results/exit-polls* and *https://www.cnn.com/election/2020/exit-polls/president/national-results.*

fewer people identified as Independents in the voting electorate's composition. In 2016, 31 percent of voters reported that they were Independents, and this decreased to 26 percent in 2020, making it even more important for Biden to win those who identified as Independents by a significant margin.

Table 10.3.   Swing States 2016 and 2020 National Exit Poll Independents Profiles

	2016			2020		
	% of the vote	*Clinton*	*Trump*	*% of the vote*	*Biden*	*Trump*
Nat'l	31	42	46	26	54	41
AZ	40	44	47	39	53	44
FL	34	43	47	32	54	43
GA	30	41	52	28	53	44
IA	35	38	51	38	50	46
ME	39	46	41	41	59	35
MI	29	36	52	23	51	45
MN	28	42	44	31	55	40
NE	—	—	—	—	—	—
NV	36	37	50	30	50	44
NH	44	45	45	46	62	35
NC	33	37	53	30	50	46
OH	29	37	51	30	48	48
PA	20	41	48	19	52	44
TX	33	38	52	29	51	45
WI	30	40	50	31	54	42

Sources: Numbers retrieved December 28, 2020 from *https://www.cnn.com/election/2016/results/exit-polls* and *https://www.cnn.com/election/2020/exit-polls/president/national-results.*

VOTER PERCEPTIONS ABOUT THE CANDIDATES

Political candidates are messengers who invoke issues and traits to persuade the audience or voters to support them. Issues can be used to personal qualities like commitment to change, experience, competence, leadership, vision, trust, and empathy. Voters may lack detailed issue knowledge themselves, but they can observe campaign behavior and assess how candidates fare on important personal traits. Voters may focus on the issues identified by the candidate to assess whether the candidate really cares about people like themselves or is biased toward other groups. They may also be less inclined to believe what a candidate says if he or she does not appear competent, trustworthy, or to share the voters' values. If people have serious reservations about the candidate as a messenger, they are unlikely to be persuaded by the campaign messages. There has to be some sense of source credibility for voters to accept candidate messages.

When 2020 exit poll voters were asked which candidate qualities mattered most to them, 33 percent said "is a strong leader," 24 percent said "has good judgment," 21 percent said "cares about people like me," and 19 percent said "can unite the country."[42] Of those who prioritized "strong leader," 72 percent supported Trump to 28 percent for Biden. Those selecting "cares about people like me" were nearly split between the candidates (50 percent for Trump and 49 percent for Biden). Those seeking "good judgment" chose Biden (68 percent) over Trump (26 percent). Voters wanted a candidate who "can united the country" selected Biden (75 percent) over Trump (24 percent).

A general sense of feelings toward the candidates can be assessed through candidate favorability measures. The 2020 exit polls asked voters which candidates they felt favorable toward. 49 percent of voters said they only felt favorable toward Biden, 43 percent said they only felt favorable toward Trump, 3 percent said both Biden and Trump, and 3 percent reported that they did not feel favorable toward either of them.[43] Among those who only felt favorable toward Biden, 97 percent voted for him. Among those who only felt favorable toward Trump, 98 percent voted for him.

The 2020 exit polls also asked voters who of the presidential candidates had the temperament to serve as president. 49 percent of voters said only Biden, 39 percent said only Trump, 5 percent said both Biden and Trump, and 6 percent said neither of them. As with favorability, 97 percent of people who said only Biden had the temperament to serve as president voted for Biden, while 98 percent of those who said only Trump voted for Trump. Among the 5 percent of voters who said that both candidates had the temperament to serve as president, 63 percent voted for Trump and 36 percent voted for Biden. Of those who did not feel either candidate had the right temperament, 66 percent voted for Trump and 20 percent voted for Biden.

Although candidate traits and positions on issues are related, they were pitted against each other in the 2020 exit polls asking voters which was more important to the presidential vote: candidate's positions on issues or candidate's personal qualities. Nearly three-fourths of voters (74 percent) claimed that positions on issues were more important compared to 23 percent who said candidate's personal qualities. The issue voters broke for Trump by a 6 percent margin—53 percent said Trump and 47 percent said Biden. For those voters who prioritized a candidate's personal qualities, 64 percent voted for Biden compared to 31 percent who voted for Trump—a margin of 33 percent.

VOTER PERCEPTIONS OF THE ISSUES

Messages are an essential component of the communication process. They are essential in presenting the overall campaign narratives as well as positioning candidates on the issues. When presidents run for a second term, it is common for the campaign to serve as a referendum on their performance. Reelection campaigns are often a mixture of referendum plus a choice between two (or more) candidates. Particular campaigns may be weighted more heavily to one of these campaign frames with less support for the other. The large slate of

Democratic primary candidates used the primary campaign season to attack Trump's presidential performance, and while they argued strongly as to why they were the best candidates for the Democratic nomination, they also reiterated their support for each other. Even before the pandemic took place, the Democrats had argued that Trump, who was impeached on January 16, 2020 but not removed, was not fit to be president. It was ultimately the pandemic that drove inspection of Trump's ability to lead from the American public.

When 2020 exit poll voters were asked which issue was most important to them, 35 percent said the economy, 20 percent said racial inequality, 17 percent said the coronavirus, 11 percent said crime and safety, and 11 percent said health care policy. Of those who said the economy, 83 percent voted for Trump and 17 percent voted for Biden. Of those who said racial inequality, 92 percent voted for Biden and 7 percent voted for Trump. Of those who said the coronavirus, 81 percent voted for Biden and 15 percent voted for Trump.

When asked which candidate would better handle the economy, the results were evenly split: 49 percent Biden to 49 percent Trump. When asked which candidate would better handle the coronavirus pandemic, 53 percent of voters said Biden and 43 percent said Trump. When asked whether it was more important to contain the coronavirus or to rebuild the economy, 52 percent said contain the virus and 42 percent said rebuild the economy. 55 percent of exit poll voters said that the coronavirus pandemic had caused them financial hardship. Of the 16 percent who reported "severe financial hardship," 69 percent voted for Biden while 29 percent voted for Trump. Of the 39 percent who experienced "moderate financial hardship," 59 percent voted for Biden while 39 percent voted for Trump. Of the 44 percent who said they had not experienced financial hardship, 60 percent voted for Trump and 38 percent voted for Biden.

When asked to rate the importance of racism in the United States as an issue, 18 percent of voters said it was the most important problem, 51 percent said it was an important problem, 18 percent said it was a minor problem, and 10 percent said it was not an important problem at all. Those who said that racism was the most important problem or an important problem overwhelmingly voted for Biden (87 percent to 11 percent if considered most important and 61 percent to 37 percent if considered an important problem). 91 percent of voters who said racism in the United States was not a problem at all voted for Trump.

VOTER SUPPORT

Voter characteristics are associated with different patterns of support for parties and candidates. Table 10.4 outlines a comparison for demographic

Table 10.4.   Demographic Comparison of 2016 and 2020 Presidential Vote

Category	2016 (%)			2020 (%)		
	% of 2016 Vote	Clinton	Trump	% of 2020 Vote	Biden	Trump
Urban	34	60	34	29	60	38
Suburban	49	45	49	51	50	48
Rural	17	34	61	19	42	57
Democrats	36	89	8	37	94	5
Independents	31	42	46	26	54	41
Republicans	33	8	88	36	6	94
Liberal	26	84	10	24	89	10
Moderate	39	52	40	38	64	34
Conservative	35	16	81	38	14	85
White	71	37	57	67	41	58
Black	12	89	8	13	87	12
Latino	11	66	28	13	65	32
Asian	4	65	27	4	61	34
Other racial/ethnic group	3	56	36	4	55	41
Men	47	41	52	48	45	53
Women	53	54	41	52	57	42
Protestant	27	36	59	43	39	60
Catholic	23	46	50	25	52	47
Union Household	18	51	42	20	56	40

Note: The categories in 2016 and 2020 are not the same. Protestant in 2020 included "other Christians."

Sources: Numbers retrieved December 28, 2020 from *https://www.cnn.com/election/2016/results/exit-polls* and *https://www.cnn.com/election/2020/exit-polls/president/national-results.*

categories where data are available for both the 2016 and the 2020 presidential elections. The data clearly underscore that the partisan preferences from demographic groups held for both elections, but that the Biden percentages were slightly higher than Clinton's in some key areas. Biden improved slightly in the area categories of suburban and rural support. Partisan preference within the candidates' respective parties showed an uptick in support for the Democratic candidate from 89 percent to 94 percent among Democrats from 2016 to 2020, while the Republican also increased support for their candidate from 88 to 94 percent. As previously mentioned, the percentage of voters claiming Independent identification decreased, but of importance was the major shift in Democratic candidate support resulting in a 13 percent gap between Biden and Trump.

On ideology, Biden registered higher percentages of support among liberals and moderates than did Clinton. In 2016, 52 percent of moderates supported Clinton, which increased to 64 percent for Biden in 2020.

White support for the Democratic candidate improved by 4 percent, but it is also worth noting that whites made up a smaller proportion of the electorate in 2020 than they had in 2016—71 percent to 67 percent. While all nonwhite groups help a majority preference for the Democratic candidate in both 2016 and 2020, it is worth noting that Biden lost a little ground with nonwhite groups overall in terms of percent support.

Biden increased support over Clinton's baseline with Protestants and Catholics, but Protestants preferred Trump with 60 percent support to Biden's 39 percent. Union household is one of the key groups in the Democratic coalition, and it registered an increase in support for Biden at 56 percent to Trump's 40 percent. This was an improvement from the levels of support garner by Clinton at 51 percent to Trump's 42 percent in 2016. The bottom line is that Biden was able to win various Democratic-oriented groups, and expand margins over Clinton's, and this contributed to his election win.

Moving to gender, scholars and the media have long been concerned about gender gaps in political preferences and understanding.[44] [45] The gender gap, or differences in how men and women vote, exists in elections. Gender has attracted media and scholarly attention since the election of Ronald Reagan in 1980. Beginning in 1980, differences seemed more apparent between men and women on party identification, presidential job approval, issues, and candidate choice. There is a tendency of men overall to be more Republican and women more Democratic. On issues, women are less inclined than men to favor the use of force in foreign policy and to express more support for domestic issues like education, health care, the environment, and financial support for the poor. In presidential elections, men have been more supportive of Republican candidates than have women.[46]

The gender gap was similar for Biden in 2020 as it had been for Clinton in 2016. Clinton lost men 41 percent to Trump's 52 percent but won women 54 percent to Trump's 41 percent. Biden lost men 45 percent to Trump's 53 percent but won women 57 percent to Trump's 42 percent. A similarly important marital gap is also manifest in recent elections, with Republican candidates like Trump winning married voters 53 percent to Biden's 46 percent. Biden, however, carried unmarried voters 58 percent to Trump's 40 percent.

A further consideration is a race and ethnicity by gender, as such a data disaggregation captures a more complex gender reality. Table 10.5 contains data from 2016 and 2020 but disaggregates the data by white men, white women, Latino men, Latina women, black men, and black women. White men and white women preferred Trump in both elections, with white males registering higher levels of support for Trump at 62 percent compared to women at 52 percent in the 2016 election compared to 61 percent male and 55 percent

Table 10.5.   Presidential Vote in 2016 and 2020 by Race and Gender (%)

Category	*2016 (%)*			*2020 (%)*		
	% of 2016 Total Vote	*Biden*	*Trump*	*% of 2020 Total Vote*	*Clinton*	*Trump*
White Men	34	31	62	35	38	61
White Women	37	43	52	32	44	55
Latino Men	5	63	32	5	59	36
Latina Women	6	69	25	8	69	30
Black Men	5	82	13	4	79	19
Black Women	7	94	4	8	90	9

Sources: Numbers retrieved December 28, 2020 from *https://www.cnn.com/election/2016/results/exit-polls* and *https://www.cnn.com/election/2020/exit-polls/president/national-results*.

Republican female support in 2020. Latina women preferred the Democratic candidate more than did Latino men in 2016 (69 percent to 63 percent) and 2020 (69 percent to 59 percent). Black women supported the Democratic candidate more so than did men in 2016 (94 percent to 82 percent) and 2020 (90 percent to 79 percent). The race divisions are clear, and the overall pattern in all three racial categories is that women are less likely to vote Republican than men.

CONCLUSION

In 2020, Democrat Joe Biden reclaimed the White House from Republican Donald Trump. The Democrats failed to retain the presidency in 2016. The 2016 presidential race resulted in a surprising victory for Trump as Clinton had led in the polls throughout September and October with Trump reducing her margins and finally coming close to parity by the day of the election. The accuracy of public opinion data was brought into question following the November 3, 2020 election as most polls had inflated expectations for the Democratic candidate.[47] Although Biden won, the margins in the polls were higher than the Election Day reality. Ultimately, the 2020 general election campaign was a close race.

In addition to concerns about whether there was a possible bias in the presidential campaign surveys owing to potential systematic decisions by people to not participate in them, one limitation of the analyses presented in this chapter is that they utilize exit polling data to make inferences about candidate support. Mail-in balloting increased in 2020 owing to the pandemic. As a result, the exit poll methodology changed from 2016 to 2020.[48] This limitation should be kept in mind as one reflects on the meaning of the results.

The unusual circumstances of the presidential campaign being held during a global pandemic and people being concerned about the U.S. handling of the problem appeared to widen the path for Joe Biden's victory. Most presidential campaigns with incumbent candidates involve public reflection of the president's ability to lead and how that leadership has affected them. Usually, that reflection centers on the economy, but in 2020 it appeared to involve not only the economy but public health and safety as well. The public was highly polarized going into 2020, and partisans managed to eke out additional partisan support for their side over already highly polarized numbers from 2016. Biden appeared to make inroads with members of the public who were Independents and who had supported Trump in 2016 but changed their tune in 2020 and supported Biden by a 13 percent margin. Had the pandemic not occurred, the outcome might have been different. Elections are based on the conditions that exist, not the conditions that candidates wish them to be. Under extreme conditions of public duress, Joe Biden became the 46th president, having won both the popular and the electoral vote.

Epilogue

As noted in the preface, this collection of essays focused only on elements during the traditional phases of a presidential campaign from surfacing, nomination, conventions, and general campaign ending on Election Day. Of course, it is virtually impossible to talk about the 2020 presidential campaign without acknowledging the postcampaign period, the events of January 6, and the ramifications for literally the future of our democracy. This manuscript goes into publication in the short shadow of the siege of the Capitol. Each day there are new questions raised and revelations of the motives, actors, and actions of that day. It will literally take weeks and months to begin to more fully understand what happened, why or how could it happen, and the troubling implications. While we may be horrified by the assault upon our Capitol and our democracy, sadly, we should not be surprised. As noted in the preface, Pew Research Center reported that 90 percent of Biden's supporters and 89 percent of Trump's supporters postelection indicated there would be "lasting harm" to America if the other candidate won the election.[1] And, Rasmussen found 24 percent of likely voters view Biden voters as America's greatest enemy and 22 percent view Trump voters as our largest enemy.[2] Note that those numbers are tied with China and much greater than Russia or North Korea.

In 2017, Ben Voth and I authored a book titled *Social Fragmentation and the Decline of Democracy in America: The End of the Social Contract*.[3] We noted the emergence of "anger" during the 1990s and the crisis of trust in government and politicians. Americans were reporting the highest levels of alienation in our nation's history. In the aftermath of the 2000 presidential election, we became a "red" versus "blue" nation. For two decades, the polarization of the nation deepened across political ideology, race, gender, class, and even geography. We continue to witness a decay of our culture in terms of rather fundamental beliefs, attitudes, and values. As public cynicism and distrust toward government and politics grow, there are parallel concerns about the ever-increasing coarseness and rudeness of our culture. As a society, it seems to be have collectively become more self-centered, entitled, selfish, and independent. We would argue that the balkanization of America has resulted in the decline of the "social contract" and hence very basic prerequisites and assumptions of democracy.

Our contract with the government must inherently be based on trust. A government "of the people, by the people, and for the people" means that the common good would prevail. We expect the government to be fair, just, and operate in the interests of all citizens. Today, it appears that we no longer trust government, corporations, various civic, or public institutions . . . or even each other. For too many Americans, our "social contract" has become null and void. From a 30,000-foot view, it appears we are in a mental state of psychological egoism—all interest is self-interest. Thus, the intensity of the fragmentation and polarization were decades in the making and appears to be getting worse. Sadly, for me, I do not see an easy or even an obvious path toward unification or even interest in seeking common ground or much less agreement on transcending democratic, American values.

Simultaneously, we have also witnessed the emergence of partisan media. As noted in chapter 6, political beliefs, attitudes, and values correlate to media choices as sources of news and information. Information bubbles reinforce political views (however extreme they may be) and determine perceptions and even what we believe to be true (knowledge). This is a systemic issue in today's media environment and a threat to democracy. Audience determines success or failure. How to generate and retain audiences in a fragmented media environment demands going "vertical" in programing to include news and information. How ironic that such a multitude of sources available for information has made us by every measure less politically knowledgeable or tolerant.

As social media and associated platforms continue to grow and dominate as sources of political information and action, polarization and fragmentation will intensify and so will radicalize perspectives. Issues of access, free speech, and censorship are real and clearly impact the foundations of a democracy.

The practice of contemporary journalism is at a crossroads. The distinction between news and opinion has largely evaporated. To become an informed citizen requires more than information, and it requires understanding. Instant journalism seldom provides sufficient context to enhance understanding. Certainly, the public needed to understand what constitutes "voter fraud" and the types and frequency of "voting irregularities." What were the allegations and content of all the personal "affidavits"? What were the issues related to the

court challenges? And rejections? What happened at the Capitol? Insurrec-
tion, attempted coup, rebellion, revolution, or a riot? Those who participated,
are they rioters, protesters, patriots, thugs, domestic terrorists, or murders?
Many of the same questions could be asked about the events during the racial
unrest during the summer of 2020. Do the characterizations and labels make
a difference? Of course, they do. And, all these terms were used by "journalists" without making distinctions or providing context or, from my viewpoint,
enhancing understanding.

Many claimed to be just reporting the "facts." But it is not that simple. If
I have three ounces of water in a six-ounce glass, we can easily agree on the
amount of three ounces and the volume of six ounces. Of course, the critical
question or conclusion is whether or not the glass is half empty or half full.
The facts are the same, but the beliefs, actions, and responses would differ
greatly depending upon the conclusion. And, I fear we are at a point where
there is no agreement to or trust on what are *the* "facts." I would hope that
the role of journalism would help folks understand the differences and implications, views, actions, or behavior beyond the facts. I think the practice of
journalism is very much part of our social problems today. We continue to
proclaim that a free press is essential to a democracy to provide the forum
for the exchange of ideas and to keep the public well informed to enhance
civic decision-making. The contemporary practice of journalism is failing
this nation.

A democratic government is a reflection of its citizens. And, the values
of the citizens will be reflected in the behaviors of elected officials and
government. Our body politic is fractured in many ways. There are important and systemic issues we must address. I think we are at a critical point
in our republic. I am encouraging a broader view and perspective. The last
four to five years are just a reflection and culmination of decades of political, cultural, and social fragmentation. In many ways, Trump is not "the"
or "an issue," either good or bad. He is merely a symptom of the state of
our polity. I am certainly not suggesting the demise of our nation. I am suggesting that we need a national recommitment to the core principles of the
American experiment. Although we remain divided, appeals and messages
must be grounded in the principles that created and defined America. They
are there in the Declaration of Independence and in the Constitution. We need
an understanding and some agreement on the fundamental values essential to
our nation. And, civic responsibility and initiative should once again become
a keystone of social life. Whether we like it or not, as Americans, we do
have a "social contract" with one another. We can negotiate the terms of the
contract, perhaps, but we are boned and bound together based upon national
values.

Ben Voth and I ended our volume by sharing a quote from Abraham Lincoln in an address to Congress on the challenges of a divided union:

> The dogmas of the quiet past are inadequate to the stormy present. The occasion is piled high with difficulty, and we must rise with the occasion. As our case is new, so we must think anew and act anew. . . . *We know how to save the Union. The world knows we do know how to save it. We—even we here—hold the power, and bear the responsibility.*[4]

Notes

ACKNOWLEDGMENTS

1. James David Barber, *The Pulse of Politics* (New York: W.W. Norton, 1980), 3.
2. John Gramlich, "20 Striking Findings From 2020," Pew Research Center, December 11, 2020, https://www.pewresearch.org/ft_20-12-09_strikingfindings/, retrieved December 12, 2020.
3. Ibid.
4. Rasmussen Reports, "Voters See Each Other as America's Enemy," December 1, 2020, https://www.rasmussenreports.com/public_content/politics/general_politics/november_2020/voters_see_each_other_as_america_s_enemy, retrieved December 2, 2020.
5. Bruce Gronbeck, "Functions of Presidential Campaign," in *Political Persuasion in Presidential Campaigns*, ed. Lawrence Devlin (New Brunswick, NJ: Transaction Books, 1987), 496.

CHAPTER 1

1. Judith S. Trent, "Presidential Surfacing: The Ritualistic and Crucial First Act," *Communication Monographs* 45 (1978): 282, doi: 10.1080/03637757809375974.
2. For more on rhetorical transactions in campaigns, see Craig Allen Smith, *Presidential Campaign Communication*, 2nd ed. (Cambridge: Polity, 2015), 66–68.
3. Trent, "Presidential Surfacing," 285–286.
4. Ibid., 282.
5. Lloyd F. Bitzer, "The Rhetorical Situation," *Philosophy and Rhetoric* 1 (1968): 1–14. http://jstor.org/stable/40237697 and "Functional Communication: A Situational Perspective," in *Rhetoric in Transition: Studies in the Nature and Uses of Rhetoric*, ed. Eugene E. White (University Park: Pennsylvania State University Press, 1980), 21–38.

6. Trent, "Presidential Surfacing," 283.

7. Ibid., 285–286.

8. Ibid., 283–285.

9. Ibid., 286.

10. Smith, *Presidential Campaign Communication*, 44–70.

11. Ibid., 217–225.

12. See, e.g., Maxwell E. McCombs, Donald L. Shaw, and David H. Weaver, "New Directions in Agenda-Setting Theory and Research," *Mass Communication and Society* 17:6 (2014): 781–802, doi: 10.1080/15205436.2014.964871 and Dietram Scheufele and David Tewksbury, "Framing, Agenda Setting and Priming: The Evolutions of Three Media Effects Models," *Journal of Communication* 57 (2007): 9–20, doi: 10.1111/j.0021–9916.2007.00326.x.

13. See Brian Rosenwald, *Talk Radio's America: How an Industry Took over a Political Party That Took over the United States* (Cambridge, MA: Harvard, 2019), 13–20; Natalie Jomini Stroud, *Niche News: The Politics of News Choice* (New York: Oxford, 2011); Diana C. Mutz, *In-Your-Face Politics: The Consequences of Uncivil Media* (Princeton, NJ: Princeton, 2015); Dannagal Goldthwaite Young, *Irony and Outrage: The Polarized Landscape of Rage, Fear, and Laughter in the United States* (New York: Oxford, 2020).

14. Gallup's polls can be searched at https://news.gallup.com/poll/1675/most-important-problem.aspx.

15. Pew studies can be searched at https://www.pewresearch.org.

16. Trent, "Presidential Surfacing," 286.

17. Ibid., 286.

18. Ibid., 283–287 and Smith, *Presidential Campaign Communication*, 19–27.

19. The presidential campaigns quarterly funding reports can be found at https://www.fec.gov/data/candidates/president/?election_year=2020&cycle=2020&election_full=true.

20. 538.com, "The 2020 Endorsement Primary," *FiveThirtyEight.com* (April 8, 2020), https://projects.fivethirtyeight.com/2020-endorsements/democratic-primary/.

21. Because of the great number of candidate polls, each with its own margin for error, it is safer to discuss the rolling average of polls. This chapter relied upon the rolling averages compiled by RealClearPolitics as "Democratic Presidential Polls," RealClearPolitics (2018–2020), https://www.realclearpolitics.com/epolls/2020/president/us/2020_democratic_presidential_nomination-6730.html.

22. "Republican Delegate Rules, 2020," *Ballotpedia*, 1–2, accessed October 7, 2019, https://ballotpedia.org/Republican_delegate_rules_2020.

23. For an earlier use see Craig Allen Smith, "Setting the Stage: Three Dimensions of Surfacing for 2016," in *The 2016 US Presidential Campaign: Political Communication and Practice*, ed. Robert E. Denton (Palgrave Macmillan, 2017) 3–25, doi: 10.1007/978-3-319-52599-0_1.

24. Russell Berman, "The DNC Isn't Apologizing for Its Debate Rules," *The Atlantic* (June 13, 2019), accessed June 25, 2019 https://www.theatlantic.com/politics/archive/2019/06/democratic-debate-rules/591550/.

25. Reid J. Epstein and Matt Stevens, "Democratic Debate Rules Will Make It Harder to Get Onstage," *The New York Times* (October 2, 2019), accessed November 5, 2019 https://www.nytimes.com/2019/09/23/us/politics/democratic-debate-criteria.html.

26. Amina Dunn, "Trump's Approval Ratings So Far Are Unusually Stable and Deeply Partisan," *Pew Research Center FacTank: News in the Numbers* (August 24, 2020), accessed September 15, 2020, https://www.pewresearch.org/fact-tank/2020/08/24/trumps-approval-ratings-so-far-are-unusually-stable-and-deeply-partisan/.

27. Michael Smith and Lydia Saad, "Economy Top Problem in a Crowded Field," *Gallup* (December 19, 2016), accessed June 10, 2020, https://news.gallup.com/poll/200105/economy-top-problem-crowded-field.aspx.

28. Ibid.

29. Lydia Saad, "Government Ranks as Top U.S. Problem for Third Year," *Gallup* (December 27, 2019), accessed June 10, 2020, https://news.gallup.com/poll/273110/government-ranks-top-problem-third-year.aspx.

30. Ibid.

31. Ibid.

32. Amy Mitchell, Mark Jurkowitz, J. Baxter Oliphant, and Elisa Shearer, "Americans Who Mainly Get Their News on Social Media Are Less Engaged, Less Knowledgeable," Pew Research Center (July 30, 2020), accessed September 16, 2020, https://www.journalism.org/2020/07/30/americans-who-mainly-get-their-news-on-social-media-are-less-engaged-less-knowledgeable/.

33. Elizabeth Grieco, "Americans' Main Sources for Political News Vary by Party and Age," *Pew Research Center FacTank* (April 1, 2020), accessed October 25, 2020, https://www.pewresearch.org/fact-tank/2020/04/01/americans-main-sources-for-political-news-vary-by-party-and-age/.

34. Mark Jurkowitz, Amy Mitchell, Elisa Shearer, and Mason Walker, "U.S. Media Polarization and the 2020 Election: A Nation Divided," Pew Research Center (January 24, 2020), accessed June 24, 2020, https://www.journalism.org/2020/01/24/u-s-media-polarization-and-the-2020-election-a-nation-divided/.

35. Incumbents is used here to refer to sitting presidents, whether or not they had been personally elected.

36. Dunn, "Trump's Approval Ratings."

37. Jennifer Agiesta, "CNN Poll: More See Trump Win Likely as Biden Leads Crowded Democratic Field," *CNN.com* (October 14, 2018), accessed May 17, 2020, https://amp.cnn.com/cnn/2018/10/14/politics/cnn-poll-trump-biden-bernie-sanders-2020/index.html.

38. All references to announcements and withdrawals are to https://ballotpedia.org/Timeline_of_announcements_in_the_presidential_election,_2020.

39. Benjamin Siegel and Soo Rin Kim, "Mike Bloomberg Spent More than $1 Billion on Four-month Presidential Campaign According to Filing," *ABC News* (April 4, 2020), accessed September 16, 2020, https://abcnews.go.com/Politics/mike-bloomberg-spent-billion-month-presidential-campaign-filing/story?id=70252435.

40. Agiesta, "CNN Poll."

41. Ibid.

42. "Elizabeth Is Fighting to . . . [JUMP TO ALL PLANS]," *Warren Democrats* (2020), accessed December 4, 2020), https://elizabethwarren.com/PLANS.

43. Craig Allen Smith, "The Iowa Caucuses and Super Tuesday Primaries Reconsidered: How Untenable Hypotheses Enhance the Campaign Melodrama," *Presidential Studies Quarterly* 22 (1992): 519–529, accessed December 4, 2020, http://www.jstor.org/stable/27550994.

44. Susan Davis, "Joe Biden Gets Boost with Endorsement of Influential South Carolina Democrat," *NPR: Politics* (February 26, 2020), accessed June 17, 2020, https://www. npr.org/2020/02/26/808856350/clyburn-endorses-biden-ahead-of-south-carolina-primary.

45. RealClearPolitics, "Polls: Democratic Presidential Nomination."

CHAPTER 2

1. For a detailed discussion, see Marty Cohen, et al., *The Party Decides: Presidential Nominations before and after Reform* (Chicago: University of Chicago Press, 2008).

2. Tammy R. Vigil, "National Conventions: Evolving Functions and Forms," in *Political Campaign Communication: Theory, Method, and Practice*, Robert E. Denton Jr., ed. (Lanham, MD: Lexington Books, 2017), 343–363; Tammy R. Vigil, *Connecting with Constituents: Identification Building and Blocking in Contemporary National Convention Addresses* (Lanham, MD: Lexington Books, 2015).

3. Not using the term "constitutive" but suggesting this approach is Thomas B. Farrell, "Political Conventions as Legitimation Ritual," *Communication Monographs* 45.4 (1978), 293–306.

4. For a fuller discussion, see Theodore F. Sheckels, "Orchestrating 'The Show': The 2016 Political Party Conventions in Historical Context," in *Political Campaign Communication: Theory, Method, and Practice*, ed. Robert F. Denton Jr. (Lanham, MD: Lexington Books, 2017), 327–342.

5. For a fuller discussion, see Theodore F. Sheckels, *The Rhetoric of the American Political Party Conventions, 1948–2016* (Lanham, MD: Lexington Books, 2020).

6. Sheckels, "Orchestrating," 327–342.

7. See Geoffrey Skelley, "Trump May Have Gotten a Convention Bounce, But It's Very Slight and May Already Be Fading," *FiveThirtyEight*, September 2, 2020, https://fivethirtyeight.com/features.

8. On the keynote as a genre, see Paul A. Barefield, "Republican Keynoters," *Speech Monographs* 37.4 (1970), 232–240; Edwin A. Miles, "The Keynote Speech at National Nominating Conventions," *Quarterly Journal of Speech* 46.1 (1960), 26–32; for discussions of specific keynotes, see David A. Frank and Mark L. McPhail, "Barack Obama's Address to the 2004 Democratic National Convention: Trauma, Compromise, Consilience, and the (Im)possibility of Racial Reconciliation," *Rhetoric & Public Affairs* 8.4 (2005), 571–593; Jerry K. Frye and Franklin B. Krohn, "An Analysis of Barbara Jordan's 1976 Keynote Address," *Journal of Applied Communication Research* 5.2 (1977), 73–83; David D. Henry, "The Rhetorical Dynamics of Mario Cuomo's 1984 Keynote Address: Situation, Speaker, Metaphor," *Southern Journal of Communication* 53.1 (1988), 105–120; Brian T. Kaylor, "A New Law: The Covenant Speech of Barbara Jordan," *Southern Journal of Communication* 77.1 (2012), 10–23; Sara Newell and Thomas R. King, "The Keynote Address of the Democratic National Convention, 1972: The Evolution of a Speech," *Southern Journal of Communication* 39 (1974), 346–358. For a discussion of the possible "death" of the

genre, see Theodore F. Sheckels, "The Keynotes of the 2016 Political Conventions: The Death of a Genre?" *American Behavioral Scientist* 61.4 (2017), 401–413.

9. Jeremy Barr, "Convention Ratings Favor the Democrats," *The Washington Post*, August 29, 2020, C1, 4.

10. Ibid.

11. Sheckels, "Orchestrating," 327–342.

12. In the convention rhetoric of First Ladies, see Tammy R. Vigil, "Feminine Views in the Feminine Style: Convention Speeches by Presidential Nominees' Spouses," *Southern Journal of Communication* 79.4 (2014), 327–346; more generally on women speaking at the conventions is Elizabeth A. Petre, "Understanding Epideictic Purpose as Invitational Rhetoric in Women's Political Convention Speeches," *Kaleidoscope: A Graduate Journal of Qualitative Communication Research* 6 (2007), 21–37.

13. On Fear appeals, see J. L. Hale and J. P. Dillard, "Fear Appeals in Health Promotion Campaigns: Too Much, Too Little, or Just Right?" in *Designing Health Messages: Approaches from Communication Theory and Public Health Practices*, eds. E. Maibach and R. L. Parrott (Thousand Oaks, CA: Sage, 1995), 65–80; K. Witte and M. Allen, "A Meta-analysis of Fear Appeals: Implications for Effective Public Health Campaigns," *Health Education & Behavior* 27.5 (2000), 591–615.

14. On nomination acceptance speeches as a genre, see William L. Benoit, "Acclaiming, Attacking, and Defending in Presidential Nomination Acceptance Speeches, 1960–1996," *Quarterly Journal of Speech* 85.3 (1997), 247–268; Sharon E. Jarvis, "Campaigning Alone: Partisan Versus Personal Language in Presidential Nominating Convention Acceptance Addresses, 1948–2000," *American Behavioral Scientist* 44.12 (2001), 2152–2172; Martin J. Medhurst, "The Acceptance Address: Presidential Speechwriting, 1932–2008," in *The President's Words: Speeches and Speechwriting in the Modern White House*, eds. Michael Nelson and Russell L. Riley (Lawrence, KS: University Press of Kansas, 2010), 21–40; David B. Valley, *A History and Analysis of the Democratic Presidential Nomination Acceptance Speeches to 1968* (Lanham, MD: University Press of America, 1988).

15. Sheckels, *The Rhetoric*, op cit.

16. See Megan McArdle, "What Changes after COVID-19? I'm Betting on Everything," *The Washington Post*, December 1, 2020, A23.

CHAPTER 3

1. Jurgen Habermas, *Communication and the Evolution of Society* (Boston: Beacon Press, 1979).

2. "Presidential Debates in History," *Bill of Rights Institute*, https://billofrightsinstitute.org/educate/educator-resources/lessons-plans/presidents-constitution/presidential-debates-in-history/, retrieved December 10, 2020.

3. Lydia Saad, "Presidential Debates Rarely Game-Changers But Have Moved Voter Preferences in Several Elections," *Gallup*, September 25, 2008, http://www.gallup.com/poll/110674/Presidential-Debates-Rarely-GameChangers.aspx.

4. Mitchell McKinney and Ben Warner, "Do Presidential Debates Matter? Examining a Decade of Campaign Debate Effects," *Argumentation and Advocacy* 49 (Spring 2013), 245–246.

5. Ed Hinck, "Introduction," Televised Presidential Debates (Santa Barbara, California: Praeger, 2019).

6. Erin Schaff, "Next Democratic Debate Will Have 12 Candidates Onstage, the Most Ever," *The New York Times*, October 2, 2019, https://www.nytimes.com/2019/10/02/business/media/october-democratic-debate.html?fbclid=IwAR0OfwVs1yvkzasnlsJ6asbfFRcy-WgfsRbtkOdEpO-SodNauj7D1HRhUbc.

7. Marisa Schultz, "CNN Drops Brazile for Feeding Debate Questions to Clinton," *The New York Post*, October 31, 2016, https://nypost.com/2016/10/31/cnn-drops-brazile-for-feeding-debate-questions-to-clinton/.

8. Javier Zarracina, Karina Zaiets, and Carlie Procell, "Last Night Trump Biden Debate Recap Interruptions Speaking Time," *USA Today*, October 23, 2020, https://www.usatoday.com/in-depth/news/2020/10/23/last-night-trump-biden-debate-recap-interruptions-speaking-time/3733474001/.

9. Javier Zarracina, Karina Zaiets, and Carlie Procell, "Last Night Trump Biden Debate Recap Interruptions Speaking Time," *USA Today*, October 23, 2020, https://www.usatoday.com/in-depth/news/2020/10/23/last-night-trump-biden-debate-recap-interruptions-speaking-time/3733474001/.

10. CBS DFW, "17 States Join Texas in General Election Supreme Court Lawsuit against Four Swing States," December 10, 2020, https://www.msn.com/en-us/news/us/17-states-join-texas-in-general-election-supreme-court-lawsuit-against-4-swing-states/ar-BB1bNkWB.

11. Cydney Henderson, "C-SPAN Suspends Steve Scully after Admits Lie Twitter Hack," *USA Today*, October 15, 2020, https://www.usatoday.com/story/entertainment/tv/2020/10/15/c-span-suspends-steve-scully-after-admits-lie-twitter-hack/3670507001/.

12. Javier Zarracina, Karina Zaiets, and Carlie Procell, "Last Night Trump Biden Debate Recap Interruptions Speaking Time," *USA Today*, October 23, 2020, https://www.usatoday.com/in-depth/news/2020/10/23/last-night-trump-biden-debate-recap-interruptions-speaking-time/3733474001/.

13. League of Women Voters, "The League of Women Voters and Candidate Debates: A Changing Relationship," https://www.lwv.org/league-women-voters-and-candidate-debates-changing-relationship, retrieved November 13, 2020.

14. *Reuters*, "More than 80 Million Viewers Watched First Presidential Debate," *Time*, September 27, 2016, https://time.com/4510349/80-million-viewers-presidential-debate/.

15. Timothy McNulty, "Outrageous Debate Question Angers Kitty Dukakkis," *Chicago Tribune*, October 15, 1988, https://www.chicagotribune.com/news/ct-xpm-1988-10-15-8802070550-story.html.

16. Ben Voth, "Presidential Debates," in *Studies of Communication in the 2012 Presidential Campaign*, ed. Robert E. Denton Jr. (Lanham, MD: Lexington Books, 2014).

17. Jeremy Barr, "Chris Wallace Says He Wants to Be 'Invisible' as Debate Moderator. Will Trump Let Him?" *The Washington Post*, September 29, 2020, https://www.washingtonpost.com/media/2020/09/29/chris-wallace-debate-trump/.

18. Voth, "Presidential Debates."

19. Ben Voth, "Presidential Debates," in *The 2016 US Presidential Campaign*, ed. Robert E. Denton Jr. (Lanham, MD: Lexington Books, 2017).

20. Joe Concha, "Trump Town Hall Moderator Guthrie's Performance Praised, Slammed on Twitter," *The Hill*, October 16, 2020, https://thehill.com/homenews/media/521379-trump-town-hall-moderator-guthries-performance-praised-slammed-on-twitter.

21. Ben Voth, "It's Time to Reform How Presidential Debates Go," *American Thinker*, October 3, 2020, https://www.americanthinker.com/articles/2020/10/its_time_to_reform_how_presidential_debates_go.html.

22. National Archives, "Presidential Libraries," https://www.archives.gov/presidential-libraries, retrieved December 13, 2020.

23. Jeffrey Martin, "Former Presidential Candidate Bob Dole Calls Debate Commission Biased GOP Members Don't Support," *Newsweek*, October 9, 2020, https://www.newsweek.com/former-presidential-candidate-bob-dole-calls-debate-commission-biased-gop-members-dont-support-1537976.

24. Ibid.

25. Rachel Nuwer, "Presidential Debates Have Shockingly Little Effect on Election Outcomes," *Scientific American*, October 9, 2020, https://www.scientificamerican.com/article/presidential-debates-have-shockingly-little-effect-on-election-outcomes/.

26. "National Exit Poll: President," *ABC News*, 2020, https://abcnews.go.com/Elections/exit-polls-2020-us-presidential-election-results-analysis.

27. Ben Voth, *Debate as Global Pedagogy: Rwanda Rising* (Lanham, Maryland, Lexington Books, 2021).

28. Frank Newport, "What We Learned from the People in the 2016 Election," *Gallup*, July 17, 2020, https://news.gallup.com/opinion/polling-matters/315890/learned-people-2016-election.aspx.

29. Jurgen Habermas, *Communication and the Evolution of Society* (Boston: Beacon Press, 1979).

CHAPTER 4

1. Arne Holst, "Comparison of Average Daily In-Home Data Usage in the United States by Device Type in March 2019 and March 2020," *Statista*, March 2020, https://www.statista.com/statistics/1106863/covid-19-daily-in-home-data-usage-change-us-2020/.

2. "Political Cycle in Review," *AdImpact*, November 10, 2020, https://adimpact.com/download-the-political-cycle-in-review/.

3. Howard Homonoff, "2020 Political Ad Spending Exploded: Did It Work?" *Forbes*, December 8, 2020, https://www.forbes.com/sites/howardhomonoff/2020/12/08/2020-political-ad-spending-exploded-did-it-work/?sh=38f77e7e3ce0. "Political Cycle in Review," *AdImpact*, November 10, 2020, https://adimpact.com/download-the-political-cycle-in-review/.

4. Ibid., para 2.

5. Ibid.

6. Ibid.

7. Ibid.

8. Brian Schwartz, "Pro-Trump Super PAC America First Action Raised over $42 Million in September," *CNBC*, October 20, 2020, https://www.cnbc.com/2020/10/20/pro-trump-super-pac-america-first-action-raised-over-42-million-in-september.html.

9. Lynda Lee Kaid, "Political Advertising," *Handbook of Political Communication Research*, ed. Lynda Lee Kaid (Mahwah, NJ: Lawrence Erlbaum Associates, 2004), 156.

10. Lynda Lee Kaid and Anne Johnston, *Videostyle in Presidential Campaigns: Style and Content of Televised Political Advertising* (Westport, CT: Praeger, 2001), 1.

11. Sara Morrison, "Why Are You Seeing This Digital Political Ad? No One Knows!" *Vox*, September 29, 2020, https://www.vox.com/recode/2020/9/29/21439824/online-digital-political-ads-facebook-google.

12. Tobias Konitzer, David Rothschild, Shawndra Hill, and Kenneth C. Wilbur, "Using Big Data and Algorithms to Determine the Effect of Geographically Targeted Advertising on Vote Intention: Evidence from the 2012 U.S. Presidential Election," *Political Communication* 36 (2019), 12–13.

13. Robert E. Denton Jr., Judith S. Trent, and Robert V. Friedenberg, *Political Campaign Communication: Principles & Practices* (Lanham, MD: Rowman & Littlefield, 2020), 125.

14. Kaid and Johnston, *Videostyle in Presidential Campaigns*, 110; Kaid, "Political Advertising," 163.

15. Kaid and Johnston, *Videostyle in Presidential Campaigns*, 117.

16. Cayce Myers, "Campaign Finance and Its Impact in the 2016 Presidential Campaign," in *The 2016 US Presidential Campaign: Political Communication and Practice*, ed. Robert E. Denton Jr. (Cham, Switzerland: Palgrave Macmillan, 2017), 265.

17. Federal Election Commission, "Contribution Limits," Federal Election Commission, accessed December 28, 2020, https://www.fec.gov/help-candidates-and-committees/candidate-taking-receipts/contribution-limits/.

18. Patrick C. Meirick, "Political Knowledge and Sponsorship in Backlash from Party- and Candidate-Sponsored Attacks," *Communication Reports* 18.2 (October 2005): 79, http://doi.org/10.1080/0893421050030967.

19. John C. Tedesco and Scott W. Dunn, "Political Advertising in the 2016 U.S. Presidential Election: Ad Hominem, Ad Nauseam," *American Behavioral Scientist* 63. 7 (2019), 942.

20. Ibid.

21. Erika Franklin Fowler and Travis N. Ridout, "Negative, Angry, and Ubiquitous: Political Advertising in 2012," *The Forum* 10.4, February 9, 2013, 58–89.

22. Denton, Trent, and Friedenberg, *Political Campaign Communication*, 125–126.

23. Richard Joslyn, "Political Advertising and the Meaning of Elections," in *New Perspectives on Political Advertising*, ed. Lynda Lee Kaid, Dan Nimmo, and Keith R. Sanders (Carbondale: Southern Illinois University Press, 1986), 161.

24. Denton, Trent, and Friedenberg, *Political Campaign Communication*, 131.

25. Kaid and Johnston, *Videostyle in Presidential Campaigns*, 41; Kaid, "Political Advertising," 162.

26. Tedesco and Dunn, "Political Advertising in the 2016 U.S. Presidential Election," 942.

27. Ibid.

28. Ibid., 944–945.

29. Ibid.

30. Kaid, "Political Advertising," *Handbook*, 164.

31. Lydia Saad, "Trump and Clinton Finish with Historically Poor Images," *Gallup*, November 8, 2016, https://news.gallup.com/poll/197231/trump-clinton-finish-historically-poor-images.aspx.

32. Tony Romm, "Political Ads Are Flooding Hulu, Roku and Other Streaming Services, Revealing Loopholes in Federal Election Laws," *The Washington Post*, February 20, 2020, https://www.washingtonpost.com/technology/2020/02/20/hulu-roku-political-ads-streaming/.

33. Joe Biden, "Ser Humano," YouTube video, 0:30, November 1, 2020, https://www.youtube.com/watch?app=desktop&v=lSxpV9JeI8M.

34. Joe Biden, "It's about Us," YouTube video, 0:34, September 29, 2020, https://www.youtube.com/watch?app=desktop&v=mB_dyuReekw.

35. Joe Biden, "Rising," YouTube video, 1:00, October 27, 2020, https://www.youtube.com/watch?app=desktop&v=PDJWvAKZWqQ.

36. Joe Biden, "Personal," YouTube video, 1:00, September 3, 2020, https://www.youtube.com/watch?app=desktop&v=4WMRz5fmgIw.

37. See Tedesco and Dunn, "Political Advertising in the 2016 U.S. Presidential Election," for an analysis of Trump's 2016 ads, which used this formula frequently.

38. Joe Biden, "Empty Chairs in America Because of COVID-19," YouTube video, 1:37, October 25, 2020, https://www.youtube.com/watch?app=desktop&v=bDRXt4o84Fo.

39. Joe Biden, "Vote For," YouTube video, 0:30, October 14, 2020, https://www.youtube.com/watch?app=desktop&v=BPOYVQhAuto.

40. I-Hsien Sherwood, "Nina Simone Brings Soulful Optimism to Biden Ad Asking Citizens to Vote for Respect, Honor, Decency," *Ad Age*, October 15, 2020, https://adage.com/creativity/work/joe-biden-president-i-will-vote/2288036.

41. Joe Biden, "Chris Paul and Joe Biden," YouTube video, 1:10, October 27, 2020, https://www.youtube.com/watch?app=desktop&v=Asrnd5MaLK0.

42. Joe Biden, "Michelle Obama: 'Vote like Your Life Depends on It,'" YouTube video, 1:21, October 19, 2020, https://www.youtube.com/watch?app=desktop&v=LZ_YlTThaOc.

43. Joe Biden, "We Need Your Vote/'Dream' by Nikki Giovanni," YouTube video, 1:23, November 1, 2020, https://www.youtube.com/watch?app=desktop&v=9MvKLmW__Bs.

44. Joe Biden, "Tell You," YouTube video, 0:30, October 27, 2020, https://www.youtube.com/watch?app=desktop&v=p2GeOIOff1Q.

45. Joe Biden, "Building Back Small Businesses," YouTube video, 1:00, October 29, 2020, https://www.youtube.com/watch?app=desktop&v=6Uf-QGDhUnI.

46. Mara Liasson, "Biden Faces a Convention Test, to Offer a Vision beyond Beating Trump," *Morning Edition*, August 15, 2020, https://www.npr.

org/2020/08/15/902744637/biden-faces-a-convention-test-to-offer-a-vision-beyond-beating-trump.

47. Joe Biden, "Totally Negligent," YouTube video, 1:00, September 17, 2020, https://www.youtube.com/watch?app=desktop&v=eRictod9e7w.

48. Jack Brewster, "Democratic Convention to Feature Former Trump Voters in Unity Pitch," *Forbes*, August 10, 2020, https://www.forbes.com/sites/jackbrewster/2020/08/10/democratic-convention-to-feature-former-trump-voters-in-unity-pitch/?sh=33dfa6930753.

49. Joe Biden, "Elsie," YouTube video, 1:00, October 29, 2020, https://www.youtube.com/watch?app=desktop&v=vEV0q1SWkrs.

50. IndependenceUSA, "Somos Patriotas (English Subtitles)," YouTube video, 0:30, October 28, 2020, https://www.youtube.com/watch?app=desktop&v=AjUKU uckqus.

51. George T. Conway, III, Steve Schmidt, John Weaver, and Rick Wilson, "We Are Republicans, and We Want Trump Defeated," *The New York Times*, December 17, 2019, https://www.nytimes.com/2019/12/17/opinion/lincoln-project.html.

52. The Lincoln Project, "Imagine," YouTube video, 1:00, October 20, 2020, https://www.youtube.com/watch?app=desktop&v=_uJ9p6-Ubec.

53. Donald J. Trump, "Stronger, Safer, More Prosperous," YouTube video, 0:30, January 30, 2020, https://www.youtube.com/watch?v=m4sVnOsXIAA.

54. Donald J. Trump, "American Comeback," YouTube video, 1:00, May 3, 2020, https://www.youtube.com/watch?v=Ws66liLKGzA.

55. Donald J. Trump, "Strength," YouTube video, 1:00, October 31, 2020, https://www.youtube.com/watch?v=UZZ2VGbfoLs.

56. Donald J. Trump, "911 Police Emergency Line," iSpot.TV video, 0:30, August 22, 2020, https://www.ispot.tv/ad/njeq/Donald-j-trump-for-president-911-police-emergency-line.

57. Donald J. Trump, "Break In," YouTube video, 0:30, July 20, 2020, https://www.youtube.com/watch?v=moZOrq0qL3Q.

58. Donald J. Trump, "The Real Biden Plan," YouTube video, 0:30, October 10, 2020, https://www.youtube.com/watch?v=9WPiSLJX0So.

59. Donald J. Trump, "America Can't Afford Biden," Facebook video, 0:30, August 11, 2020, https://www.facebook.com/DonaldTrump/videos/america-cant-afford-joe-biden/1034624413645531/.

60. Donald J. Trump, "Biden Lied," YouTube video, 0:30, October 17, 2020, https://www.youtube.com/watch?v=aD9KfmrDrsY&feature=youtu.be.

61. Donald J. Trump, "Biden Corruption," YouTube video, 0:30, September 27, 2019, https://www.youtube.com/watch?v=bbixdV2F6Ts.

62. Donald J. Trump, "Why Did Joe Biden Let Hunter Do It," YouTube video0:30, October 15, 2020, https://www.youtube.com/watch?v=RGkF97pMrBM.

63. Donald J. Trump, "Donald Trump Got It Done," YouTube video, 0:30, February 2, 2020, https://www.youtube.com/watch?v=Xtv_PJE8xns.

64. Donald J. Trump, "Man of His Word," YouTube video, 1:00, n.d., https://www.ispot.tv/ad/ZQCi/donald-j-trump-for-president-charlotte.

65. America First Action, "Bad Folks," iSpot.tv video, 0:30, April 16, 2020, https://www.youtube.com/watch?v=-QoUE4Gk5PM&feature=youtu.be.

66. America First Action, "Biden Origin," YouTube video, 0:30, April 16, 2020, https://www.youtube.com/watch?v=MX5XMf69_ms&feature=emb_logo.

67. America First Action, "Forty Years," YouTube video, 0:30, April 16, 2020, https://www.youtube.com/watch?v=1_hK2qis_mU&feature=emb_logo.

68. America First Action, "China Prosperity," YouTube video, 0:30, May 1, 2020, https://www.youtube.com/watch?v=m7tHsuFA94c&feature=emb_logo.

69. America First Action, "On Hold," YouTube video, 0:30, July 24, 2020, https://www.youtube.com/watch?v=zI-TjFxQBt4.

70. America First Action, "Pandemic Tax," YouTube video, 0:30, October 8, 2020, https://www.youtube.com/watch?v=tT0f3P2lKZ0&feature=emb_logo.

71. America First Action, "Joe Biden's Tax Hike," YouTube video, 0:30, August 17, 2020, https://www.youtube.com/watch?v=SgQ0x7o7rew.

72. Preserve America, "Alyssa," iSpot.tv video, 1:00, September 1, 2020, https://www.ispot.tv/ad/nmlJ/preserve-america-pac-back-the-police.

73. Preserve America, "Gillis," iSpot.tv video, 1:00, September 1, 2020, https://www.ispot.tv/ad/nmNB/preserve-america-pac-john-gillis.

74. Preserve America, "Too Weak," iSpot.tv video, 0:30, n.d., https://www.ispot.tv/ad/nmDX/preserve-america-pac-too-weak.

75. Preserve America, "Dave," iSpot.tv video, 0:30, n.d., https://www.ispot.tv/ad/tV9g/preserve-america-pac-dave.

76. John C. Tedesco and Scott W. Dunn, "Political Advertising in the 2016 U.S. Presidential Election: Ad Hominem, Ad Nauseam," *American Behavioral Scientist* 63.7 (2019), 942.

CHAPTER 5

1. Nigel Chiwaya and Corky Siemaszko, "Covid-19 Cases, Deaths Rising Rapidly Ahead of Election Day," *NBC News*, November 2, 2020, https://www.nbcnews.com/news/us-news/covid-19-cases-deaths-rising-rapid-rate-ahead-election-day-n1245780.

2. U.S. Bureau of Labor Statistics, "The Employment Situation—October 2020," *U.S. Bureau of Labor Statistics Economic News Release*, November 6, 2020, https://www.bls.gov/news.release/archives/empsit_11062020.htm.

3. Ben Popken, "Final Jobs Report before Election Day Shows Just 661,000 Positions Were Added Last Month," *NBC News*, October 2, 2020, https://www.nbcnews.com/business/economy/final-jobs-report-election-day-shows-just-661-000-positions-n1241779.

4. *BBC*, "George Floyd: What Happened in the Final Moments of His Life?" July 16, 2020, https://www.bbc.com/news/world-us-canada-52861726.

5. Larry Buchanan, Quoctrung Bui, and Jugal K. Patel, "Black Lives Matter May Be the Largest Movement in U.S. History," *The New York Times*, July 3, 2020, https://nyti.ms/2ZqRyOU.

6. John Allen Hendricks and Robert E. Denton Jr., eds., *Communicator-In-Chief: How Barack Obama Used New Media Technology to Win the White House* (Lanham, MD: Lexington Books, 2010); John Allen Hendricks and Dan Schill, eds., *Presidential Campaigning and Social Media: An Analysis of the 2012 Campaign*

(New York: Oxford University Press, 2015); Dan Schill and John Allen Hendricks, eds., *The Presidency and Social Media: Discourse, Disruption, and Digital Democracy in the 2016 Presidential Election* (New York: Routledge, 2018).

7. Ariel Procaccia, "Social Media May Have Contributed to Record Voter Turnout in the 2020 Election," *The Washington Post*, November 27, 2020, 6–7, https://www.washingtonpost.com/opinions/2020/11/27/social-media-probably-contributed-record-voter-turnout-2020-election/.

8. John Gramlich, "10 Facts about Americans and Facebook," Pew Research Center, May 16, 2019, https://www.pewresearch.org/fact-tank/2019/05/16/facts-about-americans-and-facebook/.

9. Peter Suciu, "Social Media Could Determine the Outcome of the 2020 Election," *Forbes.com*, October 26, 2020, https://www.forbes.com/sites/petersuciu/2020/10/26/social-media-could-determine-the-outcome-of-the-2020-election/.

10. Amy Mitchell, Mark Jurkowitz, J. Baxter Oliphant, and Elisa Shearer, "Americans Who Mainly Get Their News on Social Media Are Less Engaged, Less Knowledgeable," Pew Research Center, July 30, 2020, https://www.journalism.org/2020/07/30/americans-who-mainly-get-their-news-on-social-media-are-less-engaged-less-knowledgeable/.

11. Ibid.

12. Michael Barthel, Amy Mitchell, Dorene Asare-Marfo, Courtney Kennedy, and Kirsten Worden, "Measuring News Consumption in a Digital Era," Pew Research Center, December 8, 2020, https://www.journalism.org/2020/12/08/measuring-news-consumption-in-a-digital-era/.

13. Ibid.

14. Ibid.

15. Merriam-Webster, "On 'Doomsurfing' and 'Doomscrolling,'" *Words We're Watching*, accessed December 14, 2020, https://www.merriam-webster.com/words-at-play/doomsurfing-doomscrolling-words-were-watching.

16. Elahe Izadi, "The News Is Driving You Mad. And That's Why You Can't Stop Devouring It," *The Washington Post*, October 11, 2020, https://www.washingtonpost.com/lifestyle/media/the-news-is-driving-you-mad-and-thats-why-you-cant-stop-devouring-it/2020/10/09/9fef1806-08b2-11eb-a166-dc429b380d10_story.html.

17. Anna Massoglia and Karl Evers-Hillstrom, "2020 Presidential Candidates Top $100 in Digital Ad Spending as Twitter Goes Dark," *OpenSecrets.org*, November 14, 2020, https://www.opensecrets.org/news/2019/11/digital-ad-spending-2020-presidential-candidates-top-100m/.

18. Massoglia and Evers-Hillstrom, "2020 Presidential Candidates"; Latta Nott, "Political Advertising on Social Media Platforms, "*American Bar Association*, June 26, 2020, https://www.americanbar.org/groups/crsj/publications/human_rights_magazine_home/voting-in-2020/political-advertising-on-social-media-platforms/.

19. Bill Allison and Misyrlena Egkolfopoulou, "Trump Outpaces Biden in Zeroing in on Voters with Facebook Tools," *Bloomberg*, July 13, 2020, https://www.bloomberg.com/news/articles/2020-07-13/trump-more-than-biden-is-tapping-into-facebook-targeting-tools.

20. Simon Dumenco, "Here's What Trump and Biden Have Spent on Facebook and Google Ads," *AdAge*, October 30, 2020, https://adage.com/article/campaign-trail/heres-what-trump-and-biden-have-spent-facebook-and-google-ads/2291531.

21. Ibid.

22. Daisuke Wakabayashi, Cecilia Kang and Tiffany Hsu, "Trump Campaign Will Dominate the YouTube Home Page through Election Day," *The New York Times*, October 31, 2020, https://www.nytimes.com/live/2020/10/31/us/trump-biden-election/trump-campaign-will-dominate-the-youtube-home-page-through-election-day.

23. Nick Corasaniti and Maggie Haberman, "Trump Campaign Makes Huge Digital Ad Buy During Democratic Convention," *The New York Times*, August 15, 2020, https://nyti.ms/30WSIDT.

24. Mark Bergen, "YouTube Is So Flooded with Political Ads It Can't Place Them All," *Bloomberg*, October 22, 2020, https://www.bloomberg.com/news/articles/2020-10-22/youtube-is-so-flooded-with-political-ads-it-can-t-place-them-all.

25. Ibid.

26. Emily Glazer and Michael C. Bender, "Trump Campaign Weighs Alternatives to Big Social Platforms," *The Wall Street Journal*, June 24, 2020, https://www.wsj.com/articles/trump-campaign-weighs-alternatives-to-big-social-platforms-11593003602.

27. Ibid.

28. Ibid.

29. *Wesleyan Media Project*, "Presidential General Election Ad Spending Tops $1.5 Billion," October 29, 2020, https://mediaproject.wesleyan.edu/releases-102920/.

30. Ibid.

31. Alexi McCammond, "Biden's Closing Ad Campaign," *Axios*, October 29, 2020, https://www.axios.com/biden-ad-campaign-election-day-7c225b14-b5fd-47e8-ae95-a67c5d284be3.html.

32. Sara Fischer and Alayna Treene, "Trump, Biden Strategies Revealed in Final Ad Push," *Axios*, October 27, 2020, https://www.axios.com/trump-biden-strategies-facebook-584fc2b7-32d6-4786-a1bc-2d9f41333f1f.html.

33. Brad Adgate, "Kantar Estimates 2020 Election Ads Will Cost $7 Billion," *Forbes.com*, August 11, 2020, https://www.forbes.com/sites/bradadgate/2020/08/11/2020-an-election-year-like-no-other/.

34. Kevin Roose, "Trump Still Miles Ahead of Biden in Social Media Engagement," *The New York Times*, October 22, 2020, https://nyti.ms/35lzZDa.

35. Authors' analysis of CrowdTangle data.

36. Kevin Roose, "Biden Is Losing the Internet. Does That Matter?" *The New York Times*, April 16, 2020, https://nyti.ms/2RFbHxI.

37. Social Blade, "Donald J Trump's YouTube Stats (Summary Profile)," accessed December 14, 2020, https://socialblade.com/youtube/channel/UCAql2DyGU2un 1Ei2nMYsqOA; Social Blade, "Joe Biden's YouTube Stats (Summary Profile)," accessed December 14, 2020, https://socialblade.com/youtube/channel/UCWN pXitY8eJ-ku6M-v25MKw.

38. Jane Coaston, "Trump's Presidential Campaign Is Too Online," *Vox*, October 22, 2020, https://www.vox.com/21504280/trumps-2020-campaign-too-online.

39. Tina Nguyen, "Trump's Media Favorites Battle for the Trump Trophy," *Politico*, November 14, 2020, https://www.politico.com/news/2020/11/14/trumps-media-battles-for-maga-436502.

40. Ezra Klein, "How Joe Biden, the Ultimate Insider, Defeated Donald Trump, the Ultimate Outsider," *Vox*, November 6, 2020, https://www.vox.com/21545969/joe-biden-2020-election-winner-trump-vote.

41. Allison and Egkolfopoulou, "Trump Outpaces."

42. Alexandra Jaffe and Amanda Seitz, "Trump, Biden Fight for Primacy on Social Media," *Associated Press*, July 5, 2020, https://apnews.com/article/32eb6933 d8229902f3954115529977bb.

43. Authors' analysis of CrowdTangle data.

44. Craig Timberg and Elizabeth Dwoskin, "Trump's Power on Twitter, Facebook Will Outlive His Presidency," *The Washington Post*, November 7, 2020, https://www. washingtonpost.com/technology/2020/11/06/trump-twitter-megaphone/.

45. Kate Conger, "How Twitter Policed Trump during the Election," *The New York Times*, November 6, 2020, https://nyti.ms/32h5PQA.

46. Garance Burke, "Financially Troubled Startup Helped Power Trump Campaign," *Associated Press*, November 17, 2020, https://apnews.com/article/donald-trump-coronavirus-pandemic-elections-campaigns-124d914bb082575aeec8042629 aa932c.

47. Asma Khalid and Tamara Keith, "Trump and Biden Wage an Uneven Virtual Campaign," *National Public Radio*, May 21, 2020, https://www.npr.org/2020/ 05/21/859932268/trump-and-biden-wage-an-uneven-virtual-campaign.

48. Ibid.

49. Ibid.

50. Klein, "How Joe Biden."

51. Ibid.

52. Ibid.

53. Amanda Hess, "How Fan Culture Is Swallowing Democracy," *The New York Times*, September 11, 2019, https://www.nytimes.com/interactive/2019/09/11/arts/ how-fan-culture-is-swallowing-democracy.html.

54. Roose, "Biden Is Losing."

55. Klein, "How Joe Biden."

56. Kate Knibbs, "Joe Biden Is Very Offline—and That's OK," *Wired*, October 19, 2020, https://www.wired.com/story/biden-social-media/.

57. Roose, "Biden Is Losing."

58. Neal Rothschild and Sara Fischer, "The Liberal Election Is Happening on Instagram," *Axios*, October 11, 2020, https://www.axios.com/instagram-facebook-liberal-election-1e0e1fef-364e-4857-b539-a852b892d798.html; Mark Scott, "Despite Cries of Censorship, Conservatives Dominate Social Media," *Politico*, October 26, 2020, https://www.politico.com/news/2020/10/26/censorship-conservatives-social-media-432643.

59. Authors' analysis of CrowdTangle data.

60. Rothschild and Fischer, "The Liberal Election."

61. Authors' analysis of CrowdTangle data.

62. Hans Nichols, "Biden Campaign Using Instagram to Mobilize Celebrity Supporters," *Axios*, July 6, 2020, https://www.axios.com/biden-campaign-instagram-celebrity-supporters-56d15c93-6ae4-434f-99e7-1c6c9e3397da.html.

63. Kyle Orland, "AOC Makes Explosive Twitch Debut with over 435,000 *Among Us* Viewers," *Ars Technica*, October 21, 2020, https://arstechnica.com/gaming/2020/10/ aocs-twitch-streaming-debut-attracts-over-435000-among-us-viewers/.

64. Alaa Elassar, "Joe Biden Has His Own Island on 'Animal Crossing' Where You Can Learn about His Campaign," *CNN.com*, October 18, 2020, https://www.cnn.com/2020/10/18/business/biden-animal-crossing-island-trnd/index.html.

65. Spencer Dean, "Presidential Advertising by Candidates Reveals Microtargeting Tactics on Snapchat," *Wesleyan Media Project Delta Lab*, October 28, 2020, https://deltalab.research.wesleyan.edu/2020/10/28/presidential-advertising-on-snapchat/.

66. Shane Goldmacher and Rachel Shorey, "How Joe Biden Became the Unlikeliest of Online Fund-Raising Superstars," *The New York Times*, October 14, 2020, https://nyti.ms/33U59lk.

67. Ibid.

68. Sarah Ewall-Wice, "Biden Campaign Puts Up Huge Fundraising Numbers in September," *CBS News*, October 15, 2020, https://www.cbsnews.com/news/biden-campaign-fundraising-september/.

69. Kevin Schaul, Anu Narayanswamy, Lauren Tierney, and Michelle Ye Hee Lee, "Biden Has Surged Ahead of Trump in Donors—Including in the States That Matter Most," *The Washington Post*, October 23, 2020, https://www.washingtonpost.com/graphics/2020/elections/donor-enthusiasm-biden-trump/.

70. Ewall-Wice, "Biden Campaign Puts Up"; Goldmacher and Shorey, "How Joe Biden."

71. Goldmacher and Shorey, "How Joe Biden."

72. Ewall-Wice, "Biden Campaign Puts Up."

73. Charlie Warzel, "What Facebook Fed the Baby Boomers," *The New York Times*, November 24, 2020, https://nyti.ms/3mffwXX.

74. Sara Fischer, "'Unreliable' News Sources Got More Traction in 2020," *Axios Media Trends*, December 22, 2020, https://www.axios.com/unreliable-news-sources-social-media-engagement-297bf046-c1b0-4e69-9875-05443b1dca73.html.

75. Hannah Murphy and Siddharth Venkataramakrishnan, "Conspiracy and Disinformation: America's New Politics False and Misleading Claims Have Proliferated across Platforms at Unprecedented Levels," *Financial Times*, November 13, 2020, https://www.ft.com/content/c30796ca-060d-42c0-b8e0-64e401e5193d.

76. Ibid.

77. Sara Fischer, "Conspiracies Run Rampant," *Axios Media Trends*, November 3, 2020, https://www.axios.com/newsletters/axios-media-trends-1e7d541a-5952-40b6-8a20-731c4a229aa6.html.

78. Gabby Deutch, "Tracking Facebook's Election Misinformation 'Super-Spreaders,'" *NewsGuard*, October 27, 2020, https://www.newsguardtech.com/special-report-election-misinformation/.

79. Massoglia and Evers-Hillstrom, "2020 Presidential Candidates," 12.

80. Ari Levy, Salvador Rodriguez, and Megan Graham, "Why Political Campaigns Are Flooding Facebook with Ad Dollars," *CNBC.com*, October 9, 2020, https://www.cnbc.com/2020/10/08/trump-biden-pacs-spend-big-on-facebook-as-election-nears.html.

81. Levy, Rodriguez, and Graham, "Why Political Campaigns," 10.

82. Gilad Edelman, "Social Media Drops the Hammer on Team Trump," *Wired.com*, June 29, 2020, 6, https://www.wired.com/story/twitch-reddit-hammer-team-trump-social-media/.

83. Ibid., 6.

84. Ibid., 2.

85. Kate Conger, Mike Isaac, and Daisuke Wakabayashi, "Social Media Companies Survived Election Day. More Tests Loom," *The New York Times*, November 5, 2020, https://nyti.ms/362IUJP.

86. Conger, "How Twitter Policed."

87. Sarah Perez and Taylor Hatmaker, "Facebook Blocks Hashtags for #Sharpiegate, #Stopthesteal Election Conspiracies," *Tech Crunch*, November 5, 2020, https://techcrunch.com/2020/11/05/facebook-blocks-sharpiegate-hashtag-election-conspiracies/.

88. Ibid.

89. Emily Glazer and Patience Haggin, "For Sale at YouTube: Political Ad Space in 2020," *Wall Street Journal*, October 8, 2019, https://www.wsj.com/articles/youtube-tries-to-wrest-campaign-ad-dollars-from-facebook-and-local-tv-11570527000.

90. Renee DiResta, "Right-Wing Social Media Finalizes Its Divorce from Reality," *Atlantic*, November 23, 2020, https://www.theatlantic.com/ideas/archive/2020/11/right-wing-social-media-finalizes-its-divorce-reality/617177/.

91. Catherine Sanz and Catherine Thorbecke, "What Social Media Giants Are Doing to Counter Misinformation This Election," *ABC News*, October 18, 2020, https://abcn.ws/2IIEEr5.

92. Ibid.

93. Ibid.

94. Leslie Miller, "An Update on How YouTube Supports Elections," *YouTube Blog*, August 13, 2020, https://blog.youtube/news-and-events/an-update-on-how-youtube-supports-elections/.

95. Miles Parks, "Social Media Usage Is at an All-Time High: That Could Mean a Nightmare for Democracy," *National Public Radio*, May 27, 2020, https://www.npr.org/2020/05/27/860369744/social-media-usage-is-at-an-all-time-high-that-could-mean-a-nightmare-for-democr.

96. Motley Fool Transcribers, "Facebook Inc (FB) Q1 2020 Earnings," *Motley Fool*, April 29, 2020, https://www.fool.com/earnings/call-transcripts/2020/04/29/facebook-inc-fb-q1-2020-earnings-call-transcript.aspx.

97. Parks, "Social Media Usage."

98. Ibid.

99. Timberg and Dwoskin, "Trump's Power," 2.

100. Ibid.

CHAPTER 6

1. Ezra Klein, "Why the Media Is so Polarized—and How It Polarizes Us," *VOX*, January 28, 2020, https://www.vox.com/2020/1/28/21077888/why-were-polarized-media-book-ezra-news, retrieved January 29, 2020.

2. Ben Smith, "It's the End of an Era for the Media, No Matter Who Wins the Election," *The New York Times*, November 2, 2020, https://www.nytimes.com/2020/11/01/business/media/ben-smith-election.html, retrieved November 2, 2020.

3. Ethan Zuckerman, "The Amazing Disappearing Election," *The Atlantic*, August 7, 2020, https://www.theatlantic.com/politics/archive/2020/08/why-news-sounds-same/615070/, retrieved October 26, 2020.

4. Ibid.

5. Margaret Sullivan, "Media Coverage of the 2016 Campaign Was Disastrous. Now the Last Chance to Get 2020 Right," *The Washington Post*, July 25, 2020, https://www.washingtonpost.com/lifestyle/media/media-coverage-of-..._post_most&utm_medium=email&utm_source=newsletter&wpisrc=nl_most, retrieved July 25, 2020.

6. Some of the arguments appear in Robert E. Denton Jr., Judith S. Trent, and Robert Friedenberg, *Political Campaign Communication: Principles & Practices*, 9th ed. (Lanham, MD: Rowman & Littlefield, 2020), 361–367.

7. Jim A. Kuypers, *Partisan Journalism* (Lanham, MD: Rowman & Littlefield, 2014), 6.

8. Ibid.

9. Michael Delli Carpini, "When Worlds Collide: Contentious Politics in a Fragmented Media Regime" in *U.S. Election Analysis 2020: Media, Voters and the Campaign*, eds. Daniel Jackson et al. (Center for Comparative Politics and Media Research, November 2020), 77.

10. Tim Alberta, "The Deep Roots of Trump's War on the Press," *Politico*, April 26, 2018, https://www.politico.com/magazine/story/2018/04/26/the-deep-roots-trumps-war-on-the-press-218105, retrieved July 11, 2018.

11. Kevin Arceneaux and Martin Johnson, *Changing Minds or Changing Channels?* (Chicago: University of Chicago Press, 2013), 2.

12. Ibid., 3.

13. Ezra Klein, "Why the Media Is So Polarized—and How It Polarizes Us," *VOX*, January 28, 2020, https://www.vox.com/2020/1/28/21077888/why-were-polarized-media-book-ezra-news, retrieved January 29, 2020.

14. Jack Fuller, *What Is Happening to News?* (Chicago: University of Chicago Press, 2010), 12.

15. Ibid.

16. Julia Craven, "A Conversation about Being Black in the Newsroom," *Slate*, July 31, 2020, https://slate.com/news-and-politics/2020/07/wesley-lowery-talks-about-being-black-in-the-newsroom-and-the-myth-of-objectivity.html, retrieved July 14, 2020.

17. Ibid.

18. Seth Lewis, Matt Carlson, and Sue Robinson, "When Journalism's Relevance Is Also on the Ballot," in *U.S. Election Analysis 2020: Media, Voters and the Campaign*, ed. Daniel Jackson et al. (Center for Comparative Politics and Media Research, November 2020), 63.

19. Matthew Levendusky, *How Partisan Media Polarize America* (Chicago: University of Chicago Press, 2013), 8.

20. Ibid., 18.

21. Arceneaux and Johnson, *Changing Minds*, 10.

22. Ibid., 4.

23. Levendusky, *How Partisan Media Polarize America,* 4.

24. Arceneaux and Johnson, *Changing Minds*, 166.

25. Diana Owen, "Twitter Rants, Press Bashing, and Fake News," in *Trumped: The 2016 Election that Broke all the Rules*, eds. Larry J. Sabato, Kyle Kondik, and Geoffrey Skelley (Lanham, MD: Rowman & Littlefield, 2017), 175.

26. James Ceaser, Andrew E. Busch, and John J. Pitney Jr., *Defying the Odds: The 2016 Elections and American Politics* (Lanham, MD: Rowman & Littlefield, 2017), 23.

27. John Allen Hendricks and Dan Schill, "The Social Media Election of 2016," in *The 2016 US Presidential Campaign: Political Communication and Practice*, ed. Robert E. Denton Jr. (Cham, Switzerland: Palgrave Macmillan, 2017), 130–131.

28. Owen, "Twitter Rants," 176.

29. Alex Thompson, "Newsroom or PAC? Liberal Group Muddes Online Information Wars," *Politico*, July 14, 2020, https://www.politico.com/news/2020/07/14/newsroom-pac-liberal-info-wars-356800, retrieved July 15, 2020.

30. Davey Alba and Jack Nicas, "As Local News Dies, a Pay-for-Play Network Rises in Its Place," *The New York Times*, October 19, 2020, https://www.nytimes.com/2020/10/18/technology/timpone-local-news-metric-media.html?referringSource=articleShare, retrieved October 19, 2020.

31. Thompson, "Newsroom or PAC?"

32. Virginia Allen, "Sharyl Attkisson Explains How Traditional Media Abandoned Fact-Based Reporting," *The Daily Signal/Heritage Foundation*, November 24, 2020, https://www.dailysignal.com/2020/11/24/longtime-journalist-ex...4Ym5nanZsRDFcL3FhQms4MUYxcjVWU05iaG0xNUxaV1RyNGpPdnMifQ%3D%3D, retrieved November 24, 2020.

33. Ceasar et al., *Defying the Odds*, 179; and Ethan Zuckerman, "The Amazing Disappearing Election," *The Atlantic*, August 7, 2020, https://www.theatlantic.com/politics/archive/2020/08/why-news-sounds-same/615070/, retrieved October 26, 2020.

34. Amy Mitchell et al., "Americans Who Mainly Get Their News on Social Media Are Less Engaged, Less Knowledgeable," Pew Research Center, July 30, 2020, https://www.journalism.org/2020/07/30/americans-who-mainly-get-their-news-on-social-media-are-less-engaged-less-knowledgeable/, retrieved July 30, 2020.

35. "American Views 2020: Trust, Media and Democracy," Knight Foundation, August 4, 2020, https://knightfoundation.org/reports/american-views-2020-trust-media-and-democracy/, retrieved August 8, 2020.

36. Dylan Byers, "How Donald Trump Changed Political Journalism," *Money. CNN.Com*, November 2, 2016, http://money.cnn.com/2016/11/01/media/political-journalism-2016/index.html?iid=Lead, retrieved November 15, 2016.

37. Klein, "Media Is So Polarized."

38. Mark Jurkowitz, et al., "Americans Are Divided by Party in the Sources They Turn to for Political News," Pew Research Center, January 24, 2020, https://www.journalism.org/2020/01/24/americans-are-divided-by-party-in-the-sources-they-turn-to-for-political-news/, retrieved December 2, 2020.

39. Amy Mitchell et al., "Americans Who Mainly Get Their News on Social Media Are Less Engaged, Less Knowledgeable," Pew Research Center, July 30, 2020,

https://www.journalism.org/2020/07/30/americans-who-mainly-get-their-news-on-social-media-are-less-engaged-less-knowledgeable/, retrieved July 30, 2020.

40. Stephanie Edgerley, "YouTube as Space for News," in Seth Lewis, Matt Carlson, and Sue Robinson, "When Journalism's Relevance Is Also on the Ballot," in *U.S. Election Analysis 2020: Media, Voters and the Campaign*, eds. Daniel Jackson et al. (Center for Comparative Politics and Media Research, November 2020), 66.

41. Kalev Leetaru, "Visual Narratives: A Fracturing of the Nightly News," RealClearPolitics, February 13, 2020, https://www.realclearpolitics.com/articles/2020/02/13/visual_narratives_a_fracturing_of_the_nightly_news_142385.html, retrieved February 14, 2020.

42. Megan Brenan and Helen Stubbs, "News Media Viewed as Biased but Crucial to Democracy," *Gallup*, August 4, 2020, https://news.gallup.com/poll/316574/news-media-viewed-biased-crucial-democracy.aspx?utm_source=alert&utm_medium=email&utm_content=morelink&utm_campaign=syndication, retrieved August 4, 2020.

43. "American Views 2020: Trust, Media and Democracy," *Knight Foundation*, August 4, 2020, https://knightfoundation.org/reports/american-views-2020-trust-media-and-democracy/, retrieved August 8, 2020.

44. Megan Brenan, "Americans Remain Distrustful of Mass Media," *Gallup*, September 9, 2020, https://news.gallup.com/poll/321116/americans-remain-distrustful-mass-media.aspx, retrieved September 30, 2020.

45. Ibid.

46. Jeffrey McCall, "News Media Take Losing Streak in 2020," *The Hill*, January 2, 2020, https://thehill.com/opinion/technology/476470-news-media-take-losing-streak-into-2020, retrieved January 5, 2020.

47. "American Views 2020: Trust, Media and Democracy."

48. Brenan, "Distrustful of Mass Media."

49. "American Views 2020: Trust, Media and Democracy."

50. Brenan and Stubbs, "Biased but Crucial to Democracy."

51. "American Views 2020: Trust, Media and Democracy."

52. Ibid.

53. John Solomon, "MSNBC Producer Quits, Says Job 'Forces Skilled Journalists to Make Bad Decisions,'" *Just the News*, August 4, 2020, https://justthenews.com/accountability/media/msnbc-producer-quits-says-job-forces-skilled-journalists-make-bad-decisions, retrieved August 4, 2020.

54. Ibid.

55. Bari Weiss, "Resignation Letter," *Bariweiss.com*, July 14, 2020, https://www.bariweiss.com/resignation-letter, retrieved July 14, 2020.

56. Glen Greenwald, "Demanding Silicon Valley Suppress 'Hyper-Partisan Sites' in Favor of 'Mainstream News' Is a Fraud," *Greenwald.substack.com*, November 26, 2020, https://greenwald.substack.com/p/demanding-silicon-valley-suppress, retrieved November 11, 2020.

57. Bobby Burack, "Research Finds Google Election Results 'Strongly Biased in Favor of Democrats,'" *Outkick*, November 27, 2020, retrieved December 1, 2020.

58. Mason Walker and Jeffrey Gottfried, "Americans Blame Unfair News Coverage on Media Outlets, Not the Journalists Who Work for Them," Pew Research Center, October 28, 2020, https://www.pewresearch.org/fact-tank/2020/10/28/amer icans-blame-un . . . ws-coverage-on-media-outlets-not-the-journalists-who-work-for-them/, retrieved November 11, 2020.

59. Ibid.

60. Ben Voth, "Journalistic Hegemony of 'Blue Privilege,'" in *The 2016 American Presidential Campaign and the News*, ed. Jim A. Kuypers (Lanham, MD: Lexington Books, 2018), 205.

61. Ezra Klein, "America Is Changing and So Is the Media," *VOX*, June 10, 2020, https://www.vox.com/2020/6/10/21284651/new-york-times-tom-cotton-media-lib eral-conservative-black-lives-matter, retrieved June 6, 2020.

62. Elisa Shearer, "Two-Thirds of U.S. Adults Say They've Seen Their Own News Sources Report Facts Meant to Favor One Side," Pew Research Center, November 2, 2020, https://www.pewresearch.org/fact-tank/2020/11/02/two-thirds-of-u-s-a...ve-seen-their-own-news-sources-report-facts-meant-to-favor-one-side/, retrieved November 11, 2020.

63. Victor Davis Hanson, "The News as We Once Knew It Is Dead," RealClearPolitics, September 17, 2020, https://www.realclearpolitics.com/articles/2020/09/17/the_news_ as_we_once_knew_it_is_dead_144223.html, retrieved September 18, 2020.

64. Victor Joecks, "The Media's Insane Whitewashing of Portland's Violence," *Las Vegas Review Journal*, July 28, 2020, https://outline.com/Es5jMY, retrieved July 29, 2020.

65. Joseph Wulfsohn, "MSNBC Skips Coverage of Chicago Riots during Primetime, CNN Airs Less than 3 minutes," *Fox News*, August 11, 2020, https://www.foxnews.com/media/msnbc-gives-zero-coverage-chicago-riots-cnn-ignores, retrieved August 15, 2020.

66. Daniel Payne, "CNN Briefly Describes Wisconsin Protests as 'Violent' before Scrubbing Word from Broadcast," *Just the News.Com*, August 25, 2020, https://just thenews.com/accountability/media/cnn-briefly-describes-wisconsin-protests-violent-scrubbing-word-broadcast, retrieved August 28, 2020.

67. Ezra Klein, "America Is Changing and So Is the Media," *VOX*, June 10, 2020, https://www.vox.com/2020/6/10/21284651/new-york-times-tom-cotton-media-lib eral-conservative-black-lives-matter, retrieved June 11, 2020.

68. Catherine Sanz and Gatherine Thorbecke, "What Social Media Giants Are Doing to Counter Misinformation This Election," *ABC News*, October 18, 2020, https://abcnews.go.com/Technology/social-media-giants-counter-misinformation-election/story?id=73563997, retrieved October 26, 2020.

69. Corinne Weaver and Alec Schemmel, "Twitter, Facebook Censored Trump, Campaign 65 Times, Leave Biden Untouched," *News Busters.Org*, October 19, 2020, https://www.newsbusters.org/blogs/techwatch/corinne-weaver/2020/10/19/twitter-facebook-censored-trump-campaign-65-times-leave, retrieved November 2, 2020.

70. Sanz and Thorbecke, "Social Media Giants."

71. Mollie Ziegler, "Yes, Media Are Rigging the Election against Half of the Country," *The Federalist*, October 30, 2020, https://thefederalist.com/2020/10/30/

yes-media-are-rigging-election-against-half-the-country-heres-how/, retrieved October 30, 2020.

72. David Harsanyi, "How the Media Covered Up the Hunter Biden Story—Until after the Election," *New York Post,* December 10, 2020, https://nypost.com/2020/12/10/how-media-covered-up-the-hunter-biden-story-until-after-the-election/, retrieved December 12, 2020.

73. Frank Miele, "The Top 10 Suppressed News Stories of 2020," RealClearPolitics, December 29, 2020, https://www.realclearpolitics.com/articles/2020/12/29/the_top_10_suppressed_news_stories_of_2020_144929.html, retrieved December 29, 2020.

74. Valerie Richardson, "'Hunter CoverUps': Mainstream Media under Fire for Ignoring Story before Election," *The Washington Times,* December 11, 2020, https://www.washingtontimes.com/news/2020/dec/11/hunter-biden-coverup-mainstream-media-under-fire-f/, retrieved December 13, 2020.

75. Sohrab Ahmari, "Media Disgraceful in Trying to Suppress Post's Hunter Biden Reporting," *New York Post,* December 10, 2020, https://nypost.com/2020/12/10/media-disgraceful-trying-to-suppress-posts-hunter-biden-reporting/, retrieved December 12, 2020.

76. Jonathan Turley, "Censoring the Biden Story: How Social Media Becomes State Media," *The Hill,* October 17, 2020, https://thehill.com/opinion/technology/521517-censoring-the-biden-story-how-social-media-becomes-state-media, retrieved October 20, 2020.

77. Rachel del Guidice, "If Voters Had Known about 8 Stories Media Ignored, Trump Would Have Won, Says Media Watchdog," *Daily Signal,* November 25, 2020, https://www.dailysignal.com/2020/11/25/if-voters-had-known-about-8-stories-media-...hTdWE3OTBYZnZxSjh2VFgrYTlRTEFwSDVZQk1VNXl4ellCV DY3TEJVejI1c2E2cnhKcVwvbWc3In0%3D, retrieved December 1, 2020.

78. Roger Kimball, "Sleepy Campaign Strategy Mystery Solved," *American Greatness*, November 5, 2020, https://amgreatness.com/2020/11/05/sleepy-campaign-strategy-mystery-solved/, retrieved November 11, 2020.

79. Frank Miele, "Under the Media's Berlin Wall of Truth Suppression," RealClearPolitics, September 14, 2020, https://www.realclearpolitics.com/articles/2020/09/14/under_the_medias_berlin_wall_of_truth_suppression__144190.html, retrieved September 14, 2020.

80. Paul Farhi, "Stop Doing That, or This Interview Will End: How the Smackdown Took over Cable News in 2020," *The Washington Post,* October 27, 2020, https://www.washingtonpost.com/lifestyle/media/smackdown-interview-cable-news-jake-tapper-trump-meadows/2020/10/27/59129232-07f9-11eb-9be6-cf25fb429f1a_story.html, retrieved October 27, 2020.

81. Tim Graham, "The Media's Broadcast Brutality against Trump," *Townhall*, October 26, 2020, https://townhall.com/columnists/timgraham/2020/06/12/the-medias-broadcast-brutality-against-trump-n2570529, retrieved November 20, 2020.

82. Rich Noyes, "Washington Post Bashes Trump Virus Response with 25 to 1 Negative Headlines," *Media Research Center,* April 25, 2020, https://www.newsbusters.org/blogs/nb/rich-noyes/2020/04/25/study-washington-post-bashes-trump-virus-response-25-1-negative, retrieved December 1, 2020.

83. Rich Noyes, "Liberal Media Has 150 Times More Negative Coverage of President Trump than Joe Biden," *LifeNews.com*, August 17, 2020, https://www.life news.com/2020/08/17/study-liberal-media-has-150-times-more-negative-coverage-of-president-trump-than-joe-biden/, retrieved November 23, 2020.

84. "Voters Say Media Focuses on Issues with Biden, Controversy With Trump," *Rasmussen*, September 14, 2020, https://www.rasmussenreports.com/public_content/politics/general_politics/september_2...ersy_with_trump?utm_campaign=RR09142020DN&utm_source=criticalimpact&utm_medium=email, retrieved September 15, 2020.

85. Justin Vallejo, "Polling Is 'Done' after Election Misses devastate Industry," *Independent.co.uk*, November 4, 2020, https://www.independent.co.uk/news/world/americas/us-election-2020/polling-frank-luntz-us-election-2020-misses-trump-biden-b1599174.html, retrieved December 27, 2020.

86. Trent Baker, "Frank Luntz: 'Donald Trump Was Correct'—Polling Was So Wrong," *Breitbart.com*, November 4, 2020, https://www.breitbart.com/clips/2020/11/04/frank-luntz-donald-trump-was-correct-polling-was-so-wrong/, retrieved December 27, 2020.

87. Kelli Ward, "Remember the 'Psychic Friends Network' Fraud? The Pollsters Are Even Worse," *Western Journal.Com*, November 19, 2020, https://www.west ernjournal.com/kelli-ward-remember-psychic-friends-network-fraud-pollsters-even-worse/amp/?_twitter_impression=true, retrieved November 23, 2020.

88. Mollie Ziegler, "Yes, Media Are Rigging the Election against Half of the Country," *The Federalist*, October 30, 2020, https://thefederalist.com/2020/10/30/yes-media-are-rigging-election-against-half-the-country-heres-how/, retrieved October 30, 2020.

89. Virginia Allen, "Sharyl Attkisson Explains How Traditional Media Abandoned Fact-Based Reporting," *The Daily Signal/Heritage Foundation*, November 24, 2020, https://www.dailysignal.com/2020/11/24/longtime-journalist-ex...4Ym5nanZsRDFcL3FhQms4MUYxcjVWU05iaG0xNUxaV1RyNGpPdnMifQ%3D%3D, retrieved November 24, 2020.

90. "Anomalies in Vote Counts and Their Effects," *Vote Integrity*, November 24, 2020, https://votepatternanalysis.substack.com/p/voting-anomalies-2020, retrieved December 17, 2020; Julie Kelly, "Will This Texas Lawsuit Overturn the 2020 Election?" *American Greatness*, December 8, 2020, https://amgreat ness.com/2020/12/08/will-this-texas-lawsuit-overturn-the-2020-election, retrieved December 10, 2020; Fred Lucas, "7 Takeaways from a Senate Panel's Hearing on Election Fraud," *@FredLucasWH*, December 16, 2020, https://www.dailysig nal.com/2020/12/16/7-takeaways-from-a-s...w4dm9YZW9XTXVUdTZENVZDSE plQzFYWWRyVUQwRFBcL1ppOWN5Z0xhNCJ9, retrieved December 17, 2020; Patrick Basham, "Reasons Why the 2020 Presidential Election Is Deeply Puzzling," *Spectator USA*, November 30, 2020, https://spectator.us/reasons-why-the-2020-pres idential-election-is-deeply-puzzling/, retrieved November 30, 2020; "Anomalies in Vote Counts and Their Effects on Election 2020," *Voter Integrity Project*, November 24, 2020, https://votepatternanalysis.substack.com/p/voting-anomalies-2020, retrieved December 1, 2020; David Catron, "Legitimacy of Biden Win Buried by

Objective Data," *The American Spectator*, November 30, 2020, https://spectator.org/legitimacy-of-biden-win-buried-by-objective-data/, retrieved December 1, 2020.

91. Christopher Bedford, "Saturday's Media Declaration Is a Naked Attempt to Silence Republicans, and Nothing Has Changed," *The Federalist*, November 7, 2020, https://thefederalist.com/2020/11/07/saturdays-media-declaration-is-a-naked-attempt-to-silence-republicans-and-nothing-has-changed/, retrieved November 11, 2020.

92. "Vainglory of the Press," *New York Sun*, November 20, 2020, https://www.nysun.com/editorials/vainglory-of-the-press/91341/, retrieved November 23, 2020.

93. John R. Lott, "A Simple Test for the Extent of Vote Fraud with Absentee Ballots in the 2020 Presidential Election: Georgia and Pennsylvania Data," *Social Science Research Network*, December 29, 2020, https://papers.ssrn.com/sol3/papers.cfm?abstract_id=3756988, retrieved December 30, 2020.

94. Ibid.

95. Cameron Jenkins, "Trump Slams Supreme Court Decision to Throw out Election Lawsuit," *The Hill,* December 12, 2020, https://thehill.com/homenews/administration/529940-trump-slams-supreme-court-decision-to-throw-out-election-lawsuit, retrieved December 29, 2020.

96. Joe Ferullo, "The Tribal Journalism of Cable News Is at a Crossroads," *The Hill,* November 8, 2020, https://thehill.com/opinion/technology/525004-the-tribal-journalism-of-cable-news-is-at-a-crossroads, retrieved November 29, 2020.

97. Allen, "Sharyl Attkisson."

98. Frank Miele, "Propaganda, Election Fraud and the Death of Journalism," RealClearPolitics, November 23, 2020, https://www.realclearpolitics.com/articles/2020/11/23/propaganda_election_fraud_and_the_death_of_journalism_144705.html, retrieved November 23, 2020.

99. Jim VandelHel, "Blunt 2020 Lessons for Media, America," *Axios*, November 20, 2020, https://www.axios.com/2020-lessons-media-america-b6b6c184-ea46-4fc5-a6dd-0f5ad3dda082.html, retrieved November 23, 2020.

100. McKay Coppins, "The Resistance's Breakup with the Media Is at Hand," *The Atlantic*, December 29, 2020, https://www.theatlantic.com/politics/archive/2020/12/media-after-trump/617503/, retrieved December 30, 2020.

CHAPTER 7

1. Margaret Kaplan, *Words to Win by: The Slogans, Logos, and Designs of America's Presidential Elections* (New York: Apollo Publishers, 2020), 6.

2. Francisco Guzmán, Audhesh K. Paswan and Eric Van Steenburg, "Self-Referencing and Political Candidate Brands: A Congruency Perspective," *Journal of Political Marketing* 14.1–2 (2015), 176.

3. Carly Stec, "Brand Strategy 101: 7 Essentials for Strong Company Branding," *HubSpot*, October 11, 2017, https://blog.hubspot.com/blog/tabid/6307/bid/31739/7-components-that-comprise-a-comprehensive-brand-strategy.aspx.

4. Jennifer Lees-Marshment et al., *Political Marketing* (New York: Taylor and Francis, 2019), 86, 88.

5. Catherine Needham, "Brand Leaders: Clinton, Blair and the Limitations of the Permanent Campaign," *Political Studies* 53.2 (2015), 347–348.

6. Richard Nathan Rutter, Chris Hanretty and Fiona Lettice, "Political Brands: Can Parties Be Distinguished by Their Online Brand Personality?" *Journal of Political Marketing* 17.3 (2018), 196.

7. Lees-Marshment et al., *Political Marketing*, 89.

8. Sorin Nastasia, "Political Branding of Candidates," in *Encyclopedia of Social Media and Politics*, Vol. 1, ed. Kerric Harvey (Thousand Oaks, CA: Sage Reference, 2014), 225.

9. Chase Lovett, *Grocery Store Politics: How Political Brands Manipulate Voters* (Self-Published, Amazon Kindle: 2018), 1285.

10. Andrea Schneiker, "Telling the Story of the Superhero and Anti-Politician as President: Donald Trump's Branding on Twitter," *Political Studies Review*, 17.3 (2019): 212.

11. "Brand Biden vs. Brand Trump," *Ipsos,* October 21, 2020, https://www.ipsos.com/en/brand-biden-vs-brand-trump.

12. Hunter Schwarz, "Joe Biden's Branding Was Both Traditional and Trippy, and It Looks Like the Future of Politics," *Eye on Design*, December 9, 2020, accessed December 14, 2020, https://eyeondesign.aiga.org/joe-bidens-election-branding-was-both-traditional-and-trippy-and-it-looks-like-the-future-of-politics/.

13. Ibid.

14. "Symposium: The Biden-Harris Design Team," Virtual presentation, AIGA National Conference, November 13, 2020.

15. Ibid.

16. Schwarz, "Joe Biden's Branding Was Both Traditional and Trippy."

17. Ibid.

18. "Make Trump's Branding Great Again: In-House Experts Talk Campaign Design," *AIGA*, accessed December 14, 2020, https://www.aiga.org/how-to-make-trump-branding-great-again.

19. Tony Aubé, "Trump Is a F*king Amazing Designer," *Medium*, May 18, 2018, https://medium.com/swlh/donald-trump-is-a-f-king-amazing-designer-d427b7448758.

20. Ibid.

21. Ibid.

22. Diana Budds, "The Worst Design of 2016 Was Also the Most Effective," *Fast Company*, July 09, 2018, https://www.fastcompany.com/3066599/the-worst-design-of-2016-was-also-the-most-effective.

23. "Symposium: The Biden-Harris Design Team."

24. Nastasia, "Political Branding of Candidates," 224.

25. Dan Schill and John Allen Hendricks, "Discourse, Disruption, and Digital Democracy: Political Communication in the 2016 Presidential Campaign," in *The Presidency and Social Media: Discourse, Disruption, and Digital Democracy in the 2016 Presidential Election*, eds. Dan Schill and John Allen Hendricks (New York: Routledge, 2018), 4.

26. Sam Fulwell III, "Social Media Shapes Our Politics. But Does It Actually Elect Presidents?" *Think Progress*, June 5, 2019, https://thinkprogress.org/social-media-shapes-our-politics-but-does-it-actually-elect-presidents-597e0f615725/.

27. Dan Schill and John Allen Hendricks, "Preface," in *The Presidency and Social Media: Discourse, Disruption, and Digital Democracy in the 2016 Presidential Election*, eds. Dan Schill and John Allen Hendricks (New York: Routledge, 2018), xvii.

28. Tom Infield, "Americans Who Get News Mainly on Social Media Are Less Knowledgeable and Less Engaged," *Pew Trust Magazine*, November 16, 2020, https://www.pewtrusts.org/en/trust/archive/fall-2020/americans-who-get-news-mainly-on-social-media-are-less-knowledgeable-and-less-engaged.

29. Anna Bredava, "Biden's and Trump's Election Campaigns: A Social Media Analysis," *Awario*, November 2, 2020, https://awario.com/blog/elections-2020-social-media/.

30. Schill and Hendricks, "Discourse, Disruption, and Digital Democracy," 19.

31. Zeke Miller and Alexandra Jaffe, "In a Pandemic, How US Presidential Campaign Strategies Diverge," *Christian Science Monitor*, September 9, 2020, https://www.csmonitor.com/USA/Politics/2020/0909/In-a-pandemic-how-US-presidential-campaign-strategies-diverge.

32. Bredava, "Biden's and Trump's Election Campaigns."

33. Jordan Williams, "Trump Mocks Joe Biden's Drive-in Rallies at North Carolina Event," *The Hill*, October 24, 2020, https://thehill.com/homenews/campaign/522593-trump-mocks-joe-bidens-drive-in-rallies-at-north-carolina-event.

34. John Fritze and David Jackson, "Trump Mocks Biden for Mask-Wearing, Dismisses Health Questions in Pennsylvania Rally," *USA Today*, September 3, 2020, https://www.usatoday.com/story/news/2020/09/03/trump-rally-latrobe-pennsylvania-race-biden-tightens/5701191002/.

35. Robin Foster and E.J. Mundell, "CDC Urges All Americans to Wear Face Masks," *U.S. News and World Report*, April 4, 2020, https://www.usnews.com/news/health-news/articles/2020-04-04/cdc-urges-all-americans-to-wear-face-masks.

36. "CDC Calls on Americans to Wear Masks to Prevent COVID-19 Spread," Centers for Disease Control and Prevention, July 14, 2020, https://www.cdc.gov/media/releases/2020/p0714-americans-to-wear-masks.html.

37. Nadia Kounang, "Many Counties That Hosted Trump Rallies Had a Significant Increase in Covid-19 Cases," *CNN*, October 30 2020, https://www.cnn.com/2020/10/29/health/covid-trump-rallies-counties-cases/index.html.

38. Kevin Liptak and Maeve Reston, "Trump Returns to White House and Removes Mask Despite Having COVID," *CNN*, October 5, 2020, https://www.cnn.com/2020/10/05/politics/donald-trump-covid-condition-walter-reed/index.html.

39. Charlotte Alter, "Inside the Democrat's Plans to Win Back the Internet," *Time*, August 6, 2020, https://time.com/5876600/JOE-BIDEN-INTERNET-2020-ELECTION/.

40. Bredava, "Biden's and Trump's Election Campaigns."

41. Rebecca Heilweil, "Inside the Biden Campaign's Surprising Influencer Strategy," *Vox*, September 22, 2020, https://www.vox.com/recode/21429755/influencers-joe-biden-democrats-pacs-social-media-facebook-instagram-campaign.

42. Alter, "Inside the Democrat's Plans to Win Back the Internet."

43. Miller and Jaffe, "In a Pandemic, How US Presidential Campaign Strategies Diverge."

44. Alter, "Inside the Democrat's Plans to Win Back the Internet."

45. Ibid.

46. Edward Rothstein, "In a Collection of Memorabilia, Politics at its Most Bois-terous," *The New York Times*, June 28, 2008, https://www.nytimes.com/2008/06/28/arts/design/28muse.html.

47. Amanda Pampuro, "Wearing Your Candidate on Your Sleeve: Merchandising the 2020 Race," *Courthouse News Service*, September 13, 2019, https://www.courthousenews.com/wearing-your-candidate-on-your-sleeve-merchandising-the-2020-race/.

48. Sarah Ewall-Wice and Nicole Scanga, "Rallies Might Be on Pause, but Trump Campaign Merchandise Churns On," *CBS News*, May 14, 2020, https://www.cbsnews.com/news/trump-rallies-campaign-merchandise/.

49. Alex Isenstadt, "Inside Donald Trump's 'Brilliant and Sinister' Merchandis-ing Operation," *Politico*, July 29, 2019, https://www.politico.com/story/2019/07/29/trump-campaign-culture-wars-drinking-straws-1438402.

50. Cassie Spodak, "How the Trump Hat Became an Icon," *CNN*, February 17, 2017, https://www.cnn.com/2017/02/17/politics/donald-trump-make-america-great-again-iconic-hat/index.html.

51. Katie Rogers, "With Markers and Straws, Trump's Campaign Sells Defiance as a Lifestyle," *The New York Times*, September 15, 2019, https://www.nytimes.com/2019/09/13/us/politics/donald-trump-2020-campaign.html.

52. Ilyse Liffreing, "Trump Coloring Books and Biden Hand Sanitizer: Comparing Presidential Campaign Merchandise," *Ad Age*, October 7, 2020, https://adage.com/article/cmo-strategy/trump-coloring-books-and-biden-hand-sanitizer-comparing-presidential-campaign-merchandise/2285106.

53. Gregory Krieg, "Wine, Water, and (Actual) Red Meat—It's a Donald Trump Press Conference," *CNN*, March 8, 2016, https://www.cnn.com/2016/03/08/politics/donald-trump-steak-wine-water-press-conference/index.html.

54. Brad Slage, "The Good, the Bad, and the Ugly among 2020 Campaign Mer-chandise," *The Federalist*, August 2, 2019, https://thefederalist.com/2019/08/02/collective-of-democratic-hopefuls-offers-few-election-collectibles/.

55. Isenstadt, "Inside Donald Trump's 'Brilliant and Sinister' Merchandising Operation."

56. Ibid.

57. Rogers, "With Markers and Straws."

58. Nicole Gallucci, "An Inside Look at How Biden's Campaign Is Winning the Viral Merch Game," *Mashable SE Asia,* October 12, 2020, https://sea.mashable.com/culture/12766/an-inside-look-at-how-bidens-campaign-is-winning-the-viral-merch-game.

59. Willis, "The Best Campaign Merch."

60. Slage, "The Good, the Bad, and the Ugly."

61. Zoe Donaldson, "All the 2020 Presidential Campaign Swag, Ranked," *The Oprah Magazine*, June 26, 2019, https://www.oprahmag.com/life/a28196381/2020-election-campaign-swag/.

62. Chloe Foussianes, "Inside the Biden-Harris Merch Machine: Where High Fash-ion, Sweatshirts, and Flyswatters Mix," *Town and Country*, October 10, 2020, https://www.townandcountrymag.com/society/politics/a34330279/joe-biden-kamala-harris-campaign-merch-flyswatter-fashion/.

63. Emily Petrarca, "Fashion Tries to Give Joe Biden Merch a Makeover," *The Cut*, September 8, 2020, https://www.thecut.com/2020/09/joe-biden-kamala-harris-merch-fashion.html.

64. Foussianes, "Inside the Biden-Harris Merch Machine."

65. Gallucci, "An Inside Look at How Biden's Campaign Is Winning."

66. Cam Wolf, "Of Course 'Will You Shut Up, Man' Is Already a T-Shirt," *GQ*, September 30, 2020, https://www.gq.com/story/joe-biden-will-you-shut-up-man-debate-merch.

67. Alexis Benveniste, "The Biden Campaign Started Selling Fly Swatters Right after the Debate. They've Already Sold Out," *CNN*, October 8, 2020, https://www.cnn.com/2020/10/08/business/biden-campaign-fly-swatter-trnd/index.html.

68. Gallucci, "An Inside Look at How Biden's Campaign Is Winning."

69. Ibid.

70. Foussianes, "Inside the Biden-Harris Merch Machine."

71. Christopher Ruvo, "The Power of Political Promos," *Advertising Specialty Institute*, March 10, 2020, https://www.asicentral.com/news/web-exclusive/march-2020/the-power-of-political-promos/.

72. Lees-Marshment et al., *Political Marketing*, 89.

CHAPTER 8

1. JBF Editors, "The 2020 James Beard Award Nominees," James Beard Foundation, May 4, 2020, https://www.jamesbeard.org/blog/the-2020-james-beard-award-nominees.

2. Bruce Kraig, "The Election That Defined What 'Real Americans' Ate and Drank," *Atlas Obscura*, January 15, 2018, http://www.atlasobscura.com/articles/1840-election-food-william-henry-harrison.

3. Justin Irwin, "Political Foods: Food and Drink on Campaign," *The Historical Cooking Project*, October 13, 2015, http://www.historicalcookingproject.com/2015/10/political-foods-food-and-drink-on.html.

4. Michael Owen Jones, "Politics on a Plate: Uses and Abuses of Foodways on the Campaign Trail," *Journal of Folklore Research* 57.2 (2020): 41–79, https://doi.org/10.2979/jfolkrese.57.2.02; Jan Wilson, "The Politics of Food on the Campaign Trail," *Oklahoma Center for the Humanities*, November 16, 2016, https://humanities.utulsa.edu/politics-food-campaign-trail/; Fabio Parasecoli has also written a number of times on this topic on his blog, which I cite throughout this chapter.

5. Gunn Enli and Linda Therese Rosenberg, "Trust in the Age of Social Media: Populist Politicians Seem More Authentic," *Social Media + Society* 4.1 (January 1, 2018): 2056305118764430, https://doi.org/10.1177/2056305118764430.

6. Meghan McCarron, "America Will Always Want to See Politicians Stuffing Their Faces," *Eater*, December 9, 2019, https://www.eater.com/2019/12/9/20992394/election-2020-eating-biden-sanders-warren-buttigieg-politicians-diners.

7. Cited in: Merrill Perlman, "Politics for Sale," *Columbia Journalism Review*, February 1, 2016, https://www.cjr.org/language_corner/politics_for_sale.php.

8. Jones, "Politics on a Plate," 42.

9. Faith J. Kramer, "Diners," in *The Business of Food: Encyclopedia of the Food and Drink Industries*, eds. Gary J. Allen and Ken Albala (Santa Barbara, CA: ABC-CLIO, 2007), 134–38; Andrew P. Haley, *Turning the Tables: Restaurants and the Rise of the American Middle Class, 1880–1920* (Chapel Hill: University of North Carolina Press, 2013); Andrew Hurley, *Diners, Bowling Alleys, and Trailer Parks: Chasing the American Dream in Postwar Consumer Culture* (New York: Basic Books, 2001); Andrew Hurley, "From Hash House to Family Restaurant: The Transformation of the Diner and Post-World War II Consumer Culture," *Journal of American History* 83.4 (1997): 1282–1308.

10. Doug Mack, "Why Are Journalists Always Visiting Diners in Trump Country?" *The Counter*, October 22, 2020, https://thecounter.org/trump-rust-belt-diner-presidential-race-election-2020/.

11. Gary He and Meghan McCarron, "Pete Buttigieg Ate a Smorgasbord of Food at the Iowa State Fair, and We Were There to See It," *Eater*, August 14, 2019, https://www.eater.com/2019/8/14/20805052/pete-buttigieg-eats-iowa-state-fair-food.

12. Gary He, "The Pete Buttigieg Campaign Trail Diet," *Eater*, November 7, 2019, https://www.eater.com/2019/11/7/20953442/pete-buttigieg-diet-iowa-election.

13. Gary He, "There's No Elegant Way to Eat a Corn Dog: Here Are the Democratic Candidates at the Iowa State Fair," *Eater*, August 12, 2019, https://www.eater.com/2019/8/12/20802166/iowa-state-fair-democratic-candidates-2020-eating-corn-dogs-pork-chops; Emily J. H. Contois, "The Spicy Spectacular: Food, Gender, and Celebrity on Hot Ones," *Feminist Media Studies* 18.4 (July 4, 2018): 769–773, https://doi.org/10.1080/14680777.2018.1478690.

14. He, "There's No Elegant Way to Eat a Corn Dog."

15. Kate Ward, "Let Hillary Eat Cake," *The Cut*, April 10, 2016, https://www.thecut.com/2016/04/let-hillary-eat-cake.html.

16. Ingrid Kiefer, Theres Rathmanner, and Michael Kunze, "Eating and Dieting Differences in Men and Women," *Journal of Men's Health and Gender* 2.2 (2005): 194–201; Charlotte N. Markey and Patrick M. Markey, "Relations between Body Image and Dieting Behaviors: An Examination of Gender Differences," *Sex Roles* 53.7–8 (October 2005): 519–30, https://doi.org/10.1007/s11199-005-7139-3.

17. He, "There's No Elegant Way to Eat a Corn Dog."

18. Irwin, "Political Foods."

19. Dan Alexander, "The Net Worth of Every 2020 Presidential Candidate," *Forbes*, August 14, 2019, https://www.forbes.com/sites/danalexander/2019/08/14/heres-the-net-worth-of-every-2020-presidential-candidate/.

20. Andrew Tolson, "'Being Yourself': The Pursuit of Authentic Celebrity," *Discourse Studies* 3. 4 (2001): 443–457.

21. Thomas Wood, "What the Heck Are We Doing in Ottumwa, Anyway? Presidential Candidate Visits and Their Political Consequence," *The ANNALS of the American Academy of Political and Social Science* 667.1 (September 1, 2016): 111.

22. Marshall Wyatt, "How a Plate of Tamales May Have Crushed Gerald Ford's 1976 Presidential Campaign," *Vice Munchies*, November 8, 2016, https://www.vice.com/en_us/article/ezkvxk/how-a-plate-of-tamales-may-have-crushed-gerald-fords-1976-presidential-campaign.

23. Carmina Danini, "No One Told Ford Tamales Need to Be Unwrapped," *Houston Chronicle*, December 31, 2006, https://www.chron.com/news/houston-texas/article/No-one-told-Ford-tamales-need-to-be-unwrapped-1536700.php.

24. Ibid.

25. Bob Schieffer, "Dining Tips for Presidential Candidates," *CBS News*, March 29, 2012, https://www.cbsnews.com/news/dining-tips-for-presidential-candidates/.

26. Anne Noyes Saini, "When a Tamale Determines the Presidency," *The Sporkful Podcast*, July 11, 2016, http://www.sporkful.com/when-a-tamale-determines-the-presidency/.

27. Ibid.

28. He, "The Pete Buttigieg Campaign Trail Diet."

29. Patricia Sullivan and Emma Brown, "Sargent Shriver, Founding Director of Peace Corps, Dies at 95," *The Washington Post*, January 18, 2011, https://www.washingtonpost.com/local/obituaries/sargent-shriver-founding-director-of-peace-corps-dies-at-95/2011/01/18/ABqGTSR_story.html.

30. Jeva Lange, "The Democrats' Presidential Keg Stand," *The Week*, February 27, 2019, https://theweek.com/articles/825889/democrats-presidential-keg-stand.

31. Dan Balz, "Bush Begins 'Vigorous Fight' for California," *The Washington Post*, June 30, 1999; AP, "Bush Edges Kerry in 'Regular Guy' Poll," *NBC News*, May 26, 2004, http://www.nbcnews.com/id/5067874/ns/politics/t/bush-edges-kerry-regular-guy-poll/.

32. Ben Zimmer, "Elizabeth Warren and the Down-to-Earth Trap," *The Atlantic*, January 5, 2019, https://www.theatlantic.com/entertainment/archive/2019/01/why-elizabeth-warrens-beer-moment-fell-flat/579544/.

33. Tal Axelrod, "Warren Campaign Offering Supporters Chance to 'Grab a Drink with Elizabeth,'" *The Hill*, June 12, 2019, https://thehill.com/homenews/campaign/448255-warren-campaign-offering-supporters-chance-to-grab-a-drink-with-elizabeth.

34. Christina Cauterucci, "Likability Is Whatever a Woman Candidate Doesn't Have," *Slate Magazine*, November 21, 2019, https://slate.com/news-and-politics/2019/11/elizabeth-warren-likable-presidential-candidate.html.

35. He, "The Pete Buttigieg Campaign Trail Diet."

36. Julia Poska and The Civil Eats Editors, "Where the 2020 Presidential Candidates Stand on Food and Farming," *Civil Eats*, May 29, 2019, https://civileats.com/2019/05/29/where-the-2020-presidential-candidates-stand-on-food-and-farming/.

37. Nate Silver, "How Amy Klobuchar Could Win the 2020 Democratic Nomination," *FiveThirtyEight*, February 10, 2019, https://fivethirtyeight.com/features/amy-klobuchar-2020-democratic-nomination-kickoff/.

38. Jenny G. Zhang, "A Napa Valley Wine Cave Was the Hot-Button Issue of the Democratic Debate," *Eater*, December 20, 2019, https://www.eater.com/2019/12/20/21031491/wine-cave-democratic-debate-elizabeth-warren-pete-buttigieg.

39. Alexander, "The Net Worth of Every 2020 Presidential Candidate."

40. Steve Cuozzo, "Why I Vote 'Hell, No!' On a Vegan President," *New York Post*, August 13, 2019, https://nypost.com/2019/08/13/why-i-vote-hell-no-on-a-vegan-president/; Hillary Vaughn, "Iowa Voters Have Beef with Non-Meat Eaters Booker, Gabbard at Iowa State Fair," *Fox News*, August 9, 2019, https://www.foxnews.com/

politics/iowa-voters-have-beef-with-non-meat-eaters-booker-gabbard-at-iowa-state-fair; Anon., "No to a Vegan President," *Carolina Coast Online*, August 15, 2019, https://www.carolinacoastonline.com/news_times/article_f43acf82-bfab-11e9-986f-1b4666a96e78.html.

41. Vaughn, "Iowa Voters Have Beef with Non-Meat Eaters Booker, Gabbard at Iowa State Fair"; Cuozzo, "Why I Vote 'Hell, No!' On a Vegan President."

42. He, "There's No Elegant Way to Eat a Corn Dog."

43. Meghan McCarron, "So What Do Vegetarians Eat at America's Greasiest, Porkiest State Fair?" *Eater*, August 16, 2019, https://www.eater.com/2019/8/16/20808678/iowa-state-fair-the-veggie-table-vegan-presidential-candidates; James M. Winters, "At the Iowa State Fair, the Veggie Table Is an Institution," *Stay to Play*, August 17, 2019, https://staytoplay.cf/2019/08/17/at-the-iowa-state-fair-the-veggie-table-is-an-institution/.

44. Tricia Corrin and Andrew Papadopoulos, "Understanding the Attitudes and Perceptions of Vegetarian and Plant-Based Diets to Shape Future Health Promotion Programs," *Appetite* 109 (February 1, 2017): 40–47, https://doi.org/10.1016/j.appet.2016.11.018.

45. Jenny G. Zhang, "What 2020 Democratic Presidential Candidates' Comfort Food Preferences Say about Them," *Eater*, June 19, 2019, https://www.eater.com/2019/6/19/18691943/2020-democratic-presidential-candidates-favorite-comfort-foods-campaign-trail.

46. Emily J. H. Contois, "Guilt-Free and Sinfully Delicious: A Contemporary Theology of Weight Loss Dieting," *Fat Studies*, April 8, 2015, https://www.tandfonline.com/doi/abs/10.1080/21604851.2015.1015925.

47. He, "There's No Elegant Way to Eat a Corn Dog."

48. Mari Kate Mycek, "Meatless Meals and Masculinity: How Veg* Men Explain Their Plant-Based Diets," *Food and Foodways* 26, no. 3 (July 3, 2018): 223–45, https://doi.org/10.1080/07409710.2017.1420355.

49. Anon., "2020 Democrats on Campaign Food," *The New York Times*, June 19, 2019, https://www.nytimes.com/interactive/2019/us/politics/campaign-comfort-food-democratic-candidates.html.

50. Emily Contois, "At the Crossroads of Comfort TV and Comfort Food," *Nursing Clio*, March 5, 2019, https://nursingclio.org/2019/03/05/at-the-crossroads-of-comfort-tv-and-comfort-food/; Michael Owen Jones and Lucy M. Long, *Comfort Food: Meanings and Memories* (Jackson: University Press of Mississippi, 2017).

51. Jeremy Blum, "Mike Pence Says He'll Keep Kamala Harris from Meddling with America's Meat," *HuffPost*, August 14, 2020, https://www.huffpost.com/entry/mike-pence-kamala-harris-meat_n_5f3614dbc5b69fa9e2f938fc.

52. Kim Severson, "A Classic Midwestern Dish Becomes a Talking Point in Iowa," *The New York Times*, January 28, 2020, https://www.nytimes.com/2020/01/28/dining/amy-klobuchar-hotdish.html.

53. "Join Amy at the Inaugural Hot Dish House Party," Facebook event, https://www.facebook.com/events/52-stevens-dr-brentwood-nh-03833-6400-united-states/join-amy-at-the-inaugural-hot-dish-house-party/2537250096564014/.

54. Severson, "A Classic Midwestern Dish Becomes a Talking Point in Iowa."

55. Keith Brannon-Tulane, "Political Attack Ads Have More Power against Women," *Futurity*, August 2, 2017, https://www.futurity.org/attack-ads-women-1501982/.

56. Joan Williams, "How Women Can Escape the Likability Trap," *The New York Times*, August 16, 2019, https://www.nytimes.com/2019/08/16/opinion/sunday/gender-bias-work.html.

57. Kate Cairns and Josee Johnston, *Food and Femininity* (New York: Blooms-bury Academic, 2015); K. Cairns, J. Johnston, and S. Baumann, "Caring about Food: Doing Gender in the Foodie Kitchen," *Gender & Society* 24, no. 5 (October 1, 2010): 591–615, https://doi.org/10.1177/0891243210383419.

58. Bernard Weinraub, "Mississippi Farm Topic: Does She Bake Muffins?" *The New York Times*, August 2, 1984, https://www.nytimes.com/1984/08/02/us/mississippi-farm-topic-does-she-bake-muffins.html.

59. "Muffing the Muffin Test," *The Washington Post*, March 27, 1986, https://www.washingtonpost.com/archive/lifestyle/1986/03/27/muffing-the-muffin-test/744a893c-4af1-418b-98da-84658f1f5c53/.

60. Walter Mondale, "Geraldine Ferraro Changed the Way Americans Thought of Each Other," *MPR News*, March 30, 2011, https://www.mprnews.org/story/2011/03/31/mondale.

61. Ashley Parker, "Donald Trump's Diet: He'll Have Fries with That," *The New York Times*, August 8, 2016, https://www.nytimes.com/2016/08/09/us/politics/donald-trump-diet.html.

62. Ibid.

63. Ibid.

64. Jones, "Politics on a Plate," 59.

65. Tom Sietsema, "The World Is Trump's Oyster, but He Prefers Filet-O-Fish," *The Washington Post*, March 24, 2016, https://www.washingtonpost.com/lifestyle/food/trump-can-afford-to-eat-the-finest-food-instead-he-eats-the-most-generic/2016/03/24/63aedb18-eaf0–11e5-bc08–3e03a5b41910_story.html?utm_term=.8987b3141738.

66. Betsy Klein, "Fast Food Once again Served at White House Sports Event with Trump," *CNN*, March 4, 2019, https://www.cnn.com/2019/03/04/politics/trump-fast-food-white-house/index.html.

67. Parker, "Donald Trump's Diet."

68. Joel Siegel, "Sarah Palin, Donald Trump Lambasted for Pizza Faux Pas," *ABC News*, June 2, 2011, https://abcnews.go.com/Politics/donald-trump-sarah-palin-pizza-fail-knives-forks/story?id=13743490.

69. Twitter, @realDonaldTrump, August 1, 2016, 9:22 pm, https://twitter.com/realdonaldtrump/status/760299757206208512?lang=en.

70. Marc Auge, *Non-Places: An Introduction to Supermodernity* (London; New York: Verso, 1995).

71. K. Annabelle Smith, "Why Japan Is Obsessed with Kentucky Fried Chicken on Christmas," *Smithsonian Magazine*, December 14, 2012, https://www.smithsonianmag.com/arts-culture/why-japan-is-obsessed-with-kentucky-fried-chicken-on-christmas-1-161666960/.

72. Psyche A. Williams-Forson, *Building Houses out of Chicken Legs: Black Women, Food, and Power* (Chapel Hill: University of North Carolina Press, 2006).

73. Adrian Miller, *Soul Food: The Surprising Story of an American Cuisine, One Plate at a Time* (Chapel Hill: University of North Carolina Press, 2013).

74. Twitter, @JasJWright, February 10, 2019, 7:16 am.

75. Maura Judkis, "Let's Unpack That Viral (and since-Deleted) Criticism of Kamala Harris Eating Chicken and Waffles," *The Washington Post*, February 22, 2019, https://www.washingtonpost.com/news/voraciously/wp/2019/02/22/lets-unpack-that-viral-and-since-deleted-criticism-of-kamala-harris-eating-chicken-and-waffles/; Sara Dickerman, "Why We're So Obsessed With How Politicians Eat," *POLITICO Magazine*, March 17, 2019, https://politi.co/2TVqNBy.

76. Dennis Romero, "Goya Foods' CEO Said U.S. 'Blessed' to Have Trump as a Leader, and Calls for Boycott Quickly Followed," *NBC News*, July 9, 2020, https://www.nbcnews.com/news/latino/goya-food-s-ceo-said-u-s-blessed-have-trump-n1233392.

77. Rachel Hatzipanagos, "Analysis|Even before the El Paso Mass Shooting, Latinos Said Trump's Anti-Immigrant Rhetoric Made Them Feel Unsafe," *The Washington Post*, August 16, 2020, https://www.washingtonpost.com/nation/2019/08/16/even-before-el-paso-latinos-said-trumps-anti-immigrant-rhetoric-made-them-feel-unsafe/.

78. Nadra Nittle, "Julián Castro on the Goya Boycott and How to Support Communities of Color During the Pandemic," *Eater*, July 15, 2020, https://www.eater.com/2020/7/15/21324965/goya-boycott-julian-castro-interview-how-to-support-communities-of-color.

79. Twitter, @realDonaldTrump, July 20, 2020, 6:26 pm, https://twitter.com/realDonaldTrump/status/1281731565278515202.

80. Twitter, @tedcruz, July 10, 2020, 3:01 pm, https://twitter.com/tedcruz/status/1281679899607142400.

81. Twitter, @Ivankatrump, July 14, 2020, 9:05 pm, https://twitter.com/IvankaTrump/status/1283221019684110337; Fabio Parasecoli, "Beans Battles: Goya, the Trumps, and the Power of Food," *Fabio Parasecoli*, July 20, 2020, https://fabioparasecoli.com/beans-battles-goya-the-trumps-and-the-power-of-food/.

82. Instagram, @realdonaldtrump, July 15, 2020, https://www.instagram.com/p/CCrAzKiBFUQ/.

83. Farah Stockman, Kate Kelly, and Jennifer Medina, "How Buying Beans Became a Political Statement," *The New York Times*, July 19, 2020, https://www.nytimes.com/2020/07/19/us/goya-trump-hispanic-vote.html.

84. Fabio Parasecoli, "Beans Battles: Goya, the Trumps, and the Power of Food," *Fabio Parasecoli*, July 20, 2020, https://fabioparasecoli.com/beans-battles-goya-the-trumps-and-the-power-of-food/.

85. Amanda Barroso, "Gen Z Eligible Voters Reflect the Growing Racial and Ethnic Diversity of U.S. Electorate," Pew Research Center, September 23, 2020, https://www.pewresearch.org/fact-tank/2020/09/23/gen-z-eligible-voters-reflect-the-growing-racial-and-ethnic-diversity-of-u-s-electorate/.

86. Gary He, "The Andrew Yang Campaign Trail Diet," *Eater*, December 19, 2019, https://www.eater.com/2019/12/19/21025610/andrew-yang-campaign-trail-diet.

87. He, "The Pete Buttigieg Campaign Trail Diet"; Zhang, "What 2020 Democratic Presidential Candidates' Comfort Food Preferences Say About Them."

88. George Ritzer, *The McDonaldization of Society*, 3rd ed. (Thousand Oaks, CA: SAGE Publications, 2000).

89. Julia Carrie Wong, "Burritos, Bagels and $16K Worth of Sushi: How 2020 Democrats Are Feeding Their Staff," *The Guardian*, February 10, 2020, https://www.theguardian.com/us-news/2020/feb/10/pizza-sushi-ben-jerrys-what-2020-democrats-are-feeding-their-staffers.

90. Jones, "Politics on a Plate," 49.

91. Gary He, "The Lavish Spreads of Mike Bloomberg's Food-Filled Campaign," *Eater*, February 18, 2020, https://www.eater.com/2020/2/18/21140518/mike-bloomberg-campaign-spending-free-food-voting-democrat-primary.

92. Krishnendu Ray, *The Ethnic Restaurateur* (London; New York, NY: Bloomsbury Academic, 2016).

93. Fabio Parasecoli, "No Food in the US Presidential Debates," *Fabio Parasecoli*, October 19, 2020, https://fabioparasecoli.com/no-food-in-the-us-presidential-debates/.

94. Michael Pollan, "Farmer in Chief," *The New York Times*, October 9, 2008, https://www.nytimes.com/2008/10/12/magazine/12policy-t.html.

95. Emily Heil and Tom Sietsema, "Diner-in-Chief: How the Bidens Might Eat and Entertain in and out of the White House," *The Washington Post*, October 20, 2020, https://www.washingtonpost.com/food/2020/10/20/diner-in-chief-how-bidens-would-dine-entertain-white-house/; Alison Ashton, "Jill Biden Shares Her Favorite Foods, What She's Been Reading and Her Parmesan Chicken Recipe," *Parade: Entertainment, Recipes, Health, Life, Holidays*, February 28, 2020, https://parade.com/983863/alison-ashton/jill-biden-chicken-parmesan-recipe/.

96. "Joe Biden's Plan for Rural America," *Joe Biden for President: Official Campaign*, accessed August 10, 2020, https://joebiden.com/rural/.

97. Menzie Chinn and Bill Plumley, "What Is the Toll of Trade Wars on U.S. Agriculture?" *PBS NewsHour*, January 16, 2020, https://www.pbs.org/newshour/economy/making-sense/what-is-the-toll-of-trade-wars-on-u-s-agriculture.

98. Julie M. Weise, "Perspective | Trump's Latest Immigration Restriction Exposes a Key Contradiction in Policy," *The Washington Post*, June 23, 2020, https://www.washingtonpost.com/outlook/2020/06/23/trumps-latest-immigration-restriction-exposes-key-contradiction-policy/.

99. Samantha Gross, "What Is the Trump Administration's Track Record on the Environment?" *Brookings*, August 4, 2020, https://www.brookings.edu/policy2020/votervital/what-is-the-trump-administrations-track-record-on-the-environment/.

100. Poska and The Civil Eats Editors, "Where the 2020 Presidential Candidates Stand on Food and Farming."

101. Devon C. Payne-Sturges et al., "Student Hunger on Campus: Food Insecurity among College Students and Implications for Academic Institutions," *American Journal of Health Promotion* 32, no. 2 (February 1, 2018): 349–54, https://doi.org/10.1177/0890117117719620.

102. Charlie Mitchell, "Climate Town Hall Brings Food and Agriculture to Center Stage," *Civil Eats*, September 5, 2019, https://civileats.com/2019/09/05/climate-town-hall-brings-food-and-agriculture-to-center-stage/.

103. Sam Bloch, "A Handful of Companies Control American Agriculture. Cory Booker Wants to Change That," *The Counter*, August 30, 2018, https://thecounter.org/cory-booker-agribusiness-merger-moratorium-antitrust-bill/.

104. Meghan McCarron, "The Most Powerful Restaurant Workers in America," *Eater*, February 20, 2020, https://www.eater.com/2020/2/20/21144675/culinary-workers-union-local-226-nevada-caucus-bernie-sanders-healthcare-las-vegas.

105. Chris Macias, "Is the Food Supply Strong Enough to Weather the COVID-19 Pandemic?" UC Davis, Feeding a Growing Population, June 25, 2020, https://www.ucdavis.edu/food/news/is-food-supply-strong-enough-to-weather-covid-19-pandemic;

Michael Grabell Yeung Bernice, "Meatpacking Companies Dismissed Years of Warnings but Now Say Nobody Could Have Prepared for COVID-19," *ProPublica*, August 20, 2020, https://www.propublica.org/article/meatpacking-companies-dismissed-years-of-warnings-but-now-say-nobody-could-have-prepared-for-covid-19? token=k0PuAmvq_Xy63TS9ofcxNn6J431eO1RK; Kelly McCarthy, "Nearly 16,000 Restaurants Have Closed Permanently Due to the Pandemic, Yelp Data Shows," *ABC News*, July 24, 2020, https://abcnews.go.com/Business/16000-restaurants-closed-permanently-due-pandemic-yelp-data/story?id=71943970.

106. Jeff Mason Polansek Tom, "Trump Orders U.S. Meat-Processing Plants to Stay Open despite Coronavirus Fears," *Reuters*, April 29, 2020, https://www.reuters.com/article/us-health-coronavirus-trump-liability-idUSKCN22A2OB.

107. David Knowles, "Biden Says U.S. Doesn't Have a Food Shortage Problem, 'We Have a Leadership Problem,'" *Yahoo News*, May 19, 2020, https://news.yahoo.com/biden-says-america-doesnt-have-a-food-shortage-problem-we-have-a-leadership-problem-235352311.html.

108. Ibid.

CHAPTER 9

1. Brian Schwartz, "Total 2020 Election Spending to Hit Nearly \$14 Billion, More than Double 2016's Sum," *CNBC*, last modified November 1, 2020, https://www.cnbc.com/2020/10/28/2020-election-spending-to-hit-nearly-14-billion-a-record.html.

2. "About Us," *Act Blue*, accessed January 1, 2020, https://secure.actblue.com/about.

3. *Act Blue*, accessed January 2, 2021, https://secure.actblue.com/.

4. David Nickerson and Todd Rogers, "Political Campaigns and Big Data," Faculty Research Working Paper Series Harvard Kennedy School, November 2013, https://scholar.harvard.edu/files/todd_rogers/files/political_campaigns_and_big_data_0.pdf.

5. Seema Mehta and Evan Halper, "Democratic Donors Fuel Record-Breaking Fundraising in Senate Races," *Los Angeles Times*, October 17, 2020, https://www.latimes.com/politics/story/2020-10-17/record-breaking-fundraising-senate.

6. Brian Schwartz, "Mike Bloomberg Takes Big Losses after Spending over \$100 Million in Florida, Ohio, and Texas," *CNBC*, last updated November 4, 2020, https://www.cnbc.com/2020/11/04/bloomberg-sees-losses-after-spending-over-100-million-in-florida-ohio-texas.html.

7. Harry Enten, "How Republicans Nearly Pulled Off a Big Upset and Nearly Took Back the House," *CNN*, last updated November 14, 2020, https://www.cnn.com/2020/11/14/politics/house-republicans-elections-analysis/index.html.

8. Shane Goldmacher, "With Senate Control Hanging in the Balance, 'Crazytown' Cash Floods Georgia," *The New York Times*, last updated December 8, 2020, https://www.nytimes.com/2020/11/19/us/politics/georgia-senate-races-donations.html; Brooke Singman, "RNC Ramps Up Staffing, Volunteers in Georgia, Vows to Spend at

least $20M Ahead of Senate Runoffs," *Fox News*, last updated December 1, 2020, https://www.foxnews.com/politics/rnc-georgia-senate-races-staffing-volunteers-spending.

9. Cayce Myers, "Campaign Finance and Its Impact on the 2020 Campaign," in *The 2016 U.S. Presidential Campaign*, ed. Robert Denton (London: Palgrave Macmillan, 2017), 259–267.

10. Myers, "Campaign Finance," 261–262.

11. *Newberry v. U.S.*, 256 U.S. 232 (1921). *Newberry* is an interesting case because it highlights many of the issues seen in modern-day politics. It involved a law passed in Michigan that prohibited any congressional candidate from spending more than 25 percent of one year's salary on an election. The case involved a Michigan Senate Republican primary in which a candidate Truman Newberry spent $100,000 against automotive titan Henry Ford. Newberry won the Republican primary and the subsequent election.

12. Myers, "Campaign Finance and Its Impact on the 2020 Campaign," 262.

13. *Buckley v. Valeo*, 424, U.S. 1 (1976). There were multiple plaintiffs in *Buckley v. Valeo* that represented a cross section of political beliefs. The plaintiffs included not only Buckley, the brother of famed conservative writer and founder of *National Review* William F. Buckley Jr., but also former Democratic nominee for President Eugene McCarthy, the New York Civil Liberties Union, the American Conservative Union, and other plaintiffs from across the political spectrum.

14. *Buckley v. Valeo*, 424, U.S.1 (1976).

15. Ibid., 47.

16. Ibid., 44, n. 52 (1976).

17. *First National Bank of Boston v. Belotti*, 435 U.S. 765 (1978).

18. This case was about corporate spending by the First National Bank of Boston and other corporate plaintiffs on an income tax referendum issue.

19. *Federal Election Commission v. Massachusetts Citizens for Life*, 479 U.S. 278 (1986).

20. *Citizens United v. Federal Election Commission*, 558 U.S. 310 (2010).

21. Bipartisan Campaign Reform Act of 2002, Public Law 107–155.

22. Hard money is money donated directly to candidates.

23. John McCain and Russ Feingold, "A Better Way to Fix Campaign Financing," *The Washington Post*, February 20, 1996, https://www.washingtonpost.com/opinions/a-better-way-to-fix-campaign-financing/2018/08/26/b45ede68-a935-11e8-a8d7-0f63ab8b1370_story.html.

24. McCain and Feingold were specifically addressing an opinion piece by David Broder published in January of 1996 titled "A Senate of Millionaires." In that piece Broder discussed how increasingly U.S. Senators were wealthy candidates who frequently self-financed some of their own campaigns. He saw this as a bipartisan issue that spanned candidates from the left and right.

25. *McCutcheon v. FEC*, 572 U.S. 185 (2014). The decision in this case is extremely long and complex containing multiple parts written by different justices.

26. *Citizens United v. Federal Election Commission*, 558 U.S. 310 (2010).

27. During the address President Obama criticized the Court's decision, claiming that it gave corporations an unfair advantage and open the way for foreign corporations to donate money into the U.S. election system. Justice Alito, a member of the

majority in *Citizens United*, was seen to mouth a response, which some said was "not true." See Mark Memmott, "If Alito Did Say 'Not True' about Obama's Claim, He May Have Had a Point," *National Public Radio*, January 28, 2010, https://www.npr.org/sections/thetwo-way/2010/01/if_alito_did_say_not_true_abou.html.

28. At issue in this case was the FECA section 441 that limited the amount an individual donor could make to national parties and candidate committees within a two-year period. This was a 5–4 vote with Justice Clarence Thomas concurring separately arguing that all campaign contribution limits are unconstitutional.

29. For a discussion of gray money in American campaign finance, see Chisun Lee and Douglas Keith, "How Semi-Secret Spending Took Over Politics," *The Atlantic Monthly*, June 28, 2016, https://www.theatlantic.com/politics/archive/2016/06/the-rise-of-gray-money-in-politics/489002/.

30. Peter Overby, "Obama Outspending McCain in Three Key States," *National Public Radio*, October 9, 2008, https://www.npr.org/templates/story/story.php?storyId=95531831.

31. John Whitesides and Caren Bohan, "Obama Rejects Public Financing against McCain," *Reuters*, last updated June 19, 2008, https://www.reuters.com/article/us-usa-politics/obama-rejects-public-financing-against-mccain-idUSN1828132020080619. The use of public funding of presidential elections declined since 2008. In 2014 a new law went into effect eliminating public funding for presidential conventions.

32. Kathy Keily, "Public Campaign Funding Is So Broken that Candidates Turned Down $292 million in Free Money," *The Washington Post*, February 9, 2016, https://www.google.com/amp/s/www.washingtonpost.com/posteverything/wp/2016/02/09/public-campaign-funding-is-so-broken-that-candidates-turned-down-292-million-in-free-money/%3foutputType=amp.

33. Brian Slodysko, "Shadow Group Provides Sanders Super-PAC Support He Scorns," *AP News*, January 7, 2020, https://apnews.com/article/345bbd1af529cfb1e41305fa3ab1e604.

34. Chris Cilliza, "Why a Brokered Democratic Convention Could Actually Happen in 2020," *CNN*, last updated February 12, 2020, https://www.cnn.com/2020/02/12/politics/democrats-2020-brokered-convention/index.html.

35. Terenca Chea, "Buttigieg Backers Defend 'Wine Cave' Fundraiser," *AP News*, December 21, 2020, https://apnews.com/article/a74487680e39e68805b6647816abf7fe.

36. Maggie Astor, "Elizabeth Warren, Criticizing Bloomberg, Sent a Message: She Won't be Ignored," *The New York Times*, March 5, 2020, https://www.nytimes.com/2020/02/19/us/politics/elizabeth-warren-debate.html.

37. Brian Slodysko, "Shadow Group Provides Sanders Super-PAC Support He Scorns," *AP News*, January 7, 2020, https://apnews.com/article/345bbd1af529cfb1e41305fa3ab1e604.

38. Nick Corasaniti, "Buttigieg-Warren Clash Over Wine Cave Fundraiser," *The New York Times*, December 19, 2020, https://www.nytimes.com/2019/12/19/us/politics/wine-cave.html.

39. Ben Zimmer, "How the 'Purity Test' Became Political Speak," *The Atlantic Monthly*, December 19, 2019, https://www.theatlantic.com/entertainment/archive/2019/12/pbs-democratic-debate-warren-buttigieg-purity-tests/603979/.

40. Matthew Choi, "Andrew Yang Defends Random Money Giveaway," *Politico*, last updated September 15, 2019, https://www.politico.com/story/2019/09/15/andrew-yang-random-money-giveaway-snl-cast-member-1496183.

41. Holly Otterbein and David Siders, "Sanders Suspends His Presidential Campaign," *Politico*, April 8, 2020, https://www.politico.com/news/2020/04/08/bernie-sanders-suspends-his-presidential-campaign-175137; Shane Goldmacher and Astead Herndon, "Elizabeth Warren, Once a Front Runner, Drops out of Presidential Race," *The New York Times*, March 10, 2020, https://www.nytimes.com/2020/03/05/us/politics/elizabeth-warren-drops-out.html.

42. Report of Receipts and Reimbursements, Kamala Harris for the People, Federal Election Commission, accessed January 2, 2021, https://docquery.fec.gov/cgi-bin/forms/C00694455/1391949/.

43. "Presidential Candidate Map, Pete Buttigieg Spending," Federal Election Commission, accessed January 2, 2020, https://www.fec.gov/data/candidates/president/presidential-map/. Buttigieg later converted his campaign organization, Pete for America, to Win the ERA PAC.

44. "Financial Summary Mike Bloomberg 2020," Federal Election Commission, accessed January 2, 2020, https://www.fec.gov/data/candidate/P00014530/?cycle=2020&election_full=true.

45. Sarah Ewall-Wice, "How Much Did Mike Bloomberg Spend Per Delegate? About $18 Million," *CBS News*, March 4, 2020, https://www.cbsnews.com/news/bloomberg-delegate-18-million/.

46. "Financial Summary Weld Presidential Campaign Committee, Inc.," Federal Election Commission, accessed January 2, 2021, https://www.fec.gov/data/candidate/P00011239/?cycle=2020&election_full=true.

47. Alex Isenstadt, "Trump Drives Massive Turnout in Primaries Despite Token Opposition," *Politico*, last updated February 16, 2020, https://www.politico.com/news/2020/02/16/trump-campaign-voter-turnout-115338.

48. Reuters Staff, "October 15 U.S. Presidential Debate Officially Cancelled after Trump Balked," *Reuters*, October 9, 2020, https://www.reuters.com/article/uk-usa-election-debate/october-15-u-s-presidential-debate-officially-canceled-after-trump-balked-idUSKBN26U2M5.

49. "Presidential Candidate Map, All Candidates Raising," Federal Election Commission, accessed January 2, 2020, https://www.fec.gov/data/candidates/president/presidential-map/.

50. Ibid.

51. Myers, "Campaign Finance," 273–276.

CHAPTER 10

1. Kate Kenski, Christine R. Filer, and Bethany A. Conway-Silva, "Lying, Liars, and Lies: Incivility in 2016 Presidential Candidate and Campaign Tweets During the Invisible Primary," *American Behavioral Scientist* 62, no. 3 (2018): 286–299. doi:10.1177/0002764217724840.

2. Josh Holder, Trip Gabriel, and Isabella Grullón Paz, "Biden's 306 Electoral College Votes Make His Victory Official," *The New York Times*, December 14, 2020, accessed December 28, 2020, https://www.nytimes.com/interactive/2020/12/14/us/elections/electoral-college-results.html.

3. Stephen Battaglio, "How the Networks Decided to Call the Election for Joe Biden," *Los Angeles Times*, November 7, 2020, accessed December 28, 2020, https://www.latimes.com/entertainment-arts/business/story/2020-11-07/joe-biden-president-elect-television-news-networks.

4. Rosalind S. Helderman, Jon Swaine, and Michelle Ye Hee Lee, "Despite Trump's Intense Hunt for Voter Fraud, Officials in Key States Have So Far Identified Just a Small Number of Possible Cases," *The Washington Post*, December 23, 2020, accessed December 28, 2020, https://www.washingtonpost.com/politics/voter-fraud-investigations-2020/2020/12/22/bdbe541c-42de-11eb-b0e4-0f182923a025_story.html.

5. Federal Election Commission, "Federal Elections 2016: Election Results for the U.S. President, the U.S. Senate and the U.S. House of Representatives," Washington, DC, December 2017, https://www.fec.gov/resources/cms-content/documents/federalelections2016.pdf.

6. FiveThirtyEight, "How Unpopular Is Donald Trump?" updated December 20, 2020, accessed December 20, 2020, https://projects.fivethirtyeight.com/trump-approval-ratings/.

7. Shanto Iyengar, Yphtach Lelkes, Matthew Levendusky, Neil Malhotra, and Sean J. Westwood. "The Origins and Consequences of Affective Polarization in the United States," *Annual Review of Political Science* 22 (2019): 129–146. doi:10.1146/annurev-polisci-051117-073034.

8. Ibid.

9. Federal Election Commission, "Federal Elections 2000: Election Results for the U.S. President, the U.S. Senate and the U.S. House of Representatives," Washington, DC, June 2001, accessed January 26, 2021, https://www.fec.gov/resources/cms-content/documents/federalelections00.pdf.

10. Alexander Theodoridis, "The Campaign That Didn't Matter?" *Sabato's Crystal Ball*, November 2, 2020, accessed December 31, 2020, https://centerforpolitics.org/crystalball/articles/the-campaign-that-didnt-matter/.

11. Ibid.

12. Kathleen Hall Jamieson, *Cyber-war: How Russian Hackers and Trolls Helped Elect a President* (New York: Oxford University Press, 2018).

13. Pew Research Center, "Social Media Fact Sheet," *Pew Research Center Internet & Technology*, June 12, 2019, accessed December 29, 2020, https://www.pewresearch.org/internet/fact-sheet/social-media/.

14. David E. Sanger and Zolan Kanno-Youngs, "Russian Trolls' Star Content Provider Is Trump," *The New York Times*, September 23, 2020, A17.

15. Zolan Kanno-Youngs, "Russia and Supremacists Are Posing Threats to U.S., F.B.I. Chief Warns House," *The New York Times,* September 18, 2020, A16.

16. Meysam Alizadeh, Cody Buntain, Jacob N. Shapiro, and Joshua Tucker, "Are Influence Campaigns Trolling Your Social Media Feeds?" *The Washington Post*,

October 13, 2020, accessed December 29, 2020, https://www.washingtonpost.com/politics/2020/10/13/are-influence-campaigns-trolling-your-social-media-feeds/.

17. Sheera Frenkel, Ben Decker, and Davey Alba, "How the 'Plandemic' Video Went Viral Online," *The New York Times*, May 21, 2020, B1, accessed December 29, 2020, https://www.nytimes.com/2020/05/20/technology/plandemic-movie-youtube-facebook-coronavirus.html.

18. Kevin Roose, "What Is QAnon, the Viral Pro-Trump Conspiracy Theory?" *The New York Times*, October 19, 2020, accessed December 29, 2020, https://www.nytimes.com/article/what-is-qanon.html.

19. Gallup, *Most Important Problem*, December 2020, accessed December 28, 2020, https://news.gallup.com/poll/1675/most-important-problem.aspx.

20. Sarah Boseley, "Origin Story: What Do We Know Now about Where Coronavirus Came From?" *The Guardian*, December 12, 2020, accessed December 28, 2020, https://www.theguardian.com/world/2020/dec/12/where-did-coronavirus-come-from-covid.

21. Ibid.

22. Ed Yong, "How the Pandemic Defeated America," *The Atlantic*, August 4, 2020, accessed December 28, 2020, https://www.theatlantic.com/magazine/archive/2020/09/coronavirus-american-failure/614191/.

23. Sarah Kaplan, William Wan, and Joel Achenbach, "The Coronavirus Isn't Alive. That's Why It's So Hard To Kill," *The Washington Post*, March 23, 2020, accessed December 28, 2020, https://www.washingtonpost.com/health/2020/03/23/coronavirus-isnt-alive-thats-why-its-so-hard-kill/.

24. Benjamin Fearnow, "Biden Warned One Year Ago, before COVID, U.S. 'Not Prepared for a Pandemic,'" *Newsweek*, October 25, 2020, accessed December 28, 2020, https://www.newsweek.com/biden-warned-one-year-ago-before-covid-us-not-prepared-pandemic-1541995.

25. World Health Organization, *Shortage of Personal Protective Equipment Endangering Health Workers Worldwide*, March 3, 2020, accessed December 28, 2020, https://www.who.int/news/item/03-03-2020-shortage-of-personal-protective-equipment-endangering-health-workers-worldwide.

26. Marc J. Hetherington and Isaac D. Mehlhaff, "American Attitudes toward Covid-19 Are Divided by Party. The Pandemic Itself Might Undo That," *The Washington Post*, August 18, 2020, accessed December 29, 2020, https://www.washingtonpost.com/politics/2020/08/18/american-attitudes-toward-covid-19-are-divided-by-party-pandemic-itself-might-undo-that/.

27. Noah Higgins-Dunn, "U.S. Reports Second-highest Daily Number of Covid Cases on Election Day as Scientists Warn of a Dangerous Winter," *CNBC.com*, November 4, 2020, accessed December 29, 2020, https://www.cnbc.com/2020/11/04/us-reports-second-highest-daily-number-of-covid-cases-on-election-day-as-scientists-warn-of-a-dangerous-winter.html.

28. Ibid.

29. Dieter Stiers, "Beyond the Distinction between Incumbency and Opposition: Retrospective Voting at the Level of Political Parties," *Party Politics* 25, no. 6 (2019): 805–816. doi:10.1177/1354068817744201.

30. U.S. Department of the Treasury, The CARES Act Works for All Americans (2020), accessed December 29, 2020, https://home.treasury.gov/policy-issues/cares.

31. Mike Patton, "The Impact of Covid-19 on U.S. Economy and Financial Markets," *Forbes*, October 12, 2020, accessed October 12, 2020, https://www.forbes.com/sites/mikepatton/2020/10/12/the-impact-of-covid-19-on-us-economy-and-financial-markets/?sh=7d16b9f82d20.

32. Ibid.

33. Ibid.

34. "Ahmaud Arbery: What Do We Know about the Case?" *BBC.com*, June 5, 2020, accessed December 29, 2020, https://www.bbc.com/news/world-us-canada-52623151.

35. Richard A. Oppel Jr., Derrick Bryson Taylor, and Nicholas Bogel-Burroughs, "What to Know about Breonna Taylor's Death," *The New York Times*, December 28, 2020, accessed December 29, 2020, https://www.nytimes.com/article/breonna-taylor-police.html.

36. "What We Know about the Death of George Floyd in Minneapolis," *The New York Times*, December 9, 2020, accessed December 29, 2020, https://www.nytimes.com/article/george-floyd.html.

37. George Petras, "200 of Trump's Tweets Singled Out Protests, Police following George Floyd Death," *USA Today*, June 11, 2020, accessed December 29, 2020, https://www.usatoday.com/in-depth/news/2020/06/11/trump-tweets-george-floyd-protests-police/5329940002/.

38. Ballotpedia, Battleground States, 2020, accessed December 29, 2020, https://ballotpedia.org/Presidential_battleground_states,_2020.

39. Henry C. Kenski and Kate M. Kenski, "Explaining the Vote in the Election of 2016: The Remarkable Come from Behind Victory of Republican Candidate Donald Trump," in *The 2016 Presidential Campaign: Political Communication and Practice*, ed. Robert E. Denton Jr. (Palgrave Macmillan, 2017), 285–309.

40. Kate Kenski, "Arizona: Right of Center with Potential to Change," in *Presidential Swing States*, ed. David A. Schultz and Rafael Jacob (Lanham, MD: Lexington Books, 2018), 307–321.

41. Gallup, *Party Affiliation*, accessed December 29, 2020, https://news.gallup.com/poll/15370/party-affiliation.aspx.

42. CNN, *Exit Polls*, accessed December 31, 2020, https://www.cnn.com/election/2020/exit-polls/president/national-results.

43. Ibid.

44. Henry C. Kenski, "The Gender Gap in a Changing Electorate," in *The Politics of the Gender Gap: The Social Construction of Political Influence*, ed. Carol Mueller (Newbury Park, CA: Sage Publications, 1988), 36–69.

45. Kate Kenski and Kathleen Hall Jamieson, "The Gender Gap in Political Knowledge: Are Women Less Knowledgeable than Men about Politics?" in *Everything You Think You Know About Politics . . . And Why You're Wrong*, ed. Kathleen Hall Jamieson (New York: Basic Books, 2000), 83–89.

46. Henry C. Kenski and Kate M. Kenski, "Explaining the Vote in the Election of 2008," in *The 2008 Presidential Campaign: A Communication Perspective*, ed. Robert E. Denton Jr. (Lanham, MD: Rowman and Littlefield, 2009), 244–290.

47. David A. Graham, "The Polling Crisis Is a Catastrophe for American Democracy," *The Atlantic*, November 4, 2020, accessed December 31, 2020, https://www.theatlantic.com/ideas/archive/2020/11/polling-catastrophe/616986/.

48. Laura Bronner and Nathaniel Rakich, "Exit Polls Can Be Misleading—Especially This Year," *FiveThirtyEight*, November 2, 2020, accessed January 26, 2021, https://fivethirtyeight.com/features/exit-polls-can-be-misleading-especially-this-year/.

EPILOGUE

1. John Gramlich, "20 Striking Findings from 2020," Pew Research Center, December 11, 2020, https://www.pewresearch.org/fact-tank/2020/12/11/20-striking-fin...2_12&utm_medium=email&utm_term=0_3e953b9b70-4a3f02d5c1-399745905, retrieved December 12, 2020.

2. Rasmussen Reports, "Voters See Each Other as America's Enemy," December 1, 2020, https://www.rasmussenreports.com/public_content/politics/general_poli tics/november_2...merica_s_enemy?utm_campaign=RR12012020DN&utm_source= criticalimapct&utm_medium=ema, retrieved December 12, 2020.

3. Robert E. Denton Jr. and Benjamin Voth, *Social Fragmentation and the Decline of American Democracy: The End of the Social Contract* (Cham, Switzerland: Palgrave Macmillan, 2017).

4. Abraham Lincoln, "Annual Message to Congress—Concluding Remarks," *Abraham Lincoln Online*, http://www.abrahamlincolnonline.org/lincoln/speeches/congress.htm, retrieved January 10, 2021.

Index

About the Contributors 2020

Lisa M. Burns is Professor of Media Studies at Quinnipiac University. She teaches courses including "Media, History & Memory"; "Media & Society"; "Media Trend Forecasting & Strategy"; "Political Communication"; "Media Critics & Influencers"; and "Celebrity Culture." Her research interests include media history, political communication (particularly media coverage of U.S. first ladies and presidents), public/collective memory, and media criticism. Burns edited the collection *Media Relations and the Modern First Lady: From Jacqueline Kennedy to Melania Trump* was released in 2020. Her previous book, *First Ladies and the Fourth Estate: Press Framing of Presidential Wives*, was published in August 2008. She has also published several journal articles and book chapters on first ladies.

Emily J. H. Contois is Chapman Assistant Professor of Media Studies at the University of Tulsa. She is the author of *Diners, Dudes, and Diets: How Gender and Power Collide in Food Media and Culture* (2020) and numerous articles addressing food, bodies, health, and identity in media and popular culture. As a public scholar, she has appeared on CBS, NBC, BBC, and *Ugly Delicious* with chef David Chang on Netflix, among others.

Robert E. Denton Jr. holds the W. Thomas Rice Chair in the Pamplin College of Business and is Professor and Director of the School of Communication at Virginia Tech. Denton is the author, co-author, or editor of thirty books, several in multiple editions, on the presidency and political campaigns. His most recent volume is titled *Political Campaign Communication: Principles and Practices, 9th Edition* (with Judith Trent and Robert Friedenberg).

Scott Dunn is Associate Professor in the School of Communication at Radford University. He studies political communication, and his current research interest is young people's engagement with politics. He is the author of numerous articles, book chapters, and professional research papers.

John Allen Hendricks is Chair and Professor of the Department of Mass Communication (since 2009) at Stephen F. Austin State University, where he teaches courses in communication theory, research methods, and media/politics. He has authored/edited more than twelve books on the topics of media/politics, social media/new media technologies, and the broadcasting industry.

Henry C. Kenski is a retired professor, currently teaching one course each semester as an adjunct professor at the University of Arizona. His research and teaching interests are in media, public opinion, campaigns, and presidential leadership. He has published two books: *Saving the Hidden Treasure: The Evolution of Ground Water Policy* and a co-authored endeavor with Michael Pfau titled *Attack Politics: Strategy and Defense*. In addition, he has published numerous articles on different facets of political communication. Professor Kenski believes, however, that his most important contribution to the field of political communication is his daughter Kate Kenski.

Kate Kenski is Associate Professor of Communication and Government & Public Policy at the University of Arizona, where she teaches political communication, public opinion, and research methods. Her book *The Obama Victory: How Media, Money, and Message Shaped the 2008 Election* (co-authored with Bruce W. Hardy and Kathleen Hall Jamieson) has won several awards, including the 2011 ICA Outstanding Book Award and the 2012 NCA Diamond Anniversary Book Award. Kenski is also co-author of *Capturing Campaign Dynamics: The National Annenberg Election Survey* and co-editor of *The Oxford Handbook of Political Communication* with Kathleen Hall Jamieson. She has published over seventy book chapters, articles, and research papers.

Courtney Marchese is Associate Professor of Interactive Media and Design at Quinnipiac University. She teaches a wide range of design theory, research, and technical skills at the undergraduate and graduate levels. She is also a professional designer with over a decade of experience specializing in data visualization, information graphics, user experience design, and usability studies. Using a human-centered design approach, Marchese has created a number of data-based multidisciplinary projects, including a nationally recognized award-winning voter education initiative based on political data from the renowned Quinnipiac Polling Institute. Her forthcoming book from Bloomsbury Press is titled *Information Design for the Common Good.*

Cayce Myers is Associate Professor and Director of Graduate Studies at the School of Communication at Virginia Tech. Dr. Myers's research focuses on laws that affect communication practice and the historical development of American public relations, social media, and media history. Myers is the author of *Public Relations History: Theory, Practice, and Profession* and co-author of *Mass Communication Law in Virginia.* He holds a PhD and MA from the University of Georgia Grady College of Journalism and Mass Communication, an LLM from the University of Georgia School of Law, a JD from Mercer University Walter F. George School of Law, and a BA in political science and history from Emory University.

Dan Schill is Professor in the School of Communication Studies and Affiliate Professor in Political Science at James Madison University, where he teaches courses in advocacy, political communication, research methods, and media and politics. He has published several books on political communication. His most recent is *Political Communication in Real Time* (with Rita Kirk and Amy Jasperson).

Theodore F. Sheckels is the Charles Potts Professor of Social Science as well as professor of English and communication studies at Randolph-Macon College. He earned his PhD and MA from Pennsylvania State University. Dr. Sheckels has contributed numerous articles and book chapters to publications within his field and has published six books. His research interests include the political dimensions of Margaret Atwood's fiction, presidential debates, political conventions, and lesser-known political communicators from the twentieth century.

Craig Allen Smith is Professor Emeritus, North Carolina State University. He is the author of *Presidential Campaign Communication, 2nd ed.* and *Persuasion and Social Movements, 6th ed.* with Charles J. Stewart and Robert E. Denton Jr., as well as chapters and articles about American political communication for over six decades.

Kathy B. Smith is a recently retired Professor of Political Science and International Affairs at Wake Forest University. She has co-authored *The White House Speaks: Presidential Leadership as Persuasion* and *The President and the Public: Rhetoric and National Leadership.* She has published books, chapters, and articles about American political communication for over six decades.

John C. Tedesco is Professor in the School of Communication at Virginia Tech. His areas of research interests include political communication, presidential campaign communication, and public relations. He is co-author of two books, *Civic Dialogue in the 1996 Presidential Campaign: Candidate, Media, and Public Voices* and *The Internet Election: Perspectives of the Web in Campaign 2004.* He has authored numerous book chapters, articles, and research papers.

Benjamin Voth is Associate Professor and Director of Debate and Speech programs in the Dedman College of Humanities and Sciences at Southern Methodist University. He is a leading national scholar on debate and the power of the human voice. He is the author of four books on how individual communication abilities can positively change the world, including *James Farmer Jr.: The Great Debater*; *Social Fragmentation and the Decline of American Democracy: The End of the Social Contract* (with Robert E. Denton Jr.); and *The Rhetoric of Genocide: Death as a Text. The Rhetoric of Genocide* won the American Forensic Association's 2015 top national book award, the Daniel Rohrer Memorial Outstanding Research Award, for research in the field of speech and debate. His most current book is *Debate as Global Pedagogy: Rwanda Rising.* He is currently an advisor to the Bush Institute and the Debate fellow for the Calvin Coolidge Foundation in Vermont.